Business Operations Models

Business Operations Models

Becoming
a disruptive
competitor

Alan Braithwaite and
Martin Christopher

LONDON PHILADELPHIA NEW DELHI

First published in Great Britain and the United States in 2015 by Kogan Page Limited

2nd Floor, 45 Gee Street	1518 Walnut Street, Suite 1100	4737/23 Ansari Road
London EC1V 3RS	Philadelphia PA 19102	Daryaganj
United Kingdom	USA	New Delhi 110002
www.koganpage.com		India

© Alan Braithwaite and Martin Christopher, 2015

ISBN   978 0 7494 7331 0
E-ISBN   978 0 7494 7332 7

British Library Cataloguing-in-Publication Data

A CIP record for this book is available from the British Library.

Library of Congress Cataloging-in-Publication Data

Christopher, Martin.
  Business operations models : becoming a disruptive competitor / Martin Christopher, Alan Braithwaite. – 1st Edition.
    pages cm
  ISBN 978-0-7494-7331-0 (paperback) – ISBN 978-0-7494-7332-7   1. Strategic planning.
2. Production management.   I. Braithwaite, Alan.   II. Title.
  HD30.28.C546 2015
  658.4'012–dc23

                                                                            2015013524

Typeset by Graphicraft Limited, Hong Kong
Print production managed by Jellyfish
Printed and bound by CPI Group (UK) Ltd, Croydon CR0 4YY

CONTENTS

PREFACE AND ACKNOWLEDGEMENTS

This book is the result of more than 25 years of collaboration during the formative development period of our specialization, supply chain and logistics management. It has been an exciting time as the true business potential from supply chain capabilities has been increasingly recognized. In that time, Martin's work at the Cranfield School of Management's Centre for Logistics and Supply Chain Management has helped it to achieve European pre-eminence. Alan's work has been applying the academic fundamentals in real business through his consulting company, LCP Consulting. LCP has worked with more than 400 clients over that period, helping to drive major improvements in performance for many of them. The collaboration has been symbiotic, theory has both informed and been informed by practice.

In that time, many companies have appointed and integrated the position of Supply Chain Director onto their executive boards – itself a measure of the adoption of the capability. Notwithstanding those appointments, our consulting and academic experiences have led us to observe that the capability is mostly positioned as functional and executional – the focus has been on integrating across functions to address waste. We argue in this book that 'operations' has a role in strategy development and business transformation, the potential of which is often underestimated. Indeed in Chapter 4 we point to this as a gap in the management literature that is only bridged by a few authors.

At LCP Consulting, our many contacts with boards and leadership teams in our recent work in the transformation of retail by e-commerce have led us to define a business operations model framework; we have used this as a means to communicate the strategic importance of operations in the formulation of compelling customer propositions that are profitable. In this book we have adapted the model to be generic to both retail and manufacturing businesses and used it as a platform to develop narratives to describe disruptive and super-performing businesses.

We therefore have to thank the whole LCP team for their key role in providing the core model along with the practical and experiential material on which this book is based. We also have to recognize the LCP thought leadership programme, chaired by David Quarmby, that ran from 2010 to 2013 with meetings in London, supported by many seasoned executives. That led in turn to our commissioning Chris Melton to do his Master's degree research that helped to inform our work, especially in Chapters 4 and 10; a special thanks to Chris who now works for LCP doing great work with clients.

Finally, our wives and families deserve special thanks for tolerating our obsessions with our work – it is another perspective on the idea of being disruptive.

We hope that the ideas we have developed bring current and aspiring business leaders fresh perspectives and inspiration; we also hope that academics may elect to develop some of our tenets and maxims further through research and case studies.

What we mean by business operations models – and why are they important? 01

A company is nothing without customers, and customers are not stupid. They make sophisticated choices in terms of the value they expect to derive from their purchases; this applies to both consumer and business transactions. What is meant by value is a core theme of this book. Economists use the term 'time and place utility' to describe this choice; but it is more than just about having the right product in the right place and at a price that customers are prepared to pay at that point and place in time. It is about how the product or service is presented, the emotional connection that is made through the interaction with the brand and the consequential perceived or real value that is obtained. In short, the way that a business faces and services its customers reflects its brand identity every bit as much as the product itself.

For a consumer, buying a product from Amazon involves a different set of expectations to those that come when buying the same product from a retail store. And for a manufacturer, buying a product from a distributor involves different expectations and 'conditions of supply' to purchasing the same product directly from a factory in China.

The big idea behind this book is that the way a company configures its operations to deliver this brand experience to customers – while delivering viable financial performance – is an opportunity for significant competitive advantage and marketplace disruption. In other words, by balancing the operations model within the context of the company's markets and its strategy, the company's operations can create a distinctive marketplace capability that drives step change in both growth and profitability. We use the term 'business operations model' to describe the way that this balance is formulated and delivered. We argue that it is a neglected dimension of strategy and through its execution executive teams can achieve disruptive transformation.

The concept is illustrated in Figure 1.1. For any business to be successful, its operations have to deliver distinctive brand value as perceived through the customers' lens and in line with its overall strategy for the marketplace, while also doing this at a cost that makes pricing the product or service commercially viable. Product design, service development, manufacturing, logistics and marketing have to devise a single coherent value proposition for customers that is not only compelling, but which can also be delivered profitably.

FIGURE 1.1   The business operations models concept

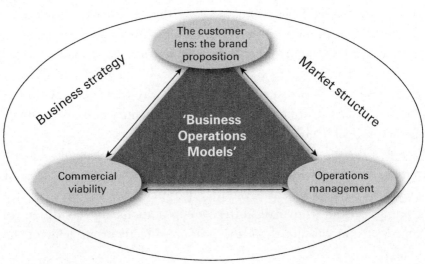

SOURCE: LCP Consulting

The resulting essence of the brand for the customer is that unique combination of the buying and service experience, the 'halo' of ownership, and the direct and consequential costs of the purchase.

As shown in Figure 1.1 there is a feedback loop between business strategy, market structure and the business operations model. But some of the most disruptive competitors have used their operations to transform markets rather than just outperform within them; in this book we use case studies to describe both approaches. Our experience is that the power of operational excellence as a strategic tool is often downplayed in both the management literature and in practice in the boardroom. Strategy statements are most usually expressed in goal-driven terms based on market size estimates, competitive structures, price points in the market and high-level views of potential; their development is normally anchored in economic or competition theory. Practical operational capabilities are often taken as read, or not seen as a source for step-change performance.

Yet what if boards could actually identify the latent potential in their operations to either do existing things dramatically better, or do new things completely differently, and thus become a disruptor? It is this question that we explore in this book, using the business operations model as a framework to do so.

Indeed, the entire foundation of this book is that operations can inform and guide strategy, building a distinctive, transformative and disruptive competence through creating compelling customer value at a profit.

In our work with executives, questions frequently arise such as: 'Who is the best, and why?' or 'What is the next big thing?' or 'Is there a single key initiative that we should be pursuing?' This search for the silver bullet or magical panacea is an understandable one, given the competitive pressures under which management teams operate. In essence it involves the desire to understand what is required in order to break away from the pack, and to put clear blue water between one's own business and those of its competitors.

But how, precisely? Whilst technology can certainly be a key component of marketplace disruption, the underlying theme of this book is that the search for an operations-led market-disrupting strategy must look beyond technical innovation, and rather focus on two core dimensions.

The first is that disruptive market leadership is about how a company configures its operations to deliver compelling value to its customers. The second is the idea that creating a distinctive competitive edge is not about exploiting a single competitive advantage; rather it is about building a unique blend of operations-led drivers and capabilities for delivering that value. That combination of capabilities is much more than the sum of its parts; it enables both people and organizations to do things differently, thereby driving both customer value and economic performance.

Business operations models is the term that we have coined to convey the multifaceted complexity of becoming an effective disruptor by creating and exploiting new ways of organizing and operating. The idea has come from research at Cranfield University, and through a thought leadership programme at LCP Consulting that is built upon 40 years of consulting experience at more than 400 companies around the world.

Every company has a business operations model; it is not just the domain of the disruptors or the high achievers. The skill is to recognize this and harness the model to rewrite the rules of competitive engagement. Our research has uncovered the fact that effective operators respond to market and technology changes – or both – by reconfiguring their business operations models in order to do just this. Sometimes the shifts in competitive stance have been highly visible, but on other occasions quite subtle and barely apparent to the uninformed observer. Nevertheless, to the customer – who is the ultimate arbiter – the changes have been sufficient to change the competitive paradigm.

The business operations model framework

So let's take a look at the business operations model in more detail. Figure 1.2 shows the framework that we refer to as we step our way through the different insights provided by a study of the business operations model.

FIGURE 1.2   The business operations model framework

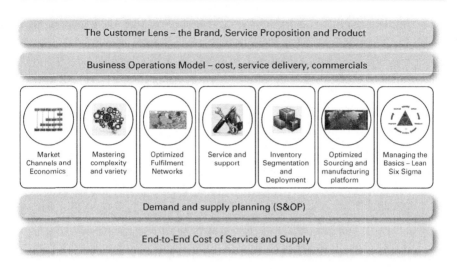

The Customer Lens – the Brand, Service Proposition and Product

Business Operations Model – cost, service delivery, commercials

| Market Channels and Economics | Mastering complexity and variety | Optimized Fulfilment Networks | Service and support | Inventory Segmentation and Deployment | Optimized Sourcing and manufacturing platform | Managing the Basics – Lean Six Sigma |

Demand and supply planning (S&OP)

End-to-End Cost of Service and Supply

SOURCE: LCP Consulting

The starting point is the customer 'lens' – namely how the customer views the brand's values, the service proposition and the product itself. Clearly, it is important that the target customer experience is defined in a way that is consistent both with the brand's positioning and with the nature of the market and the competition. As businesses aspire to do more for customers – be that in terms of products, services, prices or some combination – then the business operations model is how that distinctive customer experience is formulated and delivered. In particular, this is achieved through the unique combination of the pillars that sit beneath this customer 'lens', integrated and brought together by a process of demand and supply planning (sometimes called sales and operations planning, or S&OP) and with reference to the end-to-end cost of service and supply. In short, a business operations model succeeds if the pillars that comprise it combine together to deliver the target customer experience at both a price and cost that generates growth, margin and return.

Throughout the book we return in detail to each vertical shown in Figure 1.2, but a short summary is useful now:

- *Market and channel economics*
  This is about the routes to market that are selected. Many disruptors have disintermediated historic channels to market in order to strip out cost and achieve compelling market pricing. The growth of internet retailing, for instance, and Apple's iTunes music store are both well-known examples of this.

- *Mastering complexity and variety*
  This is about the focus on the breadth of both customers and products, and how that variety is managed. Many businesses have tried to be competitive in their markets by adding more and more products and customers, only to find that this then yields either diminishing returns or a failure to meet the brand's aspirations. A classic example of this approach to managing complexity and variety is the contrast between discount retailer Aldi and a 'full-range' supermarket such as Sainsbury or Tesco. Aldi has perhaps 3,000 products on sale, while a full-range supermarket might offer 10 times as many. It is immediately obvious that Aldi can organize its operations very differently because of this lower level of complexity, and that the 'full-range' supermarket has to find ways to organize its operations so as to prevent the additional complexity imposed by its range actually serving to erode competitiveness.

- *Optimized fulfilment networks*
  These are about how product is efficiently routed from source to destination. As such, optimized fulfilment networks go hand-in-hand with mastering complexity and channel economics, since the greater the variety and the more diverse the channels through which products reach market, the more that profits will be eroded through higher inventory levels and obsolescence. A classic example here is how the technology company Lenovo has eliminated nearly all its inventory holdings in Europe and now fulfils directly to its channels from its plants in China via overnight airfreight through Frankfurt. This greatly simplifies planning, increases demand responsiveness and reduces the propensity for stock obsolescence – and the additional cost of the airfreight is more

than offset by the competitive benefits from this 'zero inventory' model.

- *Service and support*
  This is a key part of the overall product experience, and in some cases a factor in the total cost of ownership; this total cost of owning a product can be the deciding factor in buying decisions. For example, the classic example of a market-changing disruptive service and support-led innovation is the supply of commercial jet engines on 'power by the hour' contracts, where the lifetime service and support is integrated with the supply of the engine in a single usage-based pricing model.

- *Inventory segmentation and deployment*
  This is a core skill relating to the allocation of inventory through the network in order to maximize availability and minimize obsolescence. The classic example here is the ranging of products and setting stock levels in retailing by outlet; another would be the centralization of stocks of slow-moving parts in Europe and using differential supply rules across the network.

- *Optimized sourcing and manufacturing platform*
  Companies have put a huge amount of effort into their sourcing and supply operations in order to reduce input costs. Initiatives such as strategic sourcing, globalization and value engineering are all illustrations of this. In Chapter 9 we argue that this is not about blindly pursuing functional optimization; rather it is using sourcing and supply as a key capability in building distinctive value through the business operations model. Kingfisher and Walmart have both established Asian sourcing offices in order to deal directly with factories based in Asia, while other retailers use agents such as Li & Fung. There is a trend to re-shoring and nearshoring that is already largely worked through in the automobile industry; many plants work predominantly with national and regional suppliers on lead times measured in hours, enabling plants to run with parts stocks of less than a shift.

- *Managing the basics*
  There is no substitute for doing the basics well. Achieving
  productivity and service performance levels that are in the top
  quartile can be the difference between success and failure, with
  the benefits passing through to customers in both prices and
  brand experience. Initiatives such as lean management and
  Six Sigma are well recognized as key competitive weapons
  because of their ability to deliver these enhanced productivity
  and service performances; they were the foundation of the
  global leadership of the Japanese automobile industry and are
  now emulated around the world by both manufacturers and
  retailers.

Serving to underpin and consolidate these specific operations-focused
vertical attributes of the business operations model, there are two
further aspects to creating a distinctive competitive capability that
should be addressed:

- *Integrated planning*
  The design and execution of planning processes in the context
  of the business operations model are critical to the execution
  of the end-to-end supply chain, effective stock deployment,
  and optimized sourcing and supply. Every time a business
  issues a supply order or reaches a deployment decision it is
  making a commitment that has investment and cost impacts.
  In manufacturing businesses the key concept is sales and
  operations planning (S&OP), while in retail the term is the
  weekly sales and stock intake plan (WSSI). Our experience is
  that companies that work to secure a solid process of
  integrated planning can achieve improved levels of service
  availability and reduced stockholding – thereby opening the
  door to additional revenues and lower costs. In manufacturing,
  Procter & Gamble (P&G) has reported huge benefits in
  improved availability, reduced inventory and more efficient
  manufacturing from a global and regional S&OP process.
  In retailing, the remarkable performance of Next in the UK is
  attributed to the excellence of its planning.

- *End-to-end cost and margin management of service and supply*
  Understanding how customers and products contribute to profitability is an essential part of anchoring the business operations model. The net margin contribution is the outcome of the combination of the verticals that we have just discussed with the relevant customer 'lens', together with the associated commercial conditions and the specific design of the operation. As such, it can be regarded as the internal monitoring and control process, providing essential feedback on the validity of the business operations model. The more that companies reduce their 'cost to serve' – perhaps, for instance, through reducing the proportion of loss makers in their product portfolio – the more that they will be able to apply pressure in their markets as an effective competitive disruptor.
  In Chapter 9 we bring forward the example of a health-care supplies company that used end-to-end cost management to move from loss to profit and drive profitable growth through changes to its business operations model.

Overall, the business operations model stems from our discovery – through the research that we have undertaken – that the attributes of successful, and certainly disruptive, businesses are a combination of some (but seldom all) of its elements. We also found that these attributes of success are often quite superficially interpreted and explained, with observers, commentators and academics interpreting the outcomes through the perspective of their own experiences, without necessarily seeing the full interplay between all the factors involved in that success. The value of the business operations model is that it provides a framework for more objectively analysing how operations contribute to overall business success and developing a complete narrative of how changes can impact both customers' experiences and the economics of the business.

The complexity of business is such that there is a need to generalize; competitive pressures are such that the search for a single silver bullet is understandable. Our aim in this book is to give readers – from business leaders to students – more windows through which they can interpret disruptive business success, and then consider how they might design their own distinctive capabilities. We will unpack each aspect of becoming a competitive disruptor using case studies, academic research and our own experiences, and then knit those different perspectives together to tell more complete stories. We hope that the framework we outline will provide a practical approach by which business leaders of today and tomorrow can think about the opportunities for their businesses – developing the 'narrative of success'.

Case studies are central to this book, and we use them to illustrate how business operating models have driven disruptive success in real-life business situations, unpicking each of the components of that success. In parallel we draw on academic perspectives in order to provide an interpretation of how value for both customers and companies is delivered.

CASE STUDY   The Southwest Airlines success story

As a way to start on our journey together, let's begin by looking at the growth of the low-cost airline industry. This sector has been a major disruptor to established airlines, and has reached a position of market control in both Europe and the United States. Yet low-cost airlines use the same aircraft as traditional airlines; they operate mostly through the same airports and with the same air traffic control; and they do not get any special breaks on fuel costs. So, their success is definitively not one that is driven by technology. Instead, it is the 'how' of their operations that is the critical differentiator. Low-cost airlines have redefined airline operations in order to transform them into a disruptive differentiator – or, in our terms, they have changed their business operations model to give customers fares and routes that the traditional airlines have struggled to emulate.

An example of the core concepts involved comes from one of the early adopters of the low-cost airline business operations model, Southwest Airlines in the United States. Herb Kelleher, the founder, took much of his approach at Southwest Airlines from Pacific Southwest Airlines, which lost its independence in 1988 to form US Airways. Since his stellar success at Southwest Airlines, the Southwest Airlines model has been copied by both Ryanair and EasyJet in Europe, with many other followers around the world.

The graph of the share price relative to the S&P 500 stock market index provides all the answers as to why Southwest and the other low-cost airline successes have attracted such attention. Figure 1.3 shows that Southwest has outperformed the S&P 500 by a factor of six, recording a growth since 1980 of more than 12,000 per cent. The graph shows a period of exceptional share price growth to the early 2000s, then followed by more normal market volatility. Clearly the economic downturn impacted the period between 2009 and 2012, but since then shareholder value has rocketed.

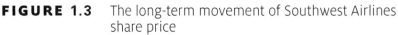

FIGURE 1.3   The long-term movement of Southwest Airlines share price

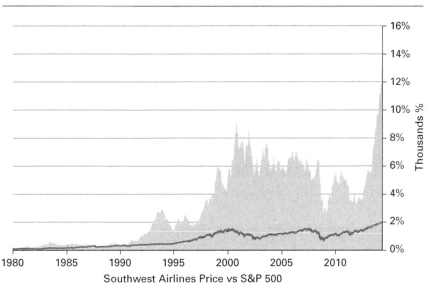

Southwest Airlines Price vs S&P 500

In contrast to this remarkable performance, the US airline industry as a whole has a heritage of serial bankruptcy. As Figure 1.4 shows, over the comparable period all the major brands have slipped into either Chapter 11 or Chapter 7 of the US bankruptcy code (some more than once). And this is just the tip of the iceberg in terms of the actual number of bankruptcy events that have been recorded. The website **www.airlines.org** reports that since 1979 there have been 196 such events, with most of the names being long forgotten. The number is a reflection of the glamorous attraction of a sector that is never short of new entrants, as well as the difficulty of making a sustainable margin.

In contrast, Southwest Airlines has been a sustained performer in terms of profits – 41 years without a loss. Table 1.1 highlights the key statistics underpinning this outperformance, showing the airline's progress in 10-year intervals from 1981, and with 2013 added.

FIGURE 1.4   The history of key US airlines bankruptcies

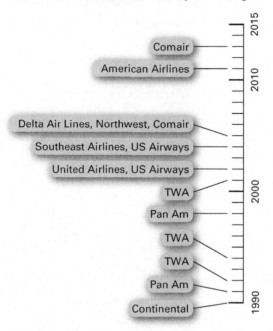

SOURCE: adapted from information on **www.airlines.org**

Clearly, there has been phenomenal growth in revenues and margin, and in passenger and aircraft numbers. But clearly, too, we can see both margin volatility and how the margins have been declining as the business moves to maturity in the market. The increasing seat utilization is equivalent to about a 15 per cent reduction in fares, and points both to scale and learning as a way to reduce the cost base. This is a classic trajectory for many successful businesses that sustain growth as they mature by leveraging their efficiency and sacrificing some gross margin in exchange for increased volume.

Bureau of Transportation statistics suggest that Southwest Airlines' domestic traffic volumes represent around 15.7 per cent of the market, achieved from zero in just over 40 years. This still leaves plenty of room for further growth in a highly fragmented market. Price competition and margin volatility can be expected to continue, since the prospect of consolidation in the airline industry to the point where there are three core players seems remote. Why three core players? Because this 'rule of three' is the level of market consolidation at which US academics Jagdish Sheth and Rajendra Sisodia hypothesize that the necessary

TABLE 1.1   Southwest Airlines financial and operational history

		1981	1991	2001	2011	2013
Passengers carried		6,792,000	22,669,942	64,446,773	103,973,000	108,075,976
Revenues '000's	$'000	$270,358	$1,319,605	$5,555,174	$15,658,000	$17,699,000
Revenues per passenger		$40	$58	$86	$151	$164
Net margin	$'000	$34,165	$26,919	$511,147	$178,000	$754,000
Margin %		12.6%	2.0%	9.2%	1.1%	4.3%
Planes at year end		27	124	355	698	681
Seat utilization	%	63.4%	61.1%	68.1%	80.9%	80.1%

SOURCE: LCP Consulting

marketplace conditions apply for oligopoly, reduced price competition and increased margin stability. So the performance of Southwest Airlines is in clear contrast to its sector – raising the question as to what is at the heart of this continuously outstanding performance.

There are ample published case studies on Southwest, presenting data, providing analysis and giving the opportunity for business-school discussion. All the points are there, but the specifi c focus of individual authors takes readers to one emphasis or another. In terms of Southwest's business operations model it can be diffi cult to pull together a complete picture. Using our model framework, the features of the airline's performance that have enabled Southwest to be a profi table low-cost leader are:

- *The brand service proposition.* Southwest's proposition – and indeed its whole strategy – is very simple: it aims to deliver compellingly competitive prices to national destinations with excellent, but not excessive, customer service. At the start, Southwest saw its competition as the car, and its twofold aim was to provide flights at a lower cost than passengers could achieve by driving to their destination, as well as saving them time. The extent of the early price competitiveness can be seen from Table 1.2, showing the average fares for some routes and the resulting cost per mile.

TABLE 1.2   Southwest Airlines fares per mile

Year	Average trip miles	Average Fare	$/mile
1984	436	$49.00	$0.11
1993	500	$60.00	$0.12
1994	1000	$135.00	$0.14 Oakland Round Trip

SOURCE: adapted from a Stanford University case study

This cost per mile can be compared to a gasoline (petrol) cost at 15 miles per gallon of around $0.08 (at the time given in the study). Since it could take many hours to drive such distances, and there are also additional vehicle running costs to consider, the value provided by Southwest's proposition was compelling. This led to Southwest rapidly growing its market, rather than simply taking market share from established players. A Stanford University case study reports that 8,000 people used to fly between Louisville and Chicago each week but that this climbed to 26,000 after Southwest Airlines entered the market.

But Southwest did not just provide low prices. It also focused on its brand, through the customer experience that it provided to its passengers. For 10 years in a row, *Fortune* magazine recognized Southwest in its survey of corporate reputations and in 1994 listed the company as number three. The airline has continued to sustain the ethic of service excellence, as can be seen in Figure 1.5, which shows JD Power surveys from 2005 to 2010 putting Southwest at the top of the pack, behind only JetBlue.

This picture of the Southwest customer proposition effectively negates the idea that low prices, cost leadership and good service are mutually exclusive. And since its unique blend of service, customer value and cost leadership is delivered through operations, it is the business operations model that is at the core of the performance of this powerful disruptive competitor.

- *Mastering complexity and variety.* Southwest has a very simple product. As at May 2014 it flew to 89 destinations in 42 American states, plus Mexico

FIGURE 1.5   Southwest Airlines service competitiveness

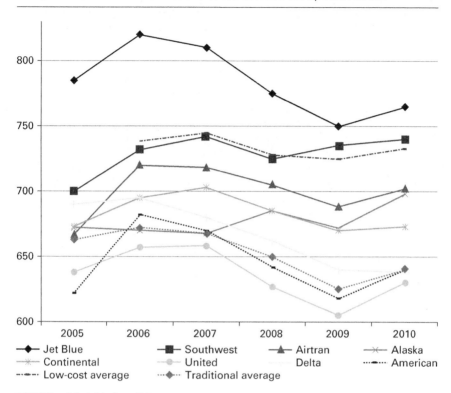

SOURCE: original data from JDPower

City, Puerto Rico and Jamaica. Services are point-to-point with no effort to link flights through interlining; customers have to do this themselves. This differs from the conventional hub-and-spoke where economic interdependence is created between routes: for southwest, the route is either profitable and it continues, or unprofitable and it does not. Customers plan their journeys based on taking advantage of attractive prices, and if necessary book onward flights with other airlines. This approach to the product avoids high complexity and interdependency, both of which tend to add to costs, while also reducing equipment utilization.

- *Market channels.* Southwest has from its inception avoided paying travel agents' commissions, and being part of the airline booking system. This avoided heavy sales channel charges, and enabled a direct go-to-market approach – initially with call centres, and latterly via the internet. Southwest was one of the first airlines to have a website, and is now the number one airline website for online booking. The cost avoided by this channel strategy

– in an industry where the gross margin per available seat is around
35 per cent of sales – could have been as high as 5 per cent of revenues,
plus the internal costs of managing the agency relationships.

- *Optimized sourcing.* Alongside its route simplicity, Southwest also operates
just a single type of aircraft: the Boeing 737, in a range of versions. This deep
relationship with Boeing on a single aircraft type reduces both engineering
and maintenance complexity as well as costs, including the holding costs of
spare parts; it avoids the resources required to train staff on different aircraft
types, and helps with equipment substitution in the event of breakdown.
Southwest is the largest operator of the 737 in the world, and this tight
relationship is reported to have also delivered buying benefits in its
negotiations with Boeing.

- *Managing the basics and operational effectiveness.* Alongside the use of the
737 as an aircraft standard, Southwest keeps its jets in the air for longer than
the competition. This is achieved both through the simplicity of its route
network, which allows it to string together sectors so as to maximize aircraft
use, as well as its famous 10-minute gate turnaround. As a result, Southwest's
aircraft are reported to spend 11 hours in the air each day as against the
industry average of 8. Additionally, the airline can use its gates 10.5 times
per day, as opposed to 4.5 for the airline industry as a whole. This rapid
turnaround has been achieved partly through slick teamwork by ground crew
– think Formula One pit stops – but also by not serving food on the aircraft,
thereby eliminating the time taken to load and stow the in-flight catering,
which also reduced costs. Today it is difficult to imagine being served
anything more than a sandwich on a short-haul flight, but when Southwest
started a meal was the standard. For their customers, serving peanuts and
a drink was just fine, as they appreciated that they were 'flying for peanuts',
as stated in Southwest's advertisements.

- *Managing the basics through attention to detail.* Cases and commentary
point to the organization taking great care over detail, specifically in the detail
that underpins staff morale, motivation and safety. At the time of writing,
Southwest has never had a fatality inside one of its aircraft resulting from
an accident, which is one of the best records in the industry. There is also
ample commentary regarding Southwest's focus on its internal culture, in
which it tries to make the airline a fun and motivating place where people
want to work. These basics – together with its advertising, promotions, pricing
and tactical competitive responses – combine to make a very successful
business operations model.

- *Managing the basics through tenacity and vision.* The case study material on Southwest Airlines points to a long legal battle to get the airline off the ground from its base at Dallas Love Field Airport, together with repeated legal challenges from competitors and regulatory challenges from authorities. Southwest has developed through an era of deregulation in the US airline industry, which has progressively removed barriers to entry and operation. Rather than accepting the status quo, it has had the tenacity to take on prolonged battles, and the vision to persevere in the face of adversity.

- *Optimized network.* A significant contributory factor to the high number of aircraft 'in-flight' hours per day achieved by Southwest Airlines is the relative ease of scheduling due to its homogeneous route structures (by that we mean many routes of similar length and flight time) alongside its point-to-point operating methods. There are fewer long sectors that are difficult to balance with short-haul sectors. Usefully, too, Southwest has also eliminated any dependency on connections with other flights, which helps to drive up asset utilization and drive down costs.

- *Total cost-to-serve.* The combination of these operational elements has made Southwest a low-cost operator with a highly competitive cost structure and value profile. The scale of that competitive advantage – even many years after the airline's inception in 1967 – is shown in Table 1.3.

TABLE 1.3   Southwest Airlines' cost advantage: ¢/seat/mile

	Q3 1993	Q3 1994	Average Southwest advantage	Average (¢)
	¢ per seat per mile			
Southwest	7.13	7.03		7.08
Continental	7.64	7.56	6.8%	7.6
United	8.11	8.32	13.8%	8.215
American	8.06	8.08	12.3%	8.07
TWA	9.23	8.66	20.8%	8.945
Delta	8.66	8.95	19.6%	8.805
Northwest	9.36	9.79	26.1%	9.575
US Air	10.94	10.74	34.7%	10.84

SOURCE: adapted from Stanford University Case HR-1A

In summary, Southwest Airlines' business operations model is a careful blend of capabilities that reduces complexity and cost, giving the airline the marketplace power to be a disruptor. And, throughout its almost 50-year history, it has successfully exploited that advantage.

It is also worth noting that Southwest got there by a combination of events that might be considered by some to be serendipity, which is something of a recurring theme in stories of business success. Getting there 'almost by accident' is surprisingly common. Southwest's famous '10-minute gate turnaround' is reported to have arisen during its early operations when it had to hand back the lease on one of its aircraft as it did not have the cash to pay for it. Rather than reduce the capacity, it set out to run a four-aircraft timetable with just three jets. Slashing turnaround times served to create a virtual fourth aircraft, but without any of the attendant running costs – a triumph out of adversity.

Throughout the chapters of this book we intend to show how the individual elements of the business operations model framework can be used to either enhance competitive advantage or, alternatively, deliver full-scale market disruption. Looking at case studies from businesses such as Dell, Aldi, Apple, Amazon and Walmart – as well as many others – we chart the root causes of their successes (and, in some cases, their demises).

Our argument is that the design and execution of operations through a combination of the elements of the business operations model is central to both a distinctive marketplace position and a business's competitive edge. But while both of these clearly lie at the heart of many business strategies, our experience suggests that an operations-led approach to achieving them is not commonly found within boardrooms. Instead, the language is of marketing and product innovation, financial engineering and technology. Operations, meanwhile, are often taken for granted: prosaic and routine until they go wrong. This is to seriously underestimate the potential they can deliver.

By providing a framework to discuss how an operations-led approach can make a genuine disruptive contribution to a business's competitive edge and marketplace perception, we hope that we can help to change perceptions, and put operations more firmly on the strategic landscape.

Taking forward the framework in your business

While this is the first chapter in the book and it is early to be starting to plan actions, here are our suggested steps from Chapter 1 for applying the framework (subsequent chapters will build on these steps and give further opportunities to apply our insights):

- Describe the narrative of your current business operations model (yes, every business has one).

- Identify your distinctive capabilities using the framework and how they come together to give customers value.

- Identify the three most important improvement initiatives that would take your company towards giving customers more compelling value: being a disruptor or transforming its performance (regardless of your business size, as smaller companies can do this too).

- Hold those descriptions and identifications for review later; you can expect to revisit them in the light of future insights.

The characteristics of super-performing businesses

Executives are captivated by the idea of super-performing businesses because they outperform their competitors to create enhanced and sustained shareholder value. Super-performers also exert power through their financial strength, and this gives executives the capacity for personal reward as well as growth, investment and acquisitions. Being a part of a super-performer is a good place to be.

In contrast, any reversal of performance is seized on by the city analysts and the press, and publicly quoted companies and their management can quickly find themselves pilloried for non-performance. This isn't pleasant in the context of personal pressure for the executives involved, let alone the challenge of fixing the business issues.

By way of illustration, Tesco's disappointing results in June 2014 were met with widespread commentary on the sudden decline in its fortunes. The company reported like-for-like sales down by more than 3.7 per cent, a much steeper decline than the previous quarter's 2.9 per cent. The chief executive officer (CEO) at the time said these results were the worst that he had seen, and came in spite of spending £200 million on price cuts to basic items.

The *Financial Times* was among many who were quick to put the knife in. An extract of their report on 4 June 2014, quoting analysts, serves to make the point:

> It leads us to be all the more concerned about Tesco's current performance in its core market and it suggests to us that the sustained poor and underperformance is most clearly because its prices remain too high...
>
> ... a clear concern about further margin and earnings erosion.

Reports at the time conveyed a sense of irremediable doom based on perceptions that Tesco would be unable to fight back against the hard-discount operators such as Aldi and Lidl and potentially Asda. The grocery retail market has faced a growth spurt from the hard-discount operators, who have been mopping up share at a rate of between 1.5 per cent and 2 per cent market share per year.

In the perception of the financial markets Tesco had moved, in the space of less than three years, from being a super-performer and a disruptor. Previously, it had achieved increased market share and sales, sustained margins and outstanding returns on investment. In 2014 it was seeing like-for-like declines in sales, reducing margins and the need to invest heavily in lower prices in order to maintain share and market position. In essence its business operations model was no longer delivering as compelling a proposition and the commercial return was being eroded. It is important to note that Tesco remains the largest player by far in the UK market, so the key term is 'not as compelling'; but it is small differences that make the difference.

Being a super-performer and marketplace disruptor are outcomes that have required inputs in the form of companies' successful business operations models in relation to their markets. As the Tesco story shows, super-performance is not a gift for life; it is ephemeral as customers' priorities change and competitors exploit relatively small gaps.

This chapter provides an overview of what is meant by super-performance, how it can emerge and disappear, and how it connects with business operations models. In writing the chapter, we have drawn on our analysis of the FT Global 500 rankings, the Gartner top 25 supply chain companies and the work of key contributors to this area, including Ram Charan and Stern Stewart.

The FT Global 500 rankings

The *Financial Times* publishes a Global 500 ranking on an annual basis, which enables an evaluation over time of the big winners and losers in corporate standings by market value, revenues and profits. We have compiled the timeline of the FT Global 500 rankings based on market value, revenues and earnings for the last 9 years focused on businesses that make and sell physical goods and services both to consumers and businesses, and we have stripped out sectors such as banking, insurance, property, utilities and media where the business operating models are different. This analysis shows a strong correlation between net income and market value and less significant correlations between revenue with market value and net income with turnover. The numbers are shown in Figure 2.1.

FIGURE 2.1   Correlation of market value with revenue and net income

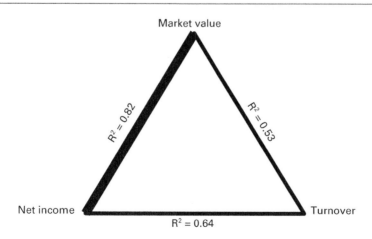

NOTE: A correlation coefficient is the statistical measure of how closely two data series for the same topic align. It is reported as a ratio called R squared (R^2) where perfect correlation gets a score of 1 and a completely random relationship scores zero. Anything above 0.75 is highly meaningful in terms of cause and effect.

This simple analysis of the leading companies in the world shows that market valuations are more highly influenced by net income (correlation coefficient of 0.82; see note to Figure 2.1) than by revenues (0.53) and that the relationship between turnover and income (0.64) is only slightly stronger. This is intuitively logical since a business that grows 10 per cent in sales at a margin of 15 per cent retains more profit that one that earns only 5 per cent net margin. The analysis bears out the old management adage 'turnover is vanity, profit is sanity and cash is reality'. Earnings and cash are what really count.

We identified some sectors where there has been disruptive competition and some big winners and losers in the rankings. The charts in Figures 2.2, 2.3 and 2.4 show some of the winners and losers in the technology hardware, general retailing and pharmaceuticals sectors.

The computer hardware story shows Apple ascending to total dominance of the rankings from around number 125 in 2006, with other former darlings of the market such as Dell, Nokia, Canon and Hewlett-Packard falling from grace.

FIGURE 2.2   Computer hardware company's movement in rankings in the FT500 by market value – 2006 to 2014

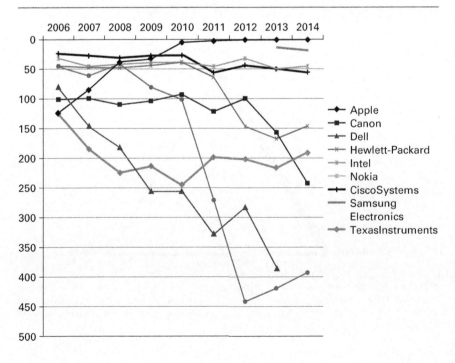

FIGURE 2.3   General retailers' movement in rankings in the FT500 by market value – 2006 to 2014

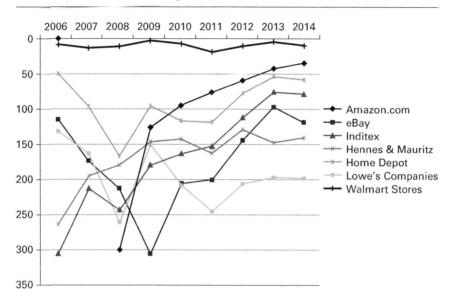

FIGURE 2.4   Pharmaceutical company movement in rankings in the FT500 by market value – 2006 to 2014

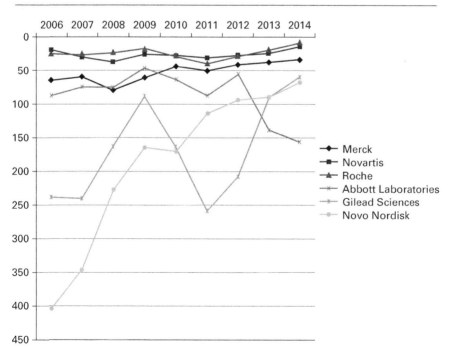

In contrast to the computer hardware sector, the impact of the 2008–09 downturn is partly apparent in this graph of general retailers standings. It also shows the sustained dominance of Walmart and the meteoric rise of Amazon, eBay, H&M and Inditex (Zara).

The changes in rankings in the pharmaceutical sector are more sedate in the sample. Figure 2.4 shows Novo Nordisk as the big winner, where the value has been accelerated because of its therapeutic specializations in diabetes treatment, which is fast becoming an epidemic. The loser in this graph is Abbott Laboratories.

These sample charts serve to illustrate some fundamentals of value creation. First, success is ephemeral; the half-life of success is shortening as new disruptors enter and make their mark for a few years. Second, a position in the top 50 seems to confer more security but the risks are still there. Third, some sectors are more volatile than others, reflecting the systemic market risk of that area of business. Fourth, companies suddenly appear or disappear from the listing based on acquisition, break-up or just new entry to the listing. This means there will be super-performers that are not visible in this analysis; indeed many smaller companies will be creating remarkable value through their operations models. Fifth, and most important, disruptors can create astonishing market value in very short periods of time.

The Gartner top 25

The Gartner top 25 ranking is prepared annually by Gartner, the leading information technology research and advisory company – 'helping its clients make the right decisions on their technology platforms', to identify benchmark leaders in supply chain management. The ranking was initiated by AMR, subsequently acquired by Gartner, and was focused on giving clients some benchmarks on their standing in terms of operational excellence. It was based on clients and recognized leaders but is not positioned as being comprehensive. It should be noted that it started with a strong US focus and Tesco was one of the early European entrants. Gartner's focus on supply chains is because supply chain design and operations models are central to companies' business systems design and configuration; success and peer group respect reflect their effective use of systems, among other factors. As a result the Gartner perspective on leaders is a good additional measure of operational excellence.

Gartner compile their rankings based on 50 per cent of the score being financial: covering inventory turns, revenue growth and return on assets. The other 50 per cent is equally divided between peer group and Gartner analysts' votes. We used the Gartner insights to understand how their rankings showed trends and then, in parallel to our purely financial FT 500 analysis, to understand how well the two perspectives tracked together. Table 2.1 shows the 10-year progression, illustrating some spectacular rises and falls as well as some sustained performers.

Inspection of the detailed results in Table 2.1 (the data for 2006 was not compiled) shows that companies come onto the radar and fall off it – sometimes lost for ever and sometimes reappearing. It also shows some interesting stories of big winners and losers.

Of the Gartner top 25, 17 feature in our operational FT top 50 (banking, utilities, financial services and insurance excluded) by market value for June 2014. Oil and gas, and pharma companies, which feature strongly in the FT Top 50, are not apparently a major focus for Gartner; together with software, such as Oracle, these make up 21 of the FT top 50. But that still leaves 12 for 2014 that do not align with the Gartner rankings. This can be attributed to the perceptual impact of peer and analyst voting and it means that some truly excellent and high-ranking businesses do not make it into to the Gartner rankings. Toyota, Volkswagen and Daimler are examples in the automotive sector; BASF and Bayer in chemicals; and L'Oréal and Home Depot are examples from other sectors. This analysis of inclusions and exclusions simply serves to show that the interpretation of business success is both quantitative and perceptual and subject to the interpretation of individuals: a point we made in Chapter 1.

However, the analysis led us to look at some specific examples to see how the Gartner rankings tracked FT 500 market value and net income and whether they led or lagged it. We selected a handful of companies for this analysis, some of which we return to with more detailed case material. The results are shown in Figures 2.5 to 2.9, as detailed below.

TABLE 2.1 The historical ranking of the Gartner top 25 supply chain companies

Rank	2014	2013	2012	2011	2010	2009	2008	2007	2005	2004
1	Apple	Apple	Apple	Apple	Apple	Apple	Apple	Nokia	Dell	Dell
2	McDonald's	McDonald's	Amazon.com	Dell	Procter & Gamble	Dell	Nokia	Apple	Procter & Gamble	Nokia
3	Amazon.com	Amazon.com	McDonald's	Procter & Gamble	Cisco Systems	Procter & Gamble	Dell	Procter & Gamble	IBM	Procter & Gamble
4	Unilever	Unilever	Dell	Research in Motion	Wal-Mart Stores	IBM	Procter & Gamble	IBM	Nokia	IBM
5	Procter & Gamble	Intel	Procter & Gamble	Amazon.com	Dell	Cisco Systems	IBM	Toyota Motor	Toyota Motor	Wal-Mart Stores
6	Samsung Electronics	Procter & Gamble	Coca-Cola Company	Cisco Systems	PepsiCo	Nokia	Wal-Mart Stores	Wal-Mart Stores	Johnson & Johnson	Toyota Motor
7	Cisco Systems	Cisco Systems	Intel	Wal-Mart Stores	Samsung Electronics	Wal-Mart Stores	Toyota Motor	Anheuser-Busch	Samsung Electronics	Johnson & Johnson
8	Intel	Samsung Electronics	Cisco Systems	McDonald's	IBM	Samsung Electronics	Cisco Systems	Tesco	Wal-Mart Stores	Johnson Controls
9	Colgate-Palmolive	Coca-Cola Company	Wal-Mart Stores	PepsiCo	Research in Motion	PepsiCo	Samsung Electronics	Best Buy	Tesco	Tesco

TABLE 2.1 *Continued*

Rank	2014	2013	2012	2011	2010	2009	2008	2007	2005	2004
10	Coca-Cola Company	Colgate-Palmolive	Unilever	Samsung Electronics	Amazon.com	Toyota Motor	Anheuser-Busch	Samsung Electronics	Johnson Controls	PepsiCo
11	Inditex	Dell	Colgate Palmolive	Coca-Cola Company	McDonald's	Schlumberger	PepsiCo	Cisco Systems	Intel	Nissan Motor
12	Nike	Inditex	PepsiCo	Microsoft	Microsoft	Johnson & Johnson	Tesco	Motorola	Anheuser-Busch	Woolworths
13	H&M	Wal-Mart Stores	Samsung Electronics	Colgate Palmolive	Coca-Cola Company	Coca-Cola Company	Coca-Cola Company	Coca-Cola Comp	Woolworths	Hewlett-Packard
14	Wal-Mart Stores	Nike	Nike	IBM	Johnson & Johnson	Nike	Best Buy	Johnson & Johnson	Home Depot	3M
15	PepsiCo	Starbucks	Inditex	Unilever	Hewlett-Packard	Tesco	Nike	PepsiCo	Motorola	GlaxoSmith Kline
16	Lenovo	PepsiCo	Starbucks	Intel	Nike	Walt Disney	SonyEricsson	Johnson Controls	PepsiCo	POSCO
17	Starbucks	H&M	H&M	Hewlett-Packard	Colgate Palmolive	Hewlett-Packard	Walt Disney	Texas Instruments	Best Buy	Coca-Cola Company
18	3M	Caterpillar	Nestlé	Nestlé	Intel	Texas Instruments	Hewlett-Packard	Nike	Cisco Systems	Best Buy

TABLE 2.1 *Continued*

Rank	2014	2013	2012	2011	2010	2009	2008	2007	2005	2004
19	Qualcomm	3M	Research in Motion	Inditex	Nokia	Lockheed Martin	Johnson & Johnson	Lowe's	Texas Instruments	Intel
20	Seagate Technology	Lenovo Group	Caterpillar	Nike	Tesco	Colgate Palmolive	Schlumberger	Glaxo Smith Kline	Lowe's	Anheuser-Busch
21	Kimberly-Clark	Nestlé	3M	Johnson & Johnson	Unilever	Best Buy	Texas Instruments	Hewlett-Packard	Nike	Home Depot
22	Johnson & Johnson	Ford Motor	Johnson & Johnson	Starbucks	Lockheed Martin	Unilever	Lockheed Martin	Lockheed Martin	L'Oréal	Lowe's
23	Caterpillar	Cummins	Cummins	Tesco	Inditex	Publix Super Markets	Johnson Controls	Publix Super Markets	Publix Super Markets	L'Oréal
24	Cummins	Qualcomm	Hewlett-Packard	3M	Best Buy	SonyEricsson	Royal Ahold	Paccar	Sysco	Canon
25	Nestlé	Johnson & Johnson	Kimberly-Clark	Kraft	Schlumberger	Intel	Publix Super Markets	AstraZeneca	Coca-Cola	Marks & Spencer

FIGURE 2.5   McDonald's market value, Gartner ranking and net income

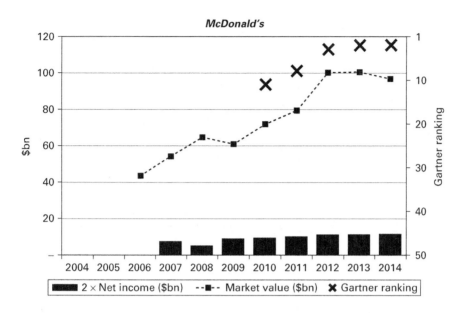

McDonald's entered the Gartner top 25 in 2010 and has risen to number 2 in the rankings behind Apple for 2013 and 2014. It was number 50 in the FT listings for 2014 by market value. Figure 2.5 shows a steady climb in market value and a corresponding climb in earnings. It is worth noting that market values have generally risen faster since the recession than earnings due to the poor returns on cash and a flight to equities, as well as bonds, which drove up values disproportionately. However, the graph shows clear visual correlations, so all is as it should be.

Amazon first appeared on the Gartner rankings at number 10 in 2010 and has been at number 2 or 3 from 2011 to 2013. As shown in Figure 2.6 its growth in market value in the same period has been meteoric. In comparison to McDonald's, its growth in market value and Gartner ranking has far outstripped its earnings growth, which over the period was essentially flat, low or negative. In the context of the analysis in Figure 2.1, Amazon's market value growth has been more tightly correlated with sales growth.

FIGURE 2.6   Amazon market value, Gartner ranking and net income

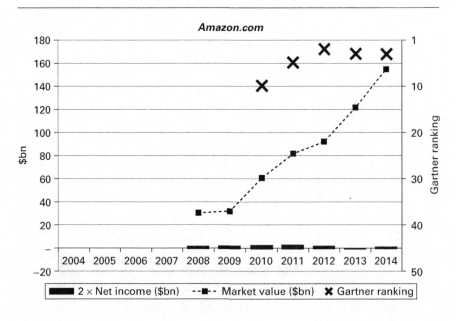

FIGURE 2.7   Dell market value, Gartner ranking and net income

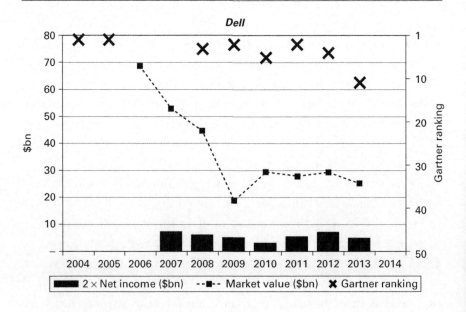

Figure 2.7 shows the performance of Dell, which ranked highly in the Gartner listings until 2013 when it fell off the scale completely. However, this lagged its decline in market value, as the chart shows, triggered by the earnings decline of 2008–10. The market value has never fully recovered albeit that the earnings trend was reversed; a situation that led to the company being taken private.

As shown in Figure 2.8, the numbers for Toyota show a rapid decline in market value preceding an earnings collapse in 2010 that corresponded to major product recalls and legal action. Market value and earnings have since recovered, but not to previous levels and the company no longer features on the Gartner rankings in spite of it being ranked number 18 in the FT 500 in 2014.

These limited analyses suggest that values and rankings may lead, lag or track earnings and revenues based on perceptions, expectations as well as macro market trends. It is also clear that the importance of perception and interpretation of a company's position cannot be understated. Mind games, a term used frequently by sporting team managers, can indeed impact competitiveness and performance alongside hard strategy.

FIGURE 2.8   Toyota market value, Gartner ranking and net income

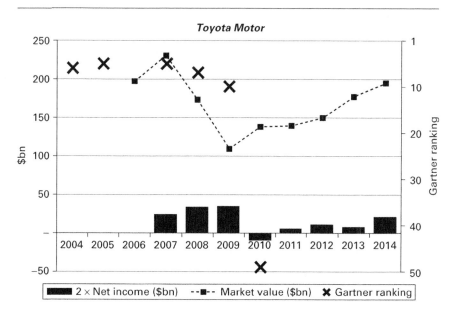

FIGURE 2.9   Inditex and H&M market value, earnings and
Gartner rankings

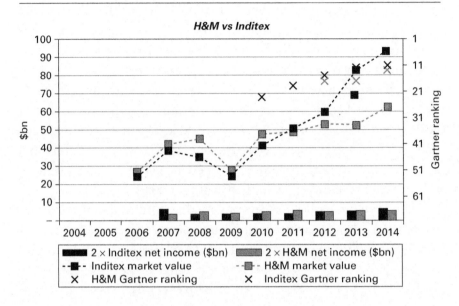

To underline this phenomenon, we looked at Inditex (the Zara holding company) and H&M – both very successful fashion retailers. Inditex featured in the FT 500 at number 76 in 2013 versus H&M at number 148. Both are ranked highly by Gartner at 12 and 17 respectively. We put the two stories together to understand their relativity in earnings and market value. This picture is shown in Figure 2.9.

The chart in Figure 2.9 shows that H&M entered the Gartner rankings only in 2012 but before that time its earnings and market value had tracked or exceeded that of Inditex. In 2013 and 2014 the market value of Inditex has powered ahead but earnings of Inditex were actually less than those of H&M in 2013; it was only overtaken in 2014. It appears that the market has consistently underestimated H&M and that Inditex/Zara has been very effective in communicating its points of difference.

The message for the boardroom from all of these examples is that ratings and rankings can apparently be perverse at many levels. However, while the formula is not consistent, empirically the fundamentals of growth, earnings and return are the key drivers on which focus should be placed. It can be difficult to manage and maintain perceptions but hard results cannot be argued with.

The five levers and the business operations model

Ram Charan in his book *What the CEO Wants You to Know* (2001) points to growth, margin and return as three of the five levers available to CEOs to enhance the value and performance of their businesses; the other two are velocity and cash. Figure 2.10 shows Charan's five levers in diagram form.

FIGURE 2.10   The five levers that the CEO cares about

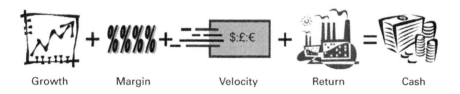

| Growth | Margin | Velocity | Return | Cash |

The impact of these levers on performance through business operations models is absolutely clear from looking at each in turn.

Growth

First, growth is important for most CEOs as the top-line revenue drives earnings and shareholder value with a significant but not dominant correlation coefficient; marketplace expectations of sales growth tend to drive elevated price earnings ratios in anticipation of increased earnings. The argument is that profit and cash will always follow, although there are some exceptions to this – as the Amazon example showed. CEOs are highly motivated by growth because it is a measure of the market acceptance of the customer proposition and the company's operational effectiveness in delivering it. A business is unlikely to grow if it is not providing compelling value to its customers, or if there are problems with its service. In Figure 1.1 (Chapter 1) this was shown as 'The customer lens – the brand proposition'. Growth is a measure of the focus of that lens; how it drives marketplace momentum through capturing share or creating entirely new demand. The business operations model sets up a successful company to face its customers through its brand positioning; in the case of Southwest Airlines their marketplace growth has been driven by compelling low prices and outstanding customer service with no frills. Super-performers get growth through giving customers great value and growing margin in parallel.

Margin

The second lever, margin, is about operating profitably and, as the earlier analysis showed, is a more crucial measure; the FT Global 500 has different leaders for revenue and profit and market valuations are more closely linked to profit than to revenues. For a business to survive and thrive it must earn the margin to give a return on the investment; super-performers achieve this through a combination of the prices they can charge and the cost-effectiveness of their operations. As a result CEOs are seriously interested in benchmarks against the competition for both gross margin and operating expenses; together these combine to give net margins, or earnings. The opportunity to create a compelling customer experience and deliver it at a profitable cost is the heart of business operations models.

Velocity

The third lever is 'velocity' and this term is used to convey the idea of the speed with which the cash and stock in the business is turned. The easiest way to represent velocity is by measuring the cash-to-cash cycle; this is the days of sale in cash terms that are locked up in the business – from the day it pays for supplies to when it gets paid by its customers, including the stock that sits in the business. The shorter the cash-to-cash cycle, the more agile and adaptable the business will be to changes in its market and the less is the risk of having to write off stock or debtors. Businesses with a short cash-to-cash cycle also require less funding for sales growth; consequently they are perceived better by the markets in terms of value. The super-performer, Inditex, has built its business operations model on speed to market, what is

TABLE 2.2   Typical sector cash-to-cash metrics by sector

Assemble-to-order computers	minus 19 days
Volume grocery	minus 8 days
Branded grocery	45 days
High-end department stores	100 days plus
Pharmaceuticals	150 days plus

called 'sketch to store'. The adaptability this gives them translates to reduced risk and increased margin.

Different sectors display quite different cash-to-cash cycles, as shown in Table 2.2. Where the cash-to-cash is negative, it means that the company is paid before it has to pay suppliers and fund the stock. The implication of a negative score is that the business can fund theoretically limitless working capital for growth.

Return on investment

This is the fourth lever and is a measure of both fixed and working capital efficiency. Measures such as return on capital employed (ROCE) and return on shareholders fund (ROSF) show how the company is returning against its invested base of buildings, equipment, vehicles, stock and net debtors together with any know-how or goodwill that it has capitalized. It is entirely possible for a company to grow in both revenue and earnings while diluting its return on investment.

Once again, the deployment of assets and their utilization is an important part of the business operations model. It is a key feature of the success of Southwest Airlines, which keeps its planes in the air for longer each day, turns the gates faster and, through equipment standardization, has less spare capacity; for Southwest Airlines, velocity drives return. Super-performers may have followed strategies of outsourcing or subcontracting asset-intensive capacity, engaging with shared services or maximizing asset utilization (these are topics to which we will return later).

Cash

This is Charan's fifth lever: 'Cash is King'. A business that is cash-generating will be generating good margins, will have excellent velocity in terms of cash-to-cash and be delivering good returns on investment. Cash is the ultimate outcome and a business that generates cash will have the capacity to invest and grow, it will be able to borrow prudently and make acquisitions. In addition, it will be able to pay substantial performance-related benefits to its executives and reward shareholders with increased dividends and share buy-backs. Super-performers have cash as well as access to cheap borrowing through bonds and bank loans; they have an established business operations model that generates cash rapidly and that in turn drives market value.

We looked earlier in this chapter at Apple as a super-performer; a report in the *Financial Times* in January 2015 emphasized the importance of cash:

> Apple shares advanced on Tuesday after an upgrade from analysts on expectations of strong sales and a boost to its cash return programme... Apple already has a $130bn capital return programme, of which $40bn is dividends and $90bn is buybacks... being returned to shareholders between 2012 and 2015.

Super-performance on the five levers is the outcome of a successful business operations model. It comes from the configuration of the blocks identified in Chapter 1 to create a unique value proposition and cost structure. It is also about exceeding the required market return for the inherent risk in the business. Capital markets make use of sophisticated statistical risk analysis of returns by sector, both to price the interest on lending and to support predictions of the share price. But we ignore the potential for apparently perverse sentiment at our peril.

Financial engineering through the business operations model

Through its business operations model, the executive team has the opportunity to engineer super-performance. There are three inter-connected perspectives available and executives can act on some or all of them: changing the risk-return profile, increasing the margin and accelerating capital velocity. The rest of this chapter looks at the opportunities to achieve this re-engineering through business operations models, applying classic financial theory and risk management. We will take forward those lessons into the cases looked at in future chapters.

Changing the risk profile in a way that either lowers the risk or increases the return on the existing risk will lead, over time, to a market revaluation. Markets value risk based on their perception of individual sectors reflecting earnings volatility and sustainability. Figure 2.11 illustrates this classic financial theory, proposing that required return is correlated with perceived risk; as the apparent risk increases so too does the requirement for a return. Even at zero risk, investors will still require a return since there is an opportunity cost involved in the investment.

Improved shareholder value can be achieved by increasing the return by more than the risk–return line, or by reducing the risk, where the return may be reduced but not proportionally to the risk–return line. Any erosion below the risk–return line will destroy market value.

This concept of value creation or erosion and its methodology for measurement was brought to prominence by the consulting firm Stern Stewart, which called it economic value added (EVA). It has been current since the mid 1980s and the methodology adopted by many hundreds of companies. The essence of EVA is that a business

FIGURE 2.11   Risk/return relationship

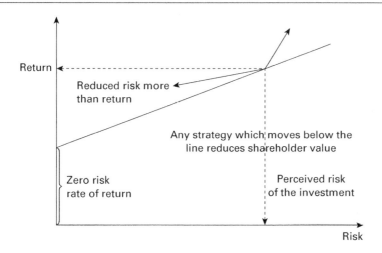

Return

Reduced risk more than return

Any strategy which moves below the line reduces shareholder value

Zero risk rate of return

Perceived risk of the investment

Risk

should return above its cost of capital for the equivalent risk; the cost of capital is the combination of debt and equity returns required by lenders and the market respectively.

The big insight is that if a company invests in a business area or project that yields below this return it will erode shareholder value and the markets will respond in due course. Conversely if a company can take specific investments off its balance sheet and onto those of suppliers who have a different risk–return ratio they can accelerate their value creation. It is this fundamental concept that has led to the boom in outsourcing.

We have used the FT Global 500 to illustrate the range of returns by sector. Figure 2.12 shows the relative market value to earnings multiples for different sectors based on the average-, upper- and

FIGURE 2.12   Value to earnings multiples by sector showing average, upper and lower quartiles

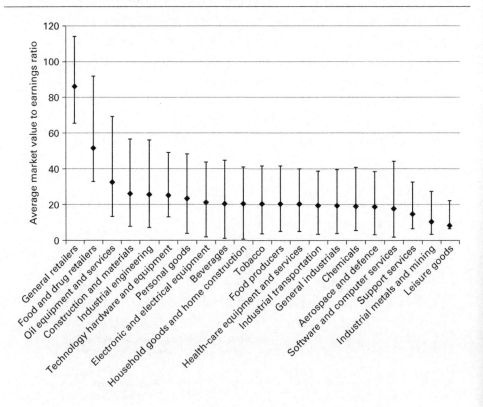

lower-quartile bands. While one might expect that the rankings would place low-risk and high-earning sectors at the upper end of market value to earnings, this is not the case. Rather it appears that the market places a premium on some combination of scale and growth potential.

Figure 2.12 shows that retailing commands a premium in the market in terms of the value–earnings ratios, along with oil equipment and industrials. At the other extreme, services, mining and leisure goods are relatively depressed. The block of sectors in the middle are relatively steady in their averages but the bands of the upper and lower quartiles show major variations. It is this variation around the averages that presents an opportunity to increase the return for the current risk or lower the market perception of risk. Companies that are in the upper quartile – and so can generate returns higher than the level of perceived risk required – are creating a 'super profit' and might be regarded as 'super-performing' companies, particularly if that premium can be sustained over a period of time. Getting into that top quartile is the goal for executive teams as they aspire to be super-performers.

Business operations models within a sector can be tailored to significantly alter the risk profile of a company. For example, companies can lock in long-term returns through contracts with market channels, reduce inventory and accelerate velocity, or cut complexity and increase focus on product and customer segments that are more reliable. These can all improve market perception of risk. The alternative of increasing return for the same risk also engages almost all the facets of the business operations model. From the perspective of return, channels to market, optimized networks and sourcing and reductions in inventory would all drive up returns for equivalent or reduced risk.

The second perspective on financial re-engineering is to improve the net margin or earnings. As we saw with the risk–return profile, this will likely increase the return for the equivalent risk; it is therefore a complementary action and this is illustrated in Figure 2.13, which shows that management teams can act on both the profit and loss (P&L) and balance sheet to increase the economic value added.

FIGURE 2.13   The determinants of economic value added

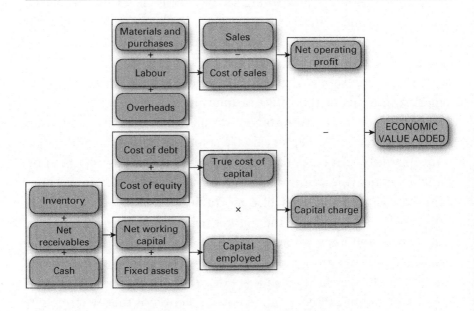

The top half of Figure 2.13 is about increasing trading margin through actions on sales and the cost of production and delivery. The lower half is about increasing capital efficiency for both fixed and working capital combined with acting on the true cost of capital. The dynamics of the model are such that quite small changes in each area can be transformational in overall performance and market value. We will return to these dynamics in Chapter 8, but it is important to note that leverage now; it is consistent with the observation from our analysis of the FT 500 listings that companies can create (or erode) super-performance in quite short timescales. The performance of some has proved to be ephemeral but the case of Southwest Airlines is one that has been sustained.

Setting aside the impact of risk and cost of capital, which are the preserves of the markets and the finance team, operations teams can act directly on the return on investment of their companies through the selection and design of the business operations model. This is a subset of Figure 2.13 and is illustrated in Figure 2.14 together with the drivers of the business operations model.

FIGURE 2.14   Improving return on investment

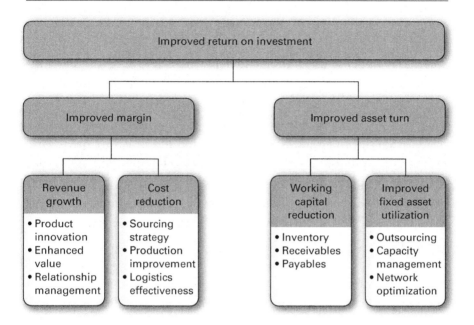

The left block in Figure 2.14 is revenue growth, which is one of the five things the CEO really cares about (as we saw in Figure 2.10). In business operations model terms this can be secured through a compelling customer offer and experience, which is at the top of our business operations model (Figure 1.2 in Chapter 1) (the customer lens is the focus of Chapter 3). Innovative products and services, delivered with excellence at compelling prices, are the key to accelerated growth; the Southwest Airlines case showed this (we will describe further cases in future chapters).

Margin is the outcome of revenues less costs; as we saw earlier it is somewhat more important for CEOs than revenue growth. In business operations model terms every area is available for acting on operating costs: channels, optimized networks and sourcing, mastering complexity, service and support, inventory management excellence, and securing excellent productivity and efficiency by managing the basics. Once again, the Southwest Airlines case showed that the company has achieved standout performance by focusing on the direct channel, reducing route and schedule complexity, optimizing its network to increase asset utilization and standardizing its sourcing. It also achieved outstanding productivity through its aircraft and gate turn-around times.

On the asset turn side, the business operations model can act on inventory and working capital through mastering complexity and variety, inventory segmentation and deployment and excellent demand–supply planning. Reduced inventory and accelerated debtors (receivables) turns improves the cash-to-cash cycle for the business and increases its velocity, hence enabling increased responsiveness because there is less capacity in the balance sheet measured in terms of time. It also reduces the potential for financial waste through margin erosion due to discounts and deals (a topic we deal with in Chapter 8). Our experience is that the opportunity cost of margin erosion due to pricing and clearance actions is the biggest hidden cost in many sectors.

Finally the company can turn its assets faster through how it runs, sources and funds its operational system. As observed earlier, this is both an operational excellence opportunity as well as an investment and risk mitigation measure. In the context of the CEO's levers it is about return but it also feeds back to margin and the potential for growth. The opportunities through the business operations model are to outsource, balance capacity with inventory holding, master complexity and manage the basics. As we saw in the Southwest Airlines case, they keep their aeroplanes in the air for longer and turn their gates faster.

A combination of growth, margin improvement, enhanced turn in both working capital and fixed assets drives better return on investment and generates cash, which is the CEO's fifth lever. Opportunities are available through the business operations model to act on every element of performance – and can be transformational. Super-performance makes the company a disruptor as it provides the opportunity to price for further growth and competitor destabilization.

Super-performers can be disruptors

The financial dimension of super-performers is where it starts and stops in terms of market value and perceived potential, and we have started to link those outcomes to operations through the drivers noted in Figures 2.13 and 2.14. Super-performance comes from driving up revenues, driving down cost (and hence margin up) while reducing the assets to achieve that and reducing levels of risk. Saying it so briefly might make it appear easy; but if this was so then everyone would be doing it. In terms of our business operations model it is about the ability to deliver superior customer value at less cost than the competition – and we will be unpacking that idea through subsequent chapters.

Our analysis on the characteristics of super-performers has shown that:

- Market value is the essence of corporate performance – the ultimate judgement of corporate effectiveness.

- Successful value creators and market disruptors can increase value in remarkably short time frames.

- Such increases are the result of a combination of market valuation and perceptions of performance of potential.

- Value can be sustained or ephemeral. The theory is empirical and apparently there can be perverse exceptions. As we saw from the analysis earlier in this chapter and the stock price graph of Southwest Airlines in Chapter 1, returns are not uniform and companies' fortunes wax and wane.

- Companies' business operations models touch every aspect of potential improvement.

Many commentators and researchers have sought to explain the reasons why some companies succeed and others do not. Whilst there are as many viewpoints as there are books and papers published on this topic, there is broad agreement on the fundamental requirements for the creation of profitable and sustainable businesses. These align to our business operations model.

First, these companies will have a compelling value proposition aimed at carefully defined target markets. By 'value proposition' we mean the intended customer benefits that are delivered through products and services. Compelling value propositions offer the promise (and the reality) of delivering superior solutions to customers' 'problems'. Whilst the 'problems' may not change that much over time, the way those problems are solved does change as product and service innovation make obsolete the previous solutions. A fundamental requirement for successful disruptive solutions is a well-executed set of processes that provide the operational support for the delivery of the value proposition. It is generally the case that most successful companies have strong value propositions underpinned by carefully designed and well-executed operational procedures. Companies such as Apple, for example, have succeeded not just because they have excellent products but because those excellent products are underpinned by world-class supply chain processes.

The challenge, therefore, to any business is to recognize the opportunities that arise to disrupt established solutions and their delivery mechanisms. As we show throughout this book, business operations models can be a fresh perspective for executives on how they can become disruptors.

Taking forward the framework in your business

This chapter has focused on the money. In the end that is the scorecard that pays the salaries and dividends, and against which a business can borrow in order to grow. From the signposts in this chapter, here are our suggested steps to start to understand the financial implications of your business operations model:

- Draw the trajectory of sales and earnings for as far back as the data is available (and share price or market value if available).
- Describe the key events that have caused changes in the terms of the business operations model framework.
- Alongside growth and margin, identify how the business is performing on the five levers and how that benchmarks against competitors in your sector.
- Step through the determinants of economic value added to identify where the greatest leverage lies in order to close any benchmark gaps identified.
- Develop a narrative for superior performance from closing the gap based on actions across the business operations model.

The customer lens – understanding compelling value

In Chapter 1 we observed that a business is nothing without its customers and customers are not stupid. They make sophisticated choices on the value they receive in the context of their purchase. The customer lens on the brand proposition is the pinnacle of the business operations model concept and the top segment of our framework. The Southwest Airlines example in Chapter 1 shows that the company has managed to combine low prices with service excellence that has driven exceptional growth and made them a long-term disruptor. In Chapter 2 we identified that sales growth at good margins is central to super-performance, which in turn is financially driven by customer attraction to the brand proposition and the value obtained by customers.

To be a disruptor, a company must listen to the voice of the customer and craft a compelling value proposition. This chapter provides perspectives and cases on how to understand and develop brand identities that can disrupt markets.

Companies compete through the creation and delivery of value to customers. That value can be defined in a number of ways but, at its simplest, customer value is created when the perceptions of the benefits to be received from a transaction or relationship exceed the total costs of ownership. One way to express this idea is as a ratio:

Customer value = perceived benefits / total cost of ownership

'Total cost of ownership' reflects the fact that in most transactions and commercial relationships the life-cycle cost will be significant in relation to the initial price. For example, when buying a car customers will be concerned about the fuel economy, the insurance rating, the taxation class, the tyre wear and the cost of maintenance; they will also be concerned about the resale value and the depreciation on their initial investment.

The perceived benefits are context sensitive and experiential as well as practical and tangible. The brand 'experience' is what attracts customers and leads to repeat purchases. This is about service and the conditions of supply, including the aura of the buying experience. Benefits go beyond the 'hard' tangible features of a product or service to include the 'softer' intangibles: for example, the brand name or reputation of the manufacturer or supplier.

Figure 3.1 develops this concept of customer value as a ratio of benefits to total costs. It makes the point that consumers and customers balance the economic and the perceptual in their purchase decisions.

FIGURE 3.1   The determinants of customer value

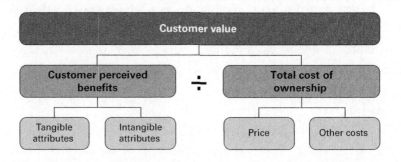

For any business to become a disruptor and super-performer in its sector, it must be able to create and deliver demonstrably more customer perceived value than its competitors. This can be achieved by either enhancing the perceived benefits or by reducing the total cost of ownership – or preferably both. It is the customers' perception of benefits that is critical; sometimes the customer may not share the same view of a benefit as the supplier and equally customers will probably differ, one to the other, in the attributes to which they attach value.

In seeking to gain competitive advantage, companies need to pay attention both to enhancing the perceived benefits derived from the offer as well as to the total costs of ownership that will be incurred by the customer. The likelihood that any company will win the sale, over a competitor, comes down to whether the customer perceives their offer to deliver a higher ratio of benefits to cost than the competitor's offer. Our experience is that customers will generally balance the price against their perception of the benefits, which includes whether their own costs in the transaction will be mitigated; the underlying question for suppliers is what benefits their customers value most and how they value them.

The fundamental change in almost all markets since the late 1970s has been that acceptable product quality, serviceability and cost of ownership has become 'normal'; markets have acquired the capacity to supply, so there is mostly no longer a shortage of choice. Markets have become more mature, trending to commoditized; as a result, buyers rather than sellers hold the power. So, the tangible benefits of the product, which make up say 80 per cent of the costs, are often not the decisive buying factor; it is the intangibles of service, experience, brand and ease of doing business that are the things that clinch the deal. These may only be 20 per cent of the costs to deliver the service but they make all the difference and effectively lower the total cost of ownership.

We have identified two underlying trends that typify current markets: 1) the emergence of the 'time-sensitive' customer; 2) customers buying 'performance' rather than products.

The 'time-sensitive' customer

Over the last few decades it has become apparent that customers are becoming increasingly time-sensitive. These time-sensitive customers can be found in every type of market, be it in high-tech markets where short life cycles demand short lead times, or in consumer durable manufacturing where just-in-time assembly requires just-in-time deliveries, or in everyday living where the pressures of managing a more complex, hectic lifestyle have led us to seek convenience in our retail shopping habits.

In these types of market environments, the winners will be those organizations that can respond more quickly to customers' requirements. To enable response times to be compressed in this way requires a strong emphasis on reducing lead times through the business operations model – particularly the time taken from when the customer need is first indicated to when that need can be fulfilled. Reduced lead times and increased demand responsiveness reduce customers' total cost of ownership; for example, this may come through eliminating their opportunity costs of being out of stock, by reducing their inventory holding and by avoiding the need to have costly administrative and control processes.

Paradoxically, companies that have learnt to do things faster often find that their costs also reduce as they eliminate activities that were not adding value; we will return to this as a business operations model design theme in Chapter 8.

Performance rather than products

Many years ago one of the founding fathers of modern marketing, Theodore Levitt, made the point that 'customers don't buy products, they buy benefits'. This simple idea has been the platform for success for companies as diverse as Procter & Gamble, Amazon and Rolls-Royce. Indeed all of the financial winners identified in Chapter 2 would be best described as selling a combination of tangible and intangible benefits alongside the physical product. What companies like these have learned is that customers seek solutions to 'problems' – indeed some marketing commentators talk about the buying process as 'problem-solving behaviour'.

Bigger, more powerful customers have become more demanding, particularly in terms of service. They are looking to suppliers for customized solutions, more frequent and just-in-time deliveries, lower transaction costs and, of course, they do not want to pay more for these services. This increased pressure on suppliers has meant that they have had to focus hard on improving their own business operations models to enable better service to be offered at lower cost.

As that competition has intensified, a growing number of companies have sought to differentiate themselves by developing this idea and increasingly are bundling services and products to focus on customer outcomes and total cost of ownership. This process, which is sometimes known as 'servitization', has led to the emergence of performance-based contracts whereby the supplier commits to deliver an agreed level of performance – and the customer doesn't necessarily ever own the product, they simply pay for the benefits they receive. Perhaps the most widely quoted example of this is the concept of 'power-by-the-hour' developed by Rolls-Royce for the marketing of aero engines. The principle underpinning this idea is that customers, primarily airlines, will pay only for every hour the engine is performing and when the engine is needed. Rolls-Royce, or its agents, are responsible for delivering that performance and the costs and investment involved. Clearly there are significant business operations model implications involved in such arrangements; channels to market, optimized fulfilment, service and support, inventory deployment, and managing the basics all come into play.

Fundamentally, the distinction between 'what is a product' and 'what is a service' has become blurred and, some might say, less relevant. Again, this is a theme to which we will return in later chapters, introducing the work of distinguished US marketing academics Stephen Vargo and Robert Lusch, and their idea of service-dominant logic as a design approach to being a disruptor.

Listening to the voice of the customer

Sam Walton, the founder of Walmart, is famously quoted as saying:

Rule 1 – the customer is always right.

Rule 2 – if the customer is wrong, refer to rule 1.

Walmart has been a regular Global 500 top 10 performer with the exception of 2011, so they must be doing it right in terms of their customers. But even a business the size of Walmart cannot be everything to everyone – the brand has to speak to its market through the delivery 'system' or business operations model in a way that customers know what to expect and self-select.

So the questions are: 'How do we identify what customers will find a compelling value proposition? What exactly drives their buying decisions?' A structured analytical process to understand customers' preferences is a vital starting point. It is the core theme of this chapter and we will show how to go about eliciting customer preferences and priorities. On the basis of 'what gets measured – gets managed', identifying both customer preferences and how they make choices is the starting point for every business operations model. Companies that can understand the 'order-winning' criteria that must be met if a sale is to be made can begin to define the business operations model changes that will make the company a disruptor; alternatively, as a minimum every company needs to know what it will have to do consistently well if it is to become the supplier of choice.

Markets are rarely homogeneous, with similar needs, requirements and preferences. Instead, what typically exists is a set of submarkets or segments that are homogeneous within each segment but will quite likely differ considerably in characteristics with other segments. A classic marketing strategy is to target a limited number of segments and to design specific marketing programmes for each segment; clearly, each may require its own unique business operations model focused on the needs of the customers within the segment.

The same principle applies to value segmentation: not all our customers value the same things or require the same level of service within a market or submarket. The challenge is therefore to understand what the different value preferences are amongst their customer base within and across markets. With that insight and knowledge, companies can craft appropriate value propositions and value delivery processes. Figure 3.2 proposes a systematic approach to developing a strategy for value delivery based on an objective assessment of customer needs and market segmentation.

We will work through each of the five steps in turn.

Step 1 – understand value preferences

The only way to understand customer value preferences is through detailed research. The first step in research of this type is to identify the sources of influence upon the purchase decision. For example, if we are selling components to a manufacturer, the question to ask is: who will make the decision on the source of supply? This is not always an easy question to answer as in many cases there will be several stakeholders involved. For example, the purchasing manager of the

FIGURE 3.2   Understanding and aligning to the voice of the customer

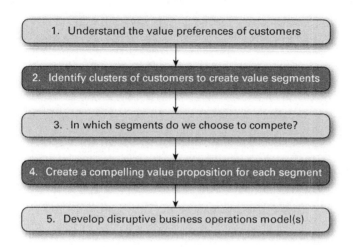

1. Understand the value preferences of customers

2. Identify clusters of customers to create value segments

3. In which segments do we choose to compete?

4. Create a compelling value proposition for each segment

5. Develop disruptive business operations model(s)

company to which we are selling may only be acting as an agent for others within the firm, whilst in some cases this manager's influence will be much greater. Alternatively, if we are manufacturing products for sale through retail outlets, is the decision to stock made centrally by a retail chain or by individual store managers? The answer can often be supplied by the sales team, who should know from experience who are the decision makers and be able to elicit their preferences. In contrast, retailers have a broader and more amorphous challenge in identifying customers' priorities and preferences, which are often captured by store exit interviews or online questionnaires. For retailers, the issue with such work is the speed with which customers can change their priorities, as the Tesco example in Chapter 1 showed.

Ideally, once the decision-making dynamics in a specific market have been identified an initial, small-scale, research programme should be initiated based upon personal interviews with a representative sample of buyers. The purpose of these interviews is to elicit, in the language of the customer, firstly the importance they attach to customer service vis-à-vis the other marketing mix elements such as price, product quality, promotion etc, and secondly, the individual components of customer service that they value and the specific importance they attach to each.

TABLE 3.1   Typical service factors

Service factors in the buying decision	
Industrial markets	**Retail consumers**
Price	Price
Quality	Quality
Order complete on time	Availability in store and online
Availability and stock visibility	Delivery options
Delivery lead time	Delivery speed
Invoice accuracy	Delivery reliability
Ease of ordering	Service charges
Expediting capabilities	Returns processing
Packaging and presentation	Credit account reliability
Special services	Responsiveness
Claims and complaint handling	Brand image
......	Retail environment
	Packaging

The key to this initial step to measuring customer service is that relevant and meaningful measures of customer service are proposed by the customers themselves. Table 3.1 shows a typical menu of selection criteria for both industrial and retail customers and from this it is quickly apparent that many of the factors overlap even if the performance measures attaching are different. With these dimensions defined, we can move on to identify the relative importance of each and the extent to which different types of customer are prepared to trade-off one aspect of service for another.

A simple way to discover the importance a customer attaches to each element of customer service is to take the components generated by means of the process above and ask a representative sample of customers to rank order them from the 'most important' to the 'least important'. This can be difficult, particularly with a large number of components, and does not give any insight into the relative importance of each element and how a selection decision would involve trade-offs. Alternatively a form of rating scale can be used. For example, the respondents could be asked to place a weight from 1 to 10 against each component according to how much importance they attach to each element. The problem here is that respondents often tend to rate most of the components as highly important. A partial solution is to ask the respondents to allocate a total of 100 points amongst all the elements listed, according to perceived importance. However, this is a fairly daunting task for the respondents and can often result in an arbitrary allocation or partial answers.

An innovation in consumer research technology now enables a deeper understanding of the psychology of customer choice; it exposes quite simply the implicit importance that a customer attaches to the separate elements of the purchase decision. The technique is a statistical one called conjoint analysis. It is based around the concept of trade-off and helps to determine how people value product and service attributes and their benefits (such as features and functions). A set of products and/or services is given to respondents; by analysis of their preferences, their motivations become apparent.

It can best be illustrated by an example from everyday life, say, the purchase of a new car. When we start our search, we might desire specific attributes such as performance in terms of speed and acceleration, economy in terms of petrol consumption, size in terms of passenger and luggage capacity and, of course, low price. However, it is unlikely that any one car will meet all of these requirements so we are forced to trade-off one or more of these attributes against the others.

The same is true for the customer faced with the alternative options of almost any brand proposition. The buyer might be prepared to sacrifice a day or two on lead time in order to gain delivery reliability, or to trade-off order completeness against improvements in order entry, or to pay a higher price for delivery speed and reliability, and so on. Essentially, the trade-off technique works by offering the respondent feasible combinations of proposition elements and asking for a specific preference for those combinations.

This is so important that we offer a simple example where a respondent is asked to choose between different levels of stock availability, order cycle time and delivery reliability. For the example, the following options are presented:

Stock availability:	75 per cent
	85 per cent
	95 per cent
Order cycle time:	2 days
	3 days
	4 days
Delivery reliability:	1 day
	3 days

The various trade-offs can be placed before the respondent as a series of matrices as shown in Figure 3.3.

Respondents complete each matrix to illustrate his/her preference for service alternatives. Thus, with the first trade-off matrix between order cycle time and stock availability, it is presumed that the most preferred combination would be an order cycle time of two days with a stock availability of 95 per cent, and the least preferred combination

FIGURE 3.3   An example of the conjoint preference analysis process

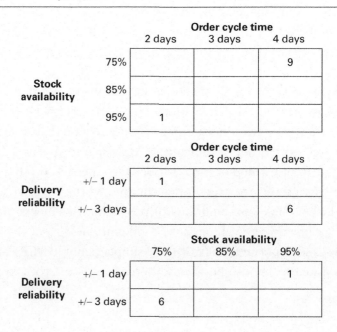

FIGURE 3.4   A completed conjoint analysis table

		Order cycle time		
		2 days	3 days	4 days
	75%	6	8	9
Stock availability	85%	3	5	7
	95%	1	2	4

		Order cycle time		
		2 days	3 days	4 days
	+/– 1 day	1	3	5
Delivery reliability	+/– 3 days	2	4	6

		Stock availability		
		75%	85%	95%
	+/– 1 day	4	2	1
Delivery reliability	+/– 3 days	6	5	3

an order cycle time of five days with a stock availability of 75 per cent. But what about the other combinations? Here the respondent is asked to complete the matrix to show his/her own preferences. An example of a typical response is given in Figure 3.4.

Using computer analysis the implicit 'importance weightings' that underlie the initial preference rankings can be generated. For the data in the simple example given above, the relative weightings in Table 3.2 emerge.

For the hypothetical respondent shown in Table 3.2, stock availability would appear to be marginally more important than delivery time and both are in the region of twice as important as delivery reliability. This information can give us vital insights into customer preferences and hence guide proposition design. For example, in this example, a stock availability of 85 per cent with 2 days' delivery and a reliability of ± 1 day is seen as being equally acceptable as a 95 per cent availability with 2 days' delivery and ± 3 days reliability (a combined weight of 0.695 compared with 0.697). Thus, this suggests that

TABLE 3.2   Customer-relative priority weightings

Service element	Importance weighting	
(1) Stock availability	75%	−0.48
	85%	0
	95%	0.48
(2) Delivery time	2 days	0.456
	3 days	0
	4 days	−0.456
(3) Delivery reliability	± 1 day	0.239
	± 3 days	−0.239

a tightening up on reliability might reduce stockholding and still provide an acceptable level of customer service.

Step 2 – identify customer value segments

Having determined the importance attached by different respondents to each of the service attributes previously identified, it is then important to understand if any groupings of similarities of preference emerge. For example, if one group of respondents have a clearly distinct set of priorities as compared to another, then it would be reasonable to think of them both as different service segments.

These segments can be identified using cluster analysis, which is a computer-based method for looking across a set of data and seeking to 'match' respondents across as many dimensions as possible. Thus if two respondents completed the trade-off matrices in a very similar way their importance scores on the various service dimensions would be similar and hence the cluster analysis would assign them to the same group. The data can be inspected to understand the customer characteristics that are represented, but it is worth noting that the service preferences may cut across traditional channel organization.

For example, a study of buyers of strip steel products found that there were a number of distinct value segments that cut across traditional industry classifications. For example, there was a 'just-in-time' segment whose primary concern was short and reliable order to delivery times; another segment that primarily was driven by technical issues such as special finishes; and, of course, there was a segment comprising buyers who were driven primarily by price.

Step 3 – choose where to compete

With these hard insights on the voice of the customer, the third question is choosing where to compete. Through the conjoint and cluster analysis, we understand the relative weighting of the 'order winners' in each of the identified segments but the company may not have the capabilities in their business operations model to compete in a specified segment. For example, in the just-in-time (JIT) segment the company may need to work out what is required to enable it to deliver highly reliable, on-time, in-full responses to customer requirements – and to do this consistently in a way superior to competitors.

It is generally unlikely that any one company will have the resources or the capabilities to try to compete effectively in all identified value segments. Successful companies are usually those who focus and concentrate their firepower on a limited number of value segments. For example, in Chapter 7 we tell the story of Dell whose first foray into the retail channel failed; value segments are often organized by channels, and channels and their economics are a key vertical in the business operations model. The generic observation is that the organization and style of a company is strongly influenced by its channel culture. The idea of 'strategic intent' is consistent with the imperative to focus (this is unpacked in Chapter 4).

Step 4 – create a compelling value proposition for each segment

The fourth step of creating compelling value propositions is so much clearer with a view of the world through the customer lens and a well-developed brand and service proposition. Ideally, companies should seek to invest in developing the competencies that would enable them to dominate their chosen value segments, remembering the need to continuously explore the opportunities for developing innovative and customized solutions within its market focus.

At its core, the idea behind a 'brand value and service proposition' is simple. Potential customers need to be given good reasons (perhaps one or two core reasons but with other influencing factors) as to why they should buy your product or service rather than another. We have often been surprised to find that companies' value propositions are not well articulated or understood within the business and that the marketplace values some quite different things to those valued inside the business. So-called mission statements that incorporate statements such as 'we want to be easy to do business with' or 'our products will have superior functionality' are unsatisfactory as they are impossible to contradict; they lack any description or measures around what is intended.

In order to formulate more tangible value propositions, the challenge is to be able to determine the impact that they will have on customers' businesses or on their individual lives in relation to the price they are prepared to pay. These choices in terms of brand positioning are reflected in the 'zone of competitive advantage' as illustrated in Figure 3.5. In essence the diagram illustrates the idea that a company can reduce the relative perceived cost by either reducing the price for the same benefits or increasing the benefits for the same price, or both would

FIGURE 3.5   The zone of competitive advantage

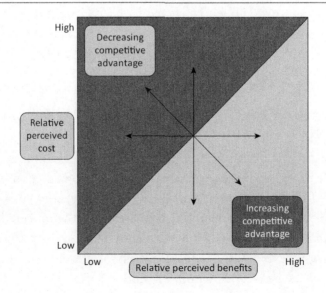

be even better. On occasions the direct price can even be increased if that adds even greater value to customers.

Clearly, this will involve appropriate value propositions for each segment and these will need to be actionable and deliverable. For them to be compelling, they must offer solutions and experiences that are clearly superior to those offered by competitors. At the end of the chapter we describe two cases that show the nuanced and detailed considerations that go with crafting compelling value propositions.

Step 5 – develop the value delivery processes to meet the goals set

The final step in our framework is about developing the value delivery processes to be able to meet the goals that have been set. This is where the pillars of our business operations model support operational design. Every super-performer competes through their capabilities. It is the vital linkage that is so often overlooked and the core thesis of this book.

The value proposition defines the nature and the shape of the underpinning business processes. Taking the example of Walmart, its value proposition is often summarized as 'everyday low prices'. To enable Walmart to deliver that proposition at a profit has required it to develop a supply chain that is able to put products on their shelves at a lower cost than most of their competitors. For this reason Walmart has consistently invested in processes and information systems that have enabled it to strip out inventories by working closely with key suppliers, and through its distribution system has implemented highly effective continuous replenishment processes.

Another good example of designing supply chain processes to enable the delivery of a compelling value proposition is provided by Dell, the computer company. Dell achieved a significant share of the global market for computers and peripherals by offering its customers a degree of product customization at a very competitive lead time from order to delivery. Dell can do this because it has created a highly synchronized supply chain whereby key suppliers are physically co-located close to Dell's assembly operations and share critical demand information across aligned business processes. As already mentioned, we tell the story of Dell in full in Chapter 7; the advantage of this model was that it gave them disruptor status, but it has become less compelling for customers in recent years.

We will return to these cases and others in later chapters. To complete our examination of the process of seeing value through the customer lens and creating tangible definitions for compelling propositions, the following case studies provide hard examples of the process from our own experience. The first is for an industrial supply chain – supplying fertilizers to farmers in Ireland. The second is a retail case looking at how customers perceive value in their e-commerce and store retail purchases. Both are grounded on detailed research and show the value of the approach.

CASE STUDY   Irish Fertilizers

This company was producing and delivering more than 700,000 tonnes of fertilizers to farmers across Ireland. With two plants providing different formulations, it held around 50 per cent of the market and was maintaining a premium price in the marketplace of about 10 per cent with a price per tonne of €110. This position was coming under increasing pressure from lower-cost competitors; so the company was understandably concerned to protect its share and price point in the face of incoming competition from across Europe. The company commissioned competitive research using the techniques described earlier in order to understand how its customers were making choices, what they thought of the business and where performance was below par. The management team wanted an objective assessment of its standing and what its customers really valued.

The fertilizer market in Ireland had some remarkable characteristics. First, the market consists of thousands of customers with many small farms working almost entirely with grass farming for livestock; their demand is on average below five tonnes per farm per year. These farms typically have no space to store the five pallets of product that this represents in conditions where the product will not be damaged by moisture. As a result the farmers depend on local wholesalers, often co-ops, to have the product available when they want to collect it to spread on their fields. And the season for the application of fertilizers is very short – perhaps only three weeks in spring and two weeks in early autumn, which extends the grass-producing life of their fields into winter.

So the profile of demand for the company was an extreme peak of final sales to farmers in spring and a smaller peak in autumn, supplied almost entirely through wholesalers and distributors because of the small volumes per customer. In contrast, the company's plants would produce and stockpile throughout the year and distribute to the wholesalers and co-ops in advance of the season; so the sales and distribution peak was focused entirely on the first four months of the year, getting product into the market at regional and customers' depots in time for the spring peak. The strategy was to maintain close relationships with the distribution channel and to also pull through the product by providing technical and agricultural advice to the farmers through a field support team. The internal values of the company really emphasized the importance of this direct contact with the farmer in order to give them advice and to reinforce the brand with the wholesalers to pull sales through.

The process of conjoint analysis described earlier elicited that customers' priorities were rather different from the company's internal view and this is shown in Table 3.3.

The company and the customers agreed on the number one priority, which was product quality, and this reflected a history of bad experience in the market with other suppliers, but not the company itself. If the product is badly produced or stored then the fertilizer granules become 'hard clumps' and these damage the blades in the farmers' tractor-mounted spreaders. The cost and time for farmers

TABLE 3.3   The customer and company lenses on the brand proposition

Rank	What the customer valued	What the company valued
1	Quality product	Quality product
2	Price	Technical support
3	Availability	Dealing with queries
4	Speed of delivery	Invoicing and delivery accuracy
5	Packaging	Price
6	Dealing with queries	Availability
7	Invoicing and delivery accuracy	Speed of delivery
8	Technical support	Packaging

to replace these during a very short spreading season was certainly greater than the price premium being paid for the product for the five tonnes or less (say €50). So the farmers were buying based on the 'total cost of ownership' approach and their perception of risk: the buying trade-offs that we introduced earlier. Furthermore, they thought that technical support was not needed and that packaging could be improved. These insights were a sobering message for the company in terms of its investments and organization.

The research went on to elicit how the company was rated against its main competitors based on the customers' priorities. The results of this are shown in Figure 3.6.

On a scale of plus four to minus four, with zero not being an allowable score, the company scored above its competitors only on quality (which customers valued) and technical support (which they did not). The implications were that a recognized and reported improvement in quality in the market by the competition

FIGURE 3.6   How the fertilizer company rated against its competitors on their preferences

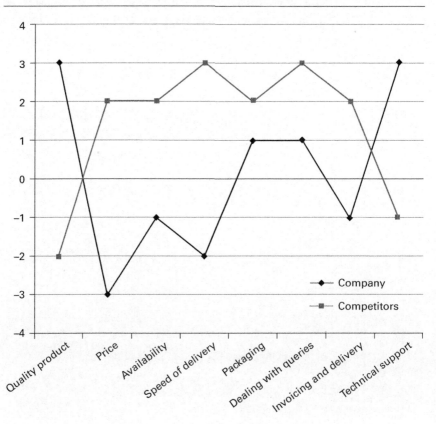

at the lower price would quickly lead to market-share erosion unless the other factors could be enhanced.

Referring back to the business operations model framework, survival would depend on coordinated changes in optimized fulfilment networks, service and support, inventory deployment and managing the basics. The calculation was that these could save around €7.50 per tonne of the €10 per tonne price difference and would close the service gap. The company took assertive actions based on the research.

However, the company was tied to two ageing plants and costly feedstock, whereas the competitors had a lower-cost sourcing and manufacturing platform in their business operations model. This gave the competition further headroom to reduce their pricing when it had fixed the largely perceptual quality issue. As a result the company is no longer in business – they were disrupted by low-cost producers in a commodity market and their defensive measures were insufficient. It is impossible to tell if an earlier understanding of the customers' preferences and trade-offs would have enabled them to counter the lower-cost producers.

CASE STUDY   e-commerce delivery models

The growth in e-commerce retailing has been inexorable with overall penetration rising to 15 per cent in the UK and forecast to grow further to as much as 25 per cent by 2020. In contrast, sales through conventional retail outlets have been flatlining or declining. The retail market has polarized into three segments: 'pureplay' online retailers who have no physical high-street presence, 'clicks and mortar' retailers who are selling both online and through stores; and traditional retailers such as discount food and pound shops who cannot make money from an online delivery model.

The 'pureplay' segment is dominated by Amazon and eBay for which low online pricing and quick deliveries are the typical brand face; indeed online pricing has set the commercial reference for the whole retail market. From an operations point of view it is broadly the same cost-to-serve through the 'pureplay' and direct retail channels; the challenge for the 'clicks and mortar' operators is that they have to maintain their store space while adding the costs of direct delivery to customers. This is eroding margins through their growth channel without reducing costs in the stores. As a result 'clicks and mortar' retailers are trying to clearly define their points of difference with customers and their brand propositions for both online and store services.

FIGURE 3.7   Increased customer acceptance under different speed and price scenarios

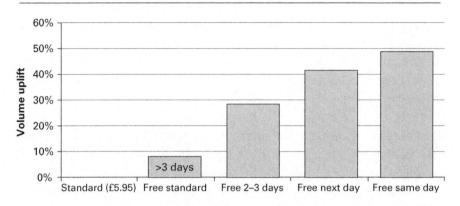

On this journey, the first discovery has been that customers who shop both in stores and online are more valuable to the company by a factor of three to eight times. Linking the online and store experiences in a seamless way is critical as footfall in stores drives additional sales. Customers express a strong preference to be able to interact with the retailers both online and in store for the same purchase, without transactional barriers: for example, buy online and return via store.

The second discovery is that customers don't like to pay extra for delivery and they specify faster delivery if there is no extra cost. Figure 3.7 shows some research into sales uplifts based on delivery cost and speed for durables. (The reader should note that this research was in a specific category context and was time specific – generalizations from this may not be safe!)

The additional costs of this growth are potentially very high and the commercial viability of the business operations model breaks down, as margin erosion for the online offer will be significant. Many clicks and mortar retailers have tried to mitigate this and increase store footfall by channelling customers to 'click and collect' services from stores. This is a much lower cost option and can be organized for next day collection. But the research shows that a significant proportion of customers choose 'click and collect' because it is free and only relatively convenient; given a zero cost for the delivery many would select the 'home' option. A major customer concern is the reliability of the home delivery experience, for example in the event that they are not at home to receive the package. For those customers, there is a perceived 'cost' from having to wait at home and/or organize another delivery event. These insights, together with recent additional customer research, point to something of a conundrum:

- Low cost mostly eclipses greater speed.

- Greater reliability mostly eclipses greater speed.

- Lower cost mostly eclipses greater reliability... and customers will make arrangements to select the most reliable and low-cost option for themselves.

The reality is that customers want it both free and super-reliable but have learnt to anticipate and compensate for unreliability by selecting the service option that is least inconvenient, in their own context. It appears that as the e-commerce market evolves and services become more reliable, customers are constantly redrawing their preferences, based on their changing perceptions and experience. For the present, retailers need to craft their core proposition around low-cost (or zero-cost) click and collect with 99.99 per cent reliability. It is these two factors that drive commercial viability. Retailers then must find ways to stamp their personality on the experience through things such as communication, packaging, returns services, gifts and the like.

Retailers' business operating models are crucial to this changing picture, with the brand proposition driving the entire commercial viability and execution engaging every single vertical in our business operations model framework.

In conclusion to our discussion of the customer lens on the brand proposition, the principle of conjoint analysis to understand the trade-offs that customers are making is crucial to building a successful and disruptive business operations model. The 'voice of the customer' needs to drive everything the company does – in order to position its brand and deliver enhanced value to its clientele. As the case studies show, it is easy to be seduced by your own self-image of the brand (the fertilizer case) or the prospect of rapid growth (in the case of retail e-commerce). Perhaps objectivity is the hardest thing to achieve when there is so much personal emotion invested in the things companies have learnt and done well over the years. The viral communications of social media platforms have the potential to neutralize such heritage in short order, but also provide instant access to the voice of the customer – listen constantly!

Taking forward the framework in your business

This chapter focused on understanding the nature of compelling value, through the lens of the customer. It is the foundation of every business operations model; it is what the company does for its customers who then drive revenue and margin. Without clear focus on what giving value looks like for the business, there can be no clarity of the model.

From the signposts in this chapter, here are our suggested steps to start to understand what value means to your customers as the key input to your business operations model:

- Even if you think you know, do the research to identify the value preferences. Use conjoint analysis if you can and discover how you stand against your competition in the market.

- Use those answers to develop the narrative as to where you need to improve and where you are vulnerable to improvements by the competition.

- Think about how customers apply your product or service and how radical changes to your proposition could transform their value chains and leapfrog the competition – develop scenarios for use later in the process.

- Once again, you need a narrative that describes the journey that you need to go through, covering improvements in both service and price to become compelling.

- Referring back to the conclusions from your analysis in Chapter 2, quantify the step changes that you will have to make in pricing, cost and hence margin in order to become a leader or, better still, a disruptor. Hold those quantum estimates for development in later stages.

The strategy operations gap 04

Business strategy is something of a holy grail for executives; the need to know where you are going and how you are going to get there is crucially important to mounting any effort to introduce change. But a search of the literature and across the internet shows that business strategy is not a clearly defined concept. Goals, means, horizons and priorities all jostle for attention – as these example quotes show:

> *Strategy is about getting from where you are now to a place where it is worthwhile being. Strategy is also about getting there through competitive advantage, with least difficulty and in least time.*
>
> Tony Grundy (1995) – academic, international
> strategy consultant and author

> *The essence of strategy is choosing what not to do.*
>
> Michael Porter (1980) – a professor at Harvard Business School and
> one of the world's leading thinkers on strategy

> *Success doesn't necessarily come from breakthrough innovation but from flawless execution. A great strategy alone won't win a game or a battle; the win comes from basic blocking and tackling.*
>
> Naveen Jain (2012) – entrepreneur and business executive
> (cited in Gladwell, 2009)

> *A strategy is something like, an innovative new product; globalization, taking your products around the world; be the low-cost producer. A strategy is something you can touch; you can motivate people with; be number one and number two in every business. You can energize people around the message.*
>
> Jack Welch (2005) – former CEO of
> General Electric (GE) and iconic business leader

Strategy provides overall direction to the enterprise and involves specifying the organization's objectives, developing policies and plans designed to achieve these objectives, and then allocating resources to implement the plans.

Pankaj Ghemawat (1991) – professor of management and strategy at New York University

Strategy is about making choices, trade-offs; it's about deliberately choosing to be different.

Michael Porter (1985)

Corporate strategy involves answering a key question from a portfolio perspective: 'What business should we be in?' Business strategy involves answering the question: 'How shall we compete in this business?'

Ellen Chaffee (1985) – distinguished business academic and leader

There are indeed countless perspectives from leading academics and successful business people as to what constitutes strategy. We have observed that management theory tends to distinguish between strategic management and operational management. The latter is considered as being primarily related to efficiency and costs within the context of the strategy; effectively a secondary consideration and a consequence of the direction set and tending to assume operational effectiveness.

As we observed in Chapter 1 and unpacked in further detail in Chapter 3, 'the entire foundation of this book is that operations can inform and guide strategy, building a distinctive, transformative and disruptive competence through creating compelling customer value at a profit'. This in turn drives financial results and business value. We do not claim that the business operations model should take a leadership role, rather that it can be a key driver of strategic difference. This is illustrated in Figure 4.1, which shows the business operations model informing strategy through building disruptive competitive capabilities as well as fulfilling the strategic goals, developed through market dynamics and benchmarks.

This chapter provides an insight into some of the core business strategy concepts from the literature and how they interact with operational strategy. We also identify some authors who have placed innovation in business operations models as a strategy in its own right, bridging the gap that disruptors have crossed. It is clear from

FIGURE 4.1   Strategy sets goals for operations but operations can inform strategy

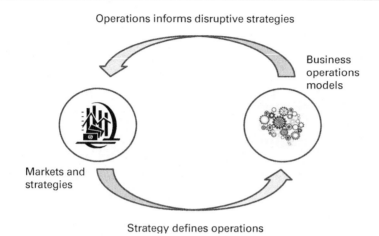

Operations informs disruptive strategies

Business operations models

Markets and strategies

Strategy defines operations

the literature that no framework currently exists to illustrate how business operations models can be a core part of strategy and its execution; we hope that our work will be seen as a useful contribution.

What is strategy?

Strategy within an enterprise can be seen to exist at three levels: corporate, business and operations:

- *Corporate strategy* is based on a set of decisions about 'what business are we in?' The answer to this question is determined in part by an understanding of the market scale and potential, aligned to the core competencies of the business and the capabilities it can apply or develop. We shall expand on this idea of competencies and capabilities in more detail later.

- Flowing from this, *business strategy* seeks to establish how the company will actually compete in that defined business. Specifically this requires the definition of the value proposition that the business intends to present to the marketplace. In other words, what are the compelling reasons why customers should buy our product or service?

- *Operations strategy*, we would argue, is concerned with identifying the means by which the value proposition is to be delivered to the chosen market(s).

We have observed that these three elements of strategy often are not systematically connected one to the other, or are treated as a top-down process. There should be a thread running through the organization that provides the linkage both up and down the elements – a thread that was termed *strategic intent* in a seminal paper by Gary Hamel and CK Prahalad (1989), distinguished US business academics and the originators of the idea of core competence. The idea behind the concept of strategic intent is that every successful organization needs to have a clearly articulated and understood vision and purpose with the means and ability to execute it. They proposed three characteristics that define strategic intent:

1 A sense of direction: where are we going?
2 A sense of discovery: where are the new opportunities?
3 A sense of destiny: is there a shared understanding of the vision and purpose of the business?

Simple though this idea might be, the reality is that for many companies there has been a failure, first to define and communicate their strategic intent and, second, to convert that intent systematically and achievably into action. It is about single-minded focus rather than qualified hedging of bets in which the 'disconnect' between strategy and the business operations model really becomes apparent.

The gap between strategy and operations

Successful companies, as all our case studies on disruptors show, tend to exhibit a strong alignment between their value proposition and their operations strategy – a realizable strategic intent. In other words, the processes that underpin their value delivery system are designed to enable the achievement of the company's strategic goals. The problem that many firms encounter is that whilst they may have developed what they consider to be achievable strategic goals they have given less thought to the specific details of the operating model that will deliver these goals. Later in this book we will show that 'the devil is in this detail'. The danger is that senior management will invest a lot of time in formulating broad or generalized 'mission statements' and less time on considering how their business operations model should be designed in order to deliver profitable value to customers.

One example of a company that has designed a well-integrated operations strategy to support its value proposition is Zara, part of Inditex, the world's biggest clothing business. Zara is a disruptor, as we showed in Chapter 2; Inditex, its parent, delivers industry-leading profits and growth. Its value proposition is that it offers fast, affordable fashion to a tightly defined demographic and lifestyle segment. To enable this, Zara has created an end-to-end, cross-functional business operations model that compresses the time from 'sketch to store' to less than a month and it does that at a cost that ensures competitive prices on the rack. For Zara, a key foundation for its business operations model is its agile supply chain. To enable greater responsiveness the company has been prepared to invest in the capabilities necessary to create agility. Thus, whilst many of their competitors have focused on cost-reduction strategies, often based upon offshore sourcing and manufacturing with consequent extended lead times, Zara has placed the emphasis on time compression. That time compression has been due in large part to the use of a myriad of small workshops in Spain and Portugal to do the final garment assembly. Even though the cost is higher, the time advantage that Zara gains enables a much more rapid response to changing market needs. The benefits are really felt in the reduction in markdowns and discounts to clear excess stock. However, it is worth noting that Zara does not apply this model to its entire range; more predictable and less risky products are still sourced in Asia, or elsewhere, on longer lead times and in larger batch quantities. This approach engages two of our verticals in the business operations model: 'inventory segmentation and deployment' and 'optimized sourcing'. We will return to these in more detail in Chapter 9.

A distinguishing feature of many of the successful 'business disruptors' who have changed the competitive landscape is that, like Zara, they have achieved a close alignment between what they want to do (strategy) and how they plan to actually do it (business operations model). For example, Expedia (the global travel business) and Amazon (the world's biggest online retailer) have developed business processes that enhance the customer experience through dramatically reducing 'search' costs and maximizing shopper convenience.

Reinventing your business model

The term 'business model' was widely used in the dot.com boom at the turn of the 21st century – many of these so-called models were found wanting as they squandered venture capital cash. Models are a recurring but not dominant theme in the literature; a particularly important set of insights came in an article by Mark Johnson, Clayton Christensen and Henning Kagermann (2008), in which their core points were:

- If you have a potential innovation on your hands, think about how it delivers value, helping customers do things that competitive offerings don't address.

- Wrap that innovation in a business model that has a clear profit formula with pricing that recognizes the value customers will receive.

- Clearly define how the business's resources and processes will engage and create that model so that it delivers the value to target customers.

This message is that the business model is both an opportunity to harness innovation as well as to think afresh about how value can be enhanced to the existing market. The examples they quoted are:

- Apple with its iPod, which established the iTunes store as the de facto standard for music, media and, more recently, app purchase.

- Hilti with its fleet management service, which put the supply of power tools for construction on to a 'just the tool when you need it, no repair or storage hassles'; this changed the company's relationship with the construction industry and kept out low-cost competition.

- Dow Corning with its new direct sales business unit – this approach offered product at a discount for customers who were prepared to order on the company's delivery terms and place their orders online with no service or support; this effectively segmented the customer base (as we discussed in Chapter 3).

In every case, customers found value in the new model and the companies found profit potential from delivering the product and service in a completely new way. The presentation of these cases in the article by Johnson and his colleagues concentrates on just three dimensions: the customer value proposition, the profit formula and the key resources and processes. This is consistent with our approach in Figure 1.1 (Chapter 1), and the business operations model framework unpacks the 'resources and processes' dimension to deliver the customer value proposition.

Value disciplines

Compelling value propositions are clearly central to success and disruptor status. One well-established framework for steering the business in a more focused and logical way towards value is that provided by Michael Treacy and Fred Wiersema, distinguished business academics and entrepreneurs. They have argued that to succeed companies need not only to have a clear value proposition and a business operating model but also a 'value discipline' (Treacy and Wiersema, 1993). The three generic value disciplines they highlighted are: operational excellence, product leadership and customer intimacy. Examining each in turn their thinking can be summarized as:

- *Operational excellence*: companies that pursue the operational excellence discipline are focused on efficient execution. They constantly seek to improve the performance of their processes, often enabling the company to become a low-cost competitor. Typically these companies are characterized by limited product ranges and standardized processes with a high degree of centralized control. They are sometimes described as 'lean'.

- *Product leadership*: innovation is the goal of companies who select product leadership as their primary value discipline. These companies place great emphasis on research and development (R&D), short time-to-market and experimentation. To encourage innovation, companies following the product leadership route will encourage risk taking and build a culture that embraces change.

- *Customer intimacy*: the focus for companies pursuing the customer intimacy value discipline is on building enduring relationships with customers. Their emphasis is on service and customization with a view to increasing customer loyalty. There is strong evidence that retained customers are more profitable than new customers, not only through the purchases they make but also through their advocacy of the company and its products. Research by John Fleming and Jim Asplund (2007), both chief scientists with Gallup, indicates that a retained customer is worth up to 1.7 times the average; these are conclusions that are supported by many others.

Whilst recognizing that any company with aspirations to become a market leader has to achieve a minimum level of performance on all three disciplines, Treacy and Wiersema (1993) asserted that companies had to really focus on just one of the three, as shown in Figure 4.2. In their terms, success was less about balance and more about focus.

The figure suggests some level of compromise in attainment between the value disciplines. But are Treacy and Wiersema correct? We disagree, arguing rather that disruptors accept no compromises – through their business operations model they redefine customer value. In today's highly competitive marketplaces customers want innovative products/services delivered by responsive supply chains and supported by high levels of service and at compelling price points. The challenge is to develop and implement a business operations model that is capable of delivering the three value disciplines simultaneously!

FIGURE 4.2   Balancing the value disciplines

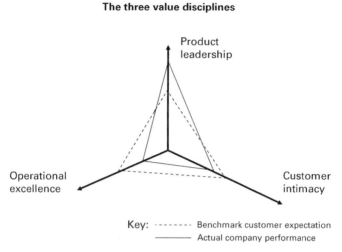

SOURCE: adapted from Treacy and Wiersema (1993)

One powerful way to address this challenge is to turn the spotlight on to the way that the key business processes that deliver customer value are structured. It is through these processes that companies compete; consequently it is vital that businesses place great emphasis on how those processes are designed and executed.

The power of process

Thomas Davenport, one of the early thought leaders on the topic of business process management, coined the following definition:

> A process is any activity or group of activities that takes an input, adds value to it, and provides an output to an internal or external customer.
>
> (Davenport, 1993)

The key point is that processes are the means by which a business creates and delivers value for customers. They are outward facing in that they respond to market needs – in contrast to the classic business functions that are internally focused. Figure 4.3 shows processes as *horizontal*, cutting across the *vertical* functions within the business.

FIGURE 4.3   Horizontal processes versus functional
organization

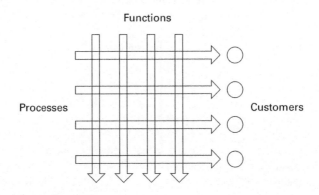

It can be argued that at a high level there are only a handful of critical business processes; of these we would suggest that the following are paramount:

- The innovation process – including new product introduction (NPI).

- The customer relationship management process – known as CRM and which includes as a subset the transactional element: order-to-cash (O2C).

- The supplier relationship management process – known as SRM and which includes as a subset the transactional element: purchase-to-pay (P2P).

- The demand management process – often known as sales and operations planning (S&OP).

- The supply chain management process – dealing with end-to-end (E2E) visibility and value chain improvement.

Let us explore each in turn.

The innovation process

Innovation is a critical requirement in every business. As competitive pressures increase and as product and service life cycles continue to shorten, the need for new solutions to customers' problems becomes ever stronger. Innovation is not just about new technology but also increasingly about new ways to deliver benefits to customers. Thus innovation applies just as much to services as to products and, indeed, to processes – ie innovation in the way that the business does things.

Innovation does not happen on its own, it requires resources and structures to enable ideas to be converted into profitable solutions. Experience has highlighted that a powerful way to facilitate high rates of successful innovation is through the use of cross-functional teams, working across organizational boundaries and empowered to commit resources that take ideas from the drawing board into the marketplace. Some companies, such as Corning and 3M, have used the concept of 'venture teams' as a way to improve the effectiveness of the innovation process. A venture team is in a sense a mini-business within the business; typically the venture team will comprise specialists from across the organization whose skills and capabilities complement each other. Thus R&D people, product engineers and market analysts will work together with other functional specialists to accelerate time-to-market and to ensure that the process is managed holistically rather than in a piecemeal and linear fashion.

The Japanese automotive industry disrupted the global market in the 1970s and 1980s and its achievement was documented in the book *The Machine that Changed the World* by James Womak, Daniel Jones and Daniel Roos (1990). One of the cornerstones of its success was the combination of faster new model introductions (down to less than 2.5 years against conventional competitors at four to five years) and at a model scale that was roughly half the industry norm (125,000 vehicles per year versus 250,000). The Japanese auto industry achieved it through very tightly organized teamwork across many technical disciplines.

The customer relationship management process

The purpose of any business is to attract and retain profitable customers. Once, this might have been seen as the responsibility of the sales and marketing functions. Now the smart companies have recognized that this vital task is a pan-company responsibility requiring the development of processes that can help to build enduring relationships with key customers.

Once again, many companies have found that a team-based approach to customer management can be highly effective. Thus, a manufacturer such as Procter & Gamble (P&G) will put together a cross-functional team to work with specific accounts. For example, P&G has created a high-level team to work closely with Tesco, the UK's biggest retailer, to ensure that the shelf space Tesco devotes to P&G's products generates maximum return for both parties. The 'Tesco Team' at P&G will include supply chain management and logistics specialists, category managers, marketing and merchandising experts – the whole team being led by a senior P&G executive. That person has the title Key Account Director. This approach is a global one at P&G with all their big customers; Walmart accounts for around 25 per cent of P&G's global revenues and this is supported by an entire team 'implanted' in Walmart's Bentonville HQ.

The idea is that by managing individual customer relationships as a process, a much more tailored set of solutions can be developed, which can lead to the delivery of greater customer value and, hopefully, result in higher levels of customer retention with a greater 'share of wallet' in terms of customer spend.

The supplier relationship management process

Not so long ago, the normal mode of working with suppliers was to keep them very much at arm's-length. In many cases the relationship was adversarial, with the emphasis on seeking to squeeze the supplier on price – often the company would have multiple suppliers for the same item or commodity in order to 'play one off against the other'. Whilst this style of supplier management is still commonplace, more enlightened companies today seek instead to become the 'customer of choice' for their suppliers.

Why has this fundamental shift in philosophy and practice occurred? One important reason is that as companies have outsourced more of the activities that they used to perform themselves, so too have the number of critical supplier dependencies increased. Companies are now part of what has been termed an 'extended enterprise' and the reality is that they compete as a supply chain rather than as individual stand-alone businesses. A further reason for this change is the recognition that a lot of innovation, particularly in technology, is supplier-originated. By forging strong relationships with key suppliers companies are often able to access new ideas sooner than their competitors. For many years, for example, Dell was able to leverage its strong relationship with Intel to ensure that it was always first in the queue when Intel introduced the latest microprocessor architecture. The Dell case study in Chapter 7 shows that Dell was an early volume customer for the Intel 486 processor – giving its machines a technical edge.

Some companies have formalized this collaborative approach through the creation of 'supplier development teams'. For example Nissan, the Japanese car manufacturer, has established teams of specialists to work closely with key suppliers. These supplier development teams comprise quality management specialists, information systems technicians as well as manufacturing experts. Their role is to find ways to help suppliers improve their processes and to ensure a better alignment with Nissan's processes. The aim is to create a seamless connection between key suppliers and Nissan's operations.

The demand management process

The idea behind demand management is that customer requirements should be anticipated and shaped to enable a more cost-effective fulfilment process to be achieved. So in many cases sales and marketing have worked to maximize demand for the company's products only to find that the ability to meet that demand is constrained because of lack of supply. The capability to match supply and demand is a fundamental foundation for success in any business and this is the role of the demand management process.

As before, the best way to achieve the goal of matching supply and demand is through a cross-functional, process-oriented approach. A widely adopted form of this idea is commonly termed 'sales and operations planning' (S&OP). We pointed to the importance of planning as a key integrating layer in our business operations model and in Chapter 2 stressed its key role in the financial engineering of super-performers. S&OP is a formalized and systematic mechanism for bringing together the key players and the vital information necessary to anticipate demand and to plan its fulfilment. At its very simplest the S&OP process will involve a regular meeting – either weekly or monthly – of the sales and marketing team with those responsible for supply: eg production and/or procurement management. The meeting will review the current order book and any backlog; it will examine the latest sales forecasts and have access to information on current inventory levels and factory capacity and upstream supply capabilities. The process will look at both a longer-term horizon (the outlook for demand, capacity and supply over 3 to 18 months) as well as the short term (how do we cope with the next few weeks?). In the short term, the team may have to prioritize orders for fulfilment as well as agreeing future schedules for sales promotions and new product launches.

There are many variations on this theme but the fundamental purpose of demand management is to ensure that customer requirements can be met in a timely and cost-effective manner – primarily by improving communication across functional boundaries. As we saw in Chapter 3, meeting customer expectations is a key part of the value proposition. We will return to this key lateral and integrating element in our business operations model in Chapter 9.

The supply chain management process

In some respects supply chain management subsumes all of the four processes discussed above. This is because supply chain management is essentially the coordinating process that ties together the demand and supply sides of the business. It is perhaps *the* fundamental business process and by definition it has a 'horizontal' orientation that requires direction at the highest level within the business. In many companies today, supply chain management is the responsibility of a 'C-level' executive, ie a vice-president with a seat on the executive board of the company.

Having a supply chain presence in the boardroom enables a stronger linkage between business strategy and operations. There are three key activities that constitute the supply chain management process:

managing the routes to market, ensuring end-to-end visibility of activity and costs, and orchestrating the supply/demand network. These are discussed below.

Managing the routes to market

This has become a pressing concern as many companies now use multiple channels to connect their enterprise to the marketplace. Decisions about the architecture of these channels will have a profound impact on profitability and market access – particularly as the 'cost-to-serve' can differ significantly channel by channel. Hence there is a strategic need for ongoing monitoring of channel costs and revenues and an understanding of the relative return on investment achieved in each channel. Market channels and economics are a key vertical in our business operations model and we will return to it in detail in Chapter 6.

End-to-end visibility of activity and costs

The second key activity of the supply chain management process is providing cost and performance visibility across the end-to-end pipeline. Companies too often have limited visibility of their upstream supply capability or indeed of their downstream demand, let alone the costs of the channels. Capturing and sharing this vital information is a prerequisite for excellence in the supply chain; the insights from this work can identify the potential to be a disruptor. Frequently today, companies are seeking to build a 'control tower' to provide the means to monitor, on a continuous basis, the performance of their supply chains.

The supply/demand network

The third element of the supply chain management process is the ongoing 'orchestration' of the different players who constitute the supply/demand network. Because modern supply chains are so reliant on other entities – such as providers of logistics services, suppliers of materials or products, distributors and stockists etc – the need for coordination and control has become paramount. This orchestration role is particularly important given the dynamic nature of supply chains: ie they are constantly changing their shape as new markets emerge and others decline, whilst at the same time the up-stream supply environment may also be changing rapidly. Managing the shifting 'centre of gravity' of the supply/demand network is in effect the real purpose of supply chain orchestration.

Business process redesign for strategic transformation

The previous section talked about processes and their importance for operational excellence. On the basis that process design and execution is the means by which strategy and operations are linked, then it is clearly important to ensure that great attention is paid to the architecture and management of business processes. The emphasis on operational processes as a key strategic component is quite limited in the strategy management literature.

The challenge is that processes are often disjointed and fragmented across a company, rather than the end-to-end concept described in the previous section. In the terms of Figure 4.3, the functions tend to win; indeed, most businesses typically still focus on managing functions rather than processes. This orientation is embedded in the corporate DNA through the classic, hierarchical organization structure supported by the corresponding performance measurement system and the general ledger. The functions are the pillars on which the business is built. Whilst there is no doubt that this makes life easier from an administrative view and simplifies the financial control of the business through the budgeting system, it does nothing to enable the creation of a customer-centric and responsive organization. Hence the need for a radical overhaul of the way in which the key business processes are designed and managed.

A key exception to the gap in the strategy literature in this area is the work of Michael Hammer, one of the early advocates of fundamenta-lly reshaping business processes in his seminal article 'Re-engineering work: don't automate, obliterate' (1990). He said that companies need to 'stop paving the cow tracks'; he meant by this that companies over the years have set their outdated process design in concrete, making radical change difficult and painful. The analogy was based on the way that many of today's roads still have twists and turns because they were once cow tracks that in a later century were paved. Even though the internal combustion engine has long transformed the speed at which vehicles can travel, trucks and cars still have to use the old roads!

This train of thought with a focus on 'business process re-engineering' enjoyed a period of great popularity in the 1990s and 2000s, but was still in tension with functionally prejudiced organizations and tended to deliver marginal gains rather than breakthrough. To attain radical change and competitive disruptor status, we prefer to argue the case for business process 'transformation'.

The approach we advocate is outlined in Figure 4.4 and begins by returning to the three business disciplines of innovation, customer intimacy and operational excellence. The first question is 'what do we want to achieve on each dimension?' The second question is 'where are we now?' and the third and perhaps most challenging question is 'how do we structure the organization to achieve the required transformation?'

FIGURE 4.4   The steps to business transformation through process

Alongside these three questions are two related and highly important issues: how do we measure success and reward performance; and what sort of management skills are required to support the new organizational structure?

What do we want to achieve?

Whilst ideally every business would like to excel on all three of the business disciplines, a distinctive and disruptive capability will have particular focus. So Southwest Airlines achieves remarkable operational efficiency at an acceptable level of customer intimacy; it is consistently ranked in the top five of the JD Power survey, but its customers do not expect first-class seats or elaborate meals. The first step is to understand what is the minimum level of performance on each of the three dimensions that is necessary to be in the market at all. This base level might be termed 'the market qualifier'. Once that is understood, the challenge then becomes one of prioritizing focus and resources in the context of existing or potential buying segments. For example, if innovation is seen as being the key dimension then this will set the agenda for how the key business processes need to be shaped and structured in order to support that goal; the processes that impact on time-to-market and the rate of new product introductions will be critical. Alternatively, companies where operational excellence is deemed to be the market winner will have a greater focus on creating lean and efficient infrastructures and be more likely to search for scale economies. Those organizations choosing to follow the road to customer intimacy will need to invest in relationship management and to create processes that maximize the customer experience.

Where are we now?

Few companies are able to provide an objective assessment of where they stand on the three business disciplines relative to their competitors. There will be many subjective opinions within the organization, but probably little hard evidence. What is needed is a robust set of metrics that can provide the insights needed. However, the reality is that there are few 'off the shelf' industry standards to enable an appropriate scorecard to be constructed. We suggest that it is both essential and possible to gain some insights into the company's standing relative to the competition on the three critical dimensions. Ideally, a mix of 'hard' and 'soft' indicators should be used to provide a composite picture of current performance. The type of performance indicators we have in mind could include:

- Innovation:
  - Hard metrics: such as the percentage of sales derived from products or services new to the market in the last three years; number of patents applied for in the last 12 months; R&D expenditure as a percentage of sales revenue.
  - Soft metrics: such as customer-derived ratings based on their perceptions of how they see us relative to the competition in terms of product leadership, as a source of new ideas/technology and as a business ready to embrace change.
- Customer intimacy:
  - Hard metrics: such as customer repeat purchase and retention; share of wallet (ie what proportion of a customer's total spend do we receive?).
  - Soft metrics: such as customer satisfaction surveys; customer advocacy (ie customer referrals and testimonials).
- Operational excellence:
  - Hard metrics: such as time-to-market; time-to-volume; set-up times; cash-to-cash cycle time; cost-to-serve and unit costs; perfect order achievement.
  - Soft metrics: such as customer complaints; website exits without purchase; employee suggestions and satisfaction; competitive benchmarking (as discussed in Chapter 3).

Ideally this assessment of performance against the three business disciplines should be conducted annually to provide an indication of the progress that is being made towards the goals that have been established. The European Foundation for Quality Management (EFQM) offers an excellent process to both measure and track changes in performance on all the soft metrics in the points above;

the challenge in its application is making internal resources available to sustain the initiative.

How do we structure the organization to achieve the transformation?

The task of getting from where we are today to where we want to be tomorrow requires a focus on the establishment of a process orientation. In effect, the task is to create an organizational structure based around managing the key processes that will be vital to the achievement of outstanding competitor and potential disruptor. Since most businesses will probably be organized along traditional functional lines, making this change will not be easy – we are in effect seeking to turn the organizational chart through 90 degrees, making the change from a 'vertical' to a 'horizontal' business. The aim should be to redesign the key business processes from the customer backwards. In other words, we need to ask the question: 'what is the value proposition that we seek to deliver to this market segment and what process architecture is required to achieve that?'

The key to successful process redesign is to start with the objective of creating a 'boundary-less business' that has no internal – or external – barriers to the seamless delivery of value to the ultimate customer. The concept of the boundary-less business owes its origins to Jack Welch whilst he was CEO at GE. He sought to establish an organizational structure that had no boundaries within the business, or externally between GE and its customers and suppliers. He was clear that by removing those boundaries a more responsive, agile and customer-centric business could be created. Siloed organizations and processes exist to promote administrative efficiency and they involve multiple hand-offs from one functional activity, none of which benefits the final customer; rather, processes become a way to protect one function from another. This organizational disconnect can only be fixed by cross-functional process re-design; this is an issue not well addressed in management research as published in the top management journals.

The idea that these processes might be the foundation for sustainable competitiveness is not widely accepted: getting this approach and practice on to companies' agendas as part of their business operations model is central to this book.

How do we measure success and reward performance?

It has long been recognized by change management specialists that the best way to encourage new ways of working is through the performance measurement and reward system. Traditionally, however, success has been measured against functional goals such as meeting the sales budget or achieving target cost reductions in the factory. Likewise, the reward system has tended to be linked to the achievement of those same functional goals.

In the conventional functional organization there can often be conflicts between the different functions as they compete for resources. Sometimes, the pursuit of internal goals may lead to suboptimal behaviour, for example if the production team are incentivized to reduce the unit cost of production they may seek to gain economies of scale through bigger batch sizes. This strategy will probably reduce unit costs but most likely will lead to a loss of flexibility as well as high inventory costs; at the same time as there is excess stock there will almost certainly be shortages and customer service failure. Thus, to ensure that the transformation of the organization from a functional to a process-oriented business actually happens, it is necessary to radically change the way that success is defined, measured and rewarded.

Ultimately, what the process-oriented business is seeking to achieve in terms of behaviour is a higher level of collaborative working, both internally within the organization and externally with customers and suppliers. The requirement is to establish a suite of metrics that are based around the achievement of internal team-based goals and external value-based goals. One such measure that goes some way to meeting this requirement is 'perfect order achievement'. A perfect order is achieved when we have met the customer's requirements completely. Clearly this measure has to be specific to individual customers and ideally should be clearly defined as part of a service level agreement with each customer. One frequently used measure of perfect order achievement is 'on-time, in-full, no invoice error' (OTIFNIE). Once the perfect order is defined, the team-based actions that drive the achievement of 'the perfect order' need to be understood along with the functional root cause measures. Thus, for example, what is the impact of the order-fulfilment team on perfect order performance? An analysis of previous failures to achieve the agreed perfect order levels will help to identify the critical cause-and-effect linkages. By understanding the connections between internal process performance and the achievement of external goals, appropriate targets for the process teams can be set, which can become the basis for the reward system (we return to this theme in Chapter 10).

What sort of management skills do we need to succeed?

It will be apparent that the transformation from a functionally based organization to one focused around process management will have implications for the skills profile of the management team. Working in the traditional functional organization requires managers to understand in detail how that function works and to develop high levels of competencies in the management of that function. On the other hand, working successfully in a process orientation needs this and much more. It is now widely accepted that the ideal skills profile for a manager in a process-oriented business is 'T-shaped' and we would agree. The idea of the T-shaped person is reported to have originated at the consulting firm McKinsey in order to describe the attributes of their potential recruits; management consultants need spatial awareness and the ability to work with people, alongside specific, deep technical know-how and functional experience. The term T-shaped was first documented by Tim Brown, CEO of the renowned design and innovation firm IDEO, initially in an article and then in his book *Change by Design* (2009).

What this means is that as well as having in-depth knowledge of a particular functional area – say purchasing – the manager will also have significant exposure to the other activities that are critical to the effective achievement of the goals of the process team of which he or she is a member. Let's say that the person in question was a member of an 'order-to-cash' process team (ie the process that begins with the capture of an order and ends with collection of the money from a satisfied customer) in a make-to-order business. In this case that manager would need to have an understanding of how orders enter the system, how they are processed and how they are scheduled for production, as well as the delivery and installation activities.

Clearly from a management development point of view there are implications for being T-shaped. The requirement for formal and continuing training interventions will entail a significant investment. For example, Jack Welch, who we quoted at the start of this chapter, drove remarkable growth at GE over the 20 years to 2001 and aimed to create a 'boundary-less' business; he realized that, to achieve his ambitious goals, managers at every level in the company would need an ongoing programme of skills and knowledge development. To make this possible he established GE University – a bricks and mortar campus with a faculty drawn from within the company and outside. Many other companies have also created 'universities' or 'academies' – some virtual – in order to ensure that a much broader process perspective can be engendered and nourished within the organization. Companies also need to recognize that some people will not make the journey; Jack Welch famously fired the bottom 10 per cent of GE's managers every year as a way to make the point.

The balanced scorecard

Robert Kaplan and David Norton first published their balanced scorecard concept in 1992 in the *Harvard Business Review*; it arose from their research with the Nolan Institute and is now widely adopted by Global FT 500 businesses. Their seminal book is *The Balanced Scorecard: Translating strategy to action* (1996). It is perhaps the only framework that formally links strategy with operations and its approach is entirely consistent with our analysis both in this chapter and previous chapters. Figure 4.5 shows a version of their scorecard map adapted to the language that we have used in earlier chapters as well as the emphasis on process in this chapter.

Stepping through Figure 4.5, the creation of business value is based on growth and margin (as we showed in Chapter 2). That in turn comes from a compelling customer value proposition, driven by both the

FIGURE 4.5   The balanced scorecard map

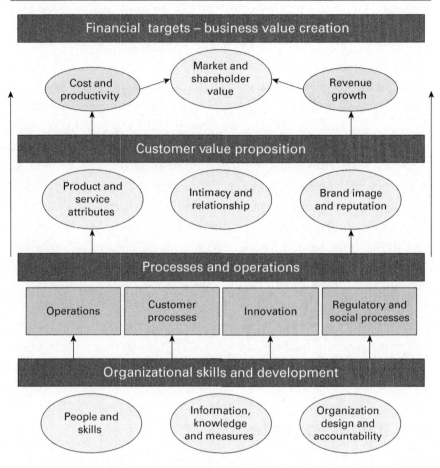

SOURCE: adapted from Kaplan and Norton (1996)

product/service combination and how the customer is engaged and handled (we developed that thinking in Chapter 3). That compelling capability is driven in turn by the processes and operations embedded in the business; this is the thinking that we have developed in this chapter and the elements of process and operations in this chart are consistent with those of Treacy and Wiersema. These in turn are determined by the organizational skills and its development through people, knowledge and accountability.

The famous quote 'what gets measured gets managed' applies here. Figure 4.5 shows that the financial outcomes are driven from the bottom up, whereas Figure 4.1 suggests that disruptive strategies are circular. Certainly, top-down goal setting without careful process integration and alignment will be a recipe for disappointment. Kaplan and Norton clearly got it right conceptually; it is the effective application of such a road map and scorecard that is the difference between success and relative failure.

Conclusion

This chapter started by highlighting the many perspectives on what makes a business strategy. We then unpacked some work from leading thinkers who have placed operations as central to business success and transformation. We have observed that there is a relative scarcity of thinkers who focus on the power of operations to drive transformative business performance. This is what we call the 'strategy-operations gap'. This is a paradox since most businesses spend between 50 per cent and 80 per cent of their revenues on buying things or making things; it is where the money is and from where the customer experience is delivered.

The potential for operations to be a backbone of strategy may often be underplayed, but is represented best by the idea of business processes driving operational excellence. Our suggestion is that the disruptive opportunity is to improve the alignment between the intended value proposition and the key business processes necessary to deliver that proposition.

The strategic realization is that the effectiveness of these processes is a key to being an effective competitor; it is a potential strategy in its own right as it can inform and guide the entire business operations model to a new place. Ultimately it is through the architecture and management of those processes that the 'strategy-operations gap' will be closed. Performance measures relating to processes and the quality of their execution are also central to setting an organization's sights on transformation and then monitoring performance on the journey.

It is critical in the design of any business operations model that great emphasis be placed on establishing an appropriate process-based organization. We will use our framework to describe how to identify, quantify and realize operational potential for transformation and, hopefully, disruptor status in the coming chapters. We see it as the way to close the 'strategy-operations gap' that we have observed.

Taking forward the framework in your business

A chapter that focuses on the role of operations in business strategy provides the background to test how you position operations in your overall strategy determination. This focuses on how you have been thinking about the contribution of operations and gives an opportunity to look again at the narratives you have developed from the last three chapters. Answer the following questions as a team:

- Has operations (not just the function but the whole way that the business delivers) been challenged during strategy development as to how it might provide step-change in performance – in either customer service, cost or both? If not, it is time to reassess your process of strategic goal setting.

- Does the business have a process ethic? Does it recognize the power of process as the foundation of transformation, including innovation? If not, this is a chance to consider how to introduce that culture because it will be a dependency for any business model change.

- Has the business made an explicit and quantified connection between its strategic objectives and the operational metrics that need to be attained for success – a balanced scorecard? If not, then the scorecard needs to be put in place so that the cascade of performance is visible.

- If the business has a scorecard, or when you have created one, revisit and revise (or establish) the targets in the context of the goals and narratives from Chapters 2 and 3 and then improve the narratives based on any insights you have gained.

Unpacking the business operations model framework

This chapter is a brief introduction to the four following chapters, which will unpack the practicalities of applying our business operations model framework through its verticals; this will be based around four scenarios for transformation or disruption. Chapter 10 will then look at the journey to becoming a disruptor and we will close Chapter 11 by summarizing the guiding principles for building a competitive advantage.

Before introducing the scenarios, a short recap of the first four chapters will help to summarize the key ideas in finance, customer value and business strategy that are the grounding of the framework and the scenarios.

The first chapter outlined the overall concept of business operations models; it made the point that being a disruptor is about building a unique combination of capabilities that provide distinctive value for customers. We argued that not every aspect of the framework will always come into play in every case but that it will always be a combination of capabilities – there is never a single silver bullet.

For a company to secure disruptor status, the business operations model has to come together with the combination of pricing and service that gives customers compelling value proposition. And it has to be done with a cost structure that gives superior returns.

Through the case study example, we showed that Southwest Airlines derives its phenomenal success from its capability to give customers exceptional value in their travel and to do it at a margin that generates cash and market value. The case study showed the long-term creation of shareholder value through the compelling value given to customers; this has been achieved through a highly focused business operations model that keeps costs low.

Based on our core business operations model schematic, first introduced in Chapter 1 (Figure 1.2 on page 5), the Southwest Airlines story shows that it is a combination of capabilities that builds a platform for success. Southwest Airlines ticks all of the boxes:

- The customer lens shows that customers respond to the combination of low prices and good service – they buy in volume.

- Southwest does this with a cost structure that generates good profits and drives market value.

- That cost structure is achieved through linked actions across the business operations model verticals, shown in Figure 1.2 from left to right:

  - Using only direct to customer channels – no agents or commissions.

  - A simple and homogeneous route structure that maximizes aircraft utilization.

  - A route network that ensures good aircraft utilization and where non-viable routes are eliminated quickly.

  - Class-leading service within the value constraints of the brand.

  - Inventory optimization: in the airline business this is about avoiding wasted seat journeys since you can never sell them again – Southwest do this through pricing and yield management.

  - Optimized sourcing: Southwest, through using a single aircraft type with all the benefits of interchangeability and standard maintenance.

  - A relentless focus on the basics, including rapid gate turnaround, safety standards and staying the course in the face of adversity.

Demand and supply planning for Southwest Airlines is relatively simple, as interlining is removed as a dependency and routes can be tested easily for viability and rescheduled as appropriate. Its operating model delivers a very low end-to-end cost of service and supply, enabling attractive prices without sacrificing service.

The simple narrative in the points above, and more fully described in Chapter 1, shows that there is not a single dimension of success; it is the combination of a number of key operations capabilities that build the distinctive and compelling offer, drive growth and margin generation.

Every company should be able to tell the story of how it creates its unique market-facing proposition through its operational capabilities to deliver those customer benefits, and at a value that generates margin.

Michael Porter, the leading Harvard business strategy thinker on competition, introduced the idea of the value chain into management parlance and also the five forces of competition. In his early work he proposed that a company should either be niche, competing on customer value; or compete primarily on price, accepting their market was a commodity. He made the point that companies competing in commodity markets needed to be low-cost producers. In today's language this translates into the maxim 'get niche or get big or get out'. We argue that today's markets can no longer be considered as either niche or commodity. Only both will do – the combination of competitive prices and good service is the standard for mass markets; successful niche segments rapidly become mass markets

- In Chapter 3 we looked at the process of understanding how companies can identify the combinations of value that their customers find compelling. The business operations model is about designing for customer preferences in the mass market. The challenge for companies has moved on from the strategic thinking of the 1980s. So, for example, Southwest Airlines is a low-cost producer with 15 per cent of the market, which is definitely not niche.

- In contrast, the fertilizer company in Ireland (Chapter 3), surely a commodity sector, was kept in business through its quality commanding a premium price, because its customers factored in their own costs and their perception of the costs of risk. On every other service count it failed and it was not a low-cost producer; when the competition caught up, they did not survive.

- Internet retailing is also no longer niche, with many 'clicks and mortar' operators generating 15 per cent to 25 per cent of revenues online. Internet retailing demand is characterized by customers who are not prepared to pay for service as well as the goods; but those customers reward retailers that can connect emotionally with them too: by a factor of two to eight times versus the average customer.

So how can a company do more than survive? How can it configure its business operations model to, at best, become a disruptor or at least thrive? This idea of being a disruptor is as attractive as that of being a super-performer. Irwin Stelzer wrote in the *Sunday Times* on 26 October 2014 that innovators no longer want to describe themselves as entrepreneurs or capitalists, terms that he claimed had respectively 'effete' and exploitative connotations. He wrote:

> Today's innovator class prefers 'disruptor'. Nothing effete about that word which evokes tough-guy actors...
>
> The disruptors' list of achievements is considerable. They have disrupted the newspaper industry, although it is managing a longer decline than expected. They are in the process of disrupting taxi industries the world over.

Stelzer went on to list other sectors that have been disrupted such as book publishing and music, telephony, oil and gas production, shoes, clothing and furniture. And he singled out the travel agency business, which we saw from the Southwest Airlines case has been made largely redundant by online booking. He attributed some of this disruption to the effect of both the internet and lower freight transportation costs. He asserted that almost every industry is open to disruption and that the major barrier is regulation. In the end he concluded that the pace of innovation will be overwhelming.

From Stelzer's article and wider experience the conclusion is that it is a wise move to work out both how you may be disrupted and have counter-measures in place; better still if you can position to be a disruptor, then you will be ahead of the game.

Our observations in Chapter 4 are that the strategy literature is not packed with recognition of the strategic contribution of operations as a foundation to becoming a disruptor. The core operations themes from the literature for achieving transformation or potential disruptor status are channel- and business-model-focused combined with process redesign; these fit our verticals of market channels and economics, mastering complexity and managing the basics.

Scenarios for transformation or disruption

In the remaining chapters of this book, we aim to develop some narratives around different scenarios for effective disruption, or the ability to thrive in a market. In our case study examples we try to expand on the basic generalizations about successful companies, many of which have become folklore in many case examples.

The scenarios we present cut across the framework since each engages several of the verticals to deliver viable and compelling offers to customers. Each scenario will develop one or more verticals in its context and provide case examples. In this short chapter, the aim is to signpost the scenarios, so that the reader will know what to expect and how the scenarios knit with our framework. Remember that it is the combination of capabilities that makes the difference:

- The first scenario (Chapter 6) is about the application of technology to become a disruptor. This dimension featured strongly in the Irwin Stelzer article quoted above, and technology is often seen as a silver bullet for business – in his article he called it a 'killer app'. However, there is ample evidence that the business operations model design is key to the successful application of new technology. This evidence shows that just owning the intellectual property is not a sufficiency; market channels, service delivery, mastering complexity and variety, optimized networks and the basics of speed, quality and accuracy count for a lot.

- The second scenario (Chapter 7) is about the creation of market-changing transformation; this scenario is about the configuration of the channels and service models for delivery of the product and/or service in original ways to provide new and compelling value to customers. This scenario engages every vertical in the framework as well as the integrating layers of planning and end-to-end cost of supply and service. This scenario should bring inspiration to every business that may not be part of some white-hot technological innovation.

- The third scenario (Chapter 8) is about competing through the basics. Many companies have major potential to improve their performance both in terms of how they face their customers and their underlying cost structures. This may not seem to be either disruptive or transformational, but can actually provide the platform for a company to win in its markets. This is often about quite small gains right across the business operations model: subtle changes can make all the difference.

- The fourth scenario (Chapter 9) is about optimizing the business operations model. We use the term optimize with some caution, since this scenario is about radically reshaping the nature of competition rather than some formulaic optimum. This scenario is often complementary to, and incorporates, competing through the basics. But it goes one step further; here the aim is to reconfigure the business operations model to deliver true competitive advantage – doing more with less.

In Chapter 10 we look at the journey to becoming a disruptor. We look at how companies landed on the particular combination that makes up their business operations model. This chapter is based on the research for a master's thesis at Cranfield School of Management by Chris Melton, who now works with our company, LCP Consulting. Leading up to that thesis project we had engaged in a number of thought leadership meetings in London with senior business leaders; these have also informed our thinking. The discovery of that work was that outcomes are the result of both intent and serendipity, good luck or good fortune – call it what you will. We provide case studies that show how the pursuit of leadership can lead to remarkable developments that exceed the wildest dreams of the managers who initiated the original idea; experimentation is good. Also we discovered that it is never too late until it is too late. The moral of the story is that the business operations model can inform focused actions that may give surprising outcomes; it shows there are clear methods by which change can be defined and managed.

Finally, in Chapter 11 we try to summarize the guiding principles to building a competitive position or, even better, becoming a disruptor. Hopefully, the executive who dips into this book will be able to pick the point of entry for initiating disruptive change. The key here is to identify the big points of leverage in the business operations model and then build the narrative for change using established techniques to define actions of change and the road map to get there.

Taking forward the framework in your business

This is a short summary chapter that leads into our scenarios for disruption. At this point you might want to consider what radical marketplace disruption might look like in your segment. That would be a way to test if your narrative so far is sufficiently radical. As you do it, review again the narrative you have been assembling and start to think about which of the scenarios will be most appropriate for your business and which of the verticals in our business operations model will be most relevant to your business. With that thinking in place, you will be able to critically assimilate the following chapters within your own context.

The technology dimension to being a disruptor 06

Gary Hamel, in his book *What Matters Now* (2012), talks about a world of relentless change, ferocious competition and unstoppable innovation. Competitive disruption is indeed relentless in the 21st century. But this is not a new idea; Joseph Schumpeter, a 20th-century economist and political scientist and latterly a professor at Harvard, popularized the term 'creative destruction' in 1942. He used it to describe the constant change in markets, which he described as mutation – a biological and evolutionary term. He observed that it is the essence of capitalism and 'what every capitalist concern has got to live in' (Schumpeter, 1942). His emphasis was on new technologies, new commodities, new sources of supply and competing through quality rather than price.

Schumpeter wrote from a somewhat left-wing political outlook that was concerned that the pace of change would lead to a vortex of economic self-destruction through unfettered capitalism. In contrast, and some 75 years on, Stelzer (as cited in Chapter 5) is concerned that innovative disruption will be stifled by regulation, which he believes it will ultimately overcome. Given the collapse of communism and the huge expansion in global trade since the 1960s, current economic thinking is that innovation is like 'clearing the undergrowth' to release new energy and expansion. Innovation is indeed alive and well; filings for patents, which can be taken as an indicator of innovation, grew in 2013 by more than 9 per cent, resuming their pre-recession levels, and much faster than global economic growth.

What is universally agreed is that technology is a major component of being a disruptor. In this chapter we unpack how the business operations model can harness technological innovation to become a disruptor.

In Chapter 4 we referred to Johnson, Christensen and Kagermann, writing in the *Harvard Business Review*, to propose the core idea that good technology needs to go hand-in-hand with a good business model. They stated that this can be represented by a compelling customer proposition, sound economics and the right operational organization and capabilities. They also asserted the need for company leadership to regularly revisit the question of whether fundamental change is needed. This is consistent with the financial analysis of super-performers in Chapter 2, which showed that sustained super-performance is difficult to achieve and that success can be ephemeral.

One could fill an entire book with the stories of businesses that came and went based on technology. While that is not our purpose, it is worth the time, and a little entertaining, to share some heritage examples of the technological disruption of markets. Both Stelzer and Schumpeter allude to the role of transportation in industrial production and this theme fits with the business operations model concept. Transport of goods directly engages with market channels, optimized networks and sourcing as well as the end-to-end cost of supply.

Disruptive evolutions in freight

The evolution of ground freight transport has been from the beast of burden, the horse and cart, through canals, railways and, with improved roads, increasingly sophisticated trucks. Each has progressively obsoleted its predecessor, leaving a rump of activity or sometimes none – as in the case of the UK canal system. Rail freight made those canals obsolete but then declined due to capacity, service flexibility and cost. Rail freight in the UK was as high as 40 per cent of all goods moved in tonne–kilometre terms in 1953 but accounts for only around 10 per cent of all freight tonne-kilometres today moved – a level that is now stable and starting to increase. This is due to the increased movement of sea containers by rail replacing the loss of traditional cargoes such as coal for power stations.

Sea freight has undergone a parallel evolution from sailing ships to steam power to motor vessels and then by type of vessel from general cargo to container vessel. The growth shown in Figure 6.1 illustrates the massive growth in world trade in manufactured goods cross-border traffic: effectively an exponential curve, with a blip for the downturn and a growth rate of between two and four times global gross domestic product (GDP). Since the majority of these goods have to be carried by sea, it points to the contribution that sea freight has made to the global economy. This simply could not have occurred without the availability of low-cost shipping capacity.

It is worth noting that the early growth was strongly attributable to the globalization of the automotive industry when the Japanese disrupted the US model; then textiles and a whole range of other segments saw the model and adopted it. Before, and in the course of that growth, there were a whole string of disruptive technological developments that transformed the shipping market and the prospects of the actors within it. Let's look at just two.

FIGURE 6.1 Growth in global trade in manufactured goods

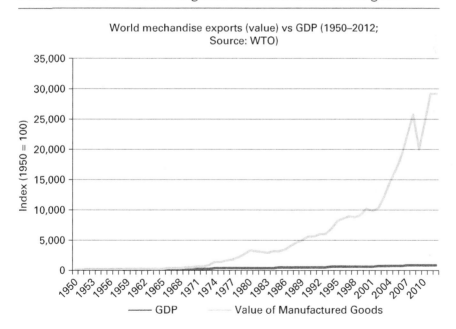

A visit to the *Cutty Sark*, in Greenwich, London, is to see one of the last sail-powered tea-clippers. The vessel was built on the River Clyde in 1869 for the China to Europe tea trade. It had a maximum speed under sail of 17.5 knots and a gross registered tonnage of 975 tons. Speed was of the essence in bringing the tea to Europe around the Cape of Good Hope. The first merchants to market secured the best prices and had the freshest product; shipowners could charge a corresponding premium, so speed was critical. However, the same year that the 'state of the art' *Cutty Sark* was constructed, the Suez Canal opened and disrupted the clipper trade as steam ships took over on the shortened route. A display on board the *Cutty Sark* reads:

> Opened in 1869, the Suez Canal shortened the route from China by 3,000 miles and steamships could now reach London in 60 days.
> The unfavourable winds in the Red Sea and the Mediterranean made the Canal impractical for sailing ships and they were gradually pushed out of the tea trade.

The *Cutty Sark* went on to carry wool from Australia where the prevailing winds and routes made it faster than steam ships, even with their improving engines. There is one report of a steam ship in the Southern Indian Ocean seeing the *Cutty Sark* sailing past in the night. The vessel lasted until 1895 in that role before being sold to a Portuguese company for general trade with South America.

In terms of our business operations model, two technical innovations – steam ships and the Suez Canal – combined to destroy the tea-clipper business. The proposition was undermined by faster ships with greater capacity sailing on a shorter route with greater reliability. The new steam ships could optimize the network better and manage the basics to be more reliable and lower cost. The value to the customer was faster transit at lower costs. Better, faster, easier and cheaper is the recurring theme to being a disruptor.

Let's carry the example of technological innovation in shipping forward to the second half of the 20th century and look at how containerization was another disruptive time for shipping. The first container ship sailed in 1960 and, after a slow start, the growth in the segment was exponential.

Figure 6.2 illustrates in two graphs the overall growth in shipping by tonnes carried and the shift in composition in the global fleet

FIGURE 6.2   Growth in the global shipping fleet and changing composition by sector

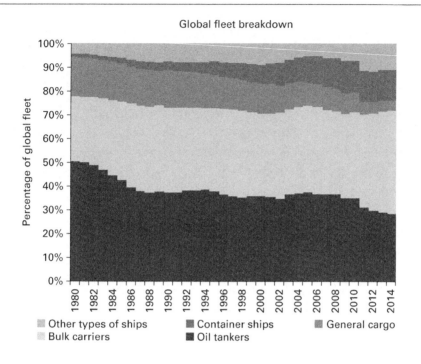

Global fleet breakdown

Other types of ships   Container ships   General cargo
Bulk carriers   Oil tankers

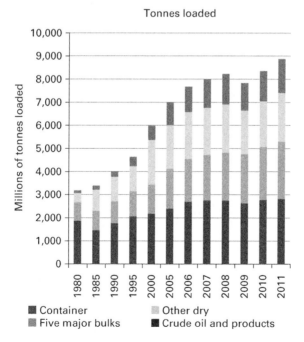

Tonnes loaded

Container   Other dry
Five major bulks   Crude oil and products

by vessel type – and it is immediately apparent that the container fleet segment has shown by far the faster growth, although all other segments have also grown in line with economic growth. However, it is important to note that it is still only 12 per cent of the total shipping market. Container ships are less than 5,000 vessels in a global fleet of just over 50,000 vessels of more than 500 gross tonnes.

The evolution of the container ship itself has led to a much more efficient design for loading, allowing a greater height of the cargo – and this supports the shipment of manufactured goods where the volume of the cargo is more important than the weight. At the time of writing, the largest ships can carry just short of 20,000 TEUs (20-foot equivalent containers); they are 400 metres long, tower 70 metres high and are operated by a crew of less than 25 sea personnel.

Container shipping as a technology (ships and containers and their handling) has led to a completely new generation of ports: highly mechanized and efficient. These ports effectively eliminated labour-intensive loading and unloading of vessels on a pallet or case basis at both origin and destination and involve very limited additional handling (or none) at the source of the goods and the receiving point.

This technology and its business operations model has been a case of creative destruction in Schumpeter's terms, not just of traditional port-handling methods but of property and consumer markets as well as factories. The key features of this destructive change are:

- Many ports and dock workers have been made redundant; albeit it took until 1989 for the UK Dock Labour Scheme to be disbanded.[1]

- Traditional port locations in cities have been repurposed as upmarket office and residential sites, after a period of sorry decay.

- Consumers have benefited from the lower prices of goods sourced from low-cost producers, helping to contain their cost of living and drive economic growth.

- Many of the people who used to work in the factories that have been offshored have been redeployed into higher-value occupations, potentially in the new offices.

There is no doubt among economists and trade experts that container freight has enabled the spectacular growth in world trade of manufactured goods by value illustrated in Figure 6.1, earlier in this chapter.

Applying our business operations model framework to this disruptive development, the narrative goes like this:

- The customer proposition is truly compelling. Anything can be shipped from anywhere to anywhere else across the globe with the security of a sealed container and at a tiny cost in comparison to the value of the goods (typically 1 per cent to 5 per cent of their cost). The end-to-end shipment costs are reduced due to the elimination of the double handling, increased shipment cube due to stacking of the containers and very limited shipping losses. And container shipping is relatively reliable. This enables low-cost sourcing and increased marketplace value for the goods.

- While container freight is a disruptive technology it is difficult to protect by patent; as a result, the growth has attracted many competitors and created a fragmented market. The resulting commercial conditions for the shipping lines have been characterized by overcapacity and volatile pricing, plunging the shipping lines into losses from time to time. This pricing volatility has been to the benefit of shippers; but it has been a tough place for the lines to secure sustained returns on investment.

- On the verticals of our business operations model framework, container shipping has disintermediated traditional high-cost port operations – putting in place a new channel with much better economics.

- It has obliterated complexity in shipping – everything goes into a container and there are very limited special handling requirements.

- It has allowed the shipping lines and their forwarders to optimize their networks by interlining containers both within their own fleet and with other lines without excessive handling costs.

- It has created vessel standards that enable optimized sourcing; ships have been constructed in quantities and hence lowered the average cost of vessel construction – successful ports have got bigger with fewer of them, as the investment in their handling equipment has become more sophisticated – and the basics of the operations have been mastered to ensure acceptable reliability and cost levels.

Container shipping has become a long-term disruptor both for shipping itself and for the manufacturing industries it serves. Its challenge, as with many disruptive models that are not protected, is how to make money from the change in the 21st-century economy. In shipping, prices are highly transparent and in periods of low demand can race to the bottom. At the same time there has been significant cash invested in capacity, anticipating growth.

The result has been that container freight has been challenged for margin and return as competitors have slugged it out, with price the main criteria in customers' minds for using any particular line. It has indeed been tough to make a satisfactory and consistent return in the sector; the individual shipping lines' propositions have not been sufficiently differentiated as that is difficult to achieve. Albeit there are some signs that this is changing for a few operators as the value of time-sensitive reliability becomes understood.

Digitization – the 21st-century 'steam engine'

Since the early 1980s when the personal computer emerged, the progression of digitization has transformed and disrupted many aspects of business. The attraction of technology as a disruptor is that it achieves amazing things and most of us struggle to understand just how it is achieved and the personal implications of the potential disruption – until of course we learn to use it. This incredulous response to technology, together with its disruptive potential, can be seen from the story of the development and introduction of the electric telegraph.

When the electric telegraph was invented and developed in the first half of the 19th century it found eager adopters. However, France had traditionally communicated using semaphore, the 'visual telegraph', using a nationwide government-owned system of stone towers along the hilltops using big windmill-like arms. This was in its time a disruptive technology, capable of outpacing a mounted despatch rider. So in France the advent of the telegraph was seen with distrust. In 1846, Dr Barbay, a semaphore specialist, produced a classic head-in-the-sand response to the telegraph system with the following commentary:

> No, the electric telegraph is not a sound invention. It will always be at the mercy of the slightest disruption, wild youths, drunkards, bums, etc... The electric telegraph meets those destructive elements with only a few meters of wire over which supervision is impossible. A single man could, without being seen, cut the telegraph wires leading to Paris, and in twenty-four hours cut in ten different places the wires of the same line, without being arrested. The visual telegraph, on the contrary, has its towers, its high walls, its gates well-guarded from inside by strong armed men. Yes, I declare, substitution of the electric telegraph for the visual one is a dreadful measure, a truly idiotic act. (cited in Martin, 1996: 48)

Referring back to Stelzer, in this example, a regulated approach was ultimately overridden. New technologies will always prevail if they enable disruptive business models; as always, the benefits are compellingly about better, faster, easier and cheaper.

The incredulity that is induced by computer technology, electronics and digitization is simply that is it is difficult to anticipate the value until it is experienced, understanding its nature and rate of evolution. Wonderful quotes from the early days include:

> Computers of the future may weigh no more than one-and-a-half tonnes.
> *Popular Mechanics*, 1949

> 'I think there is a world market for maybe five computers.'
> Thomas Watson, first CEO of IBM

Ken Olsen, the founder of Digital Equipment, is misinterpreted when he said: 'There is no reason anyone in their right mind will want a computer in their home.' He actually had a computer in his home but he was discarding the idea of computers *to run* the home. This is

FIGURE 6.3   Moore's Law diagram – logarithmic scale

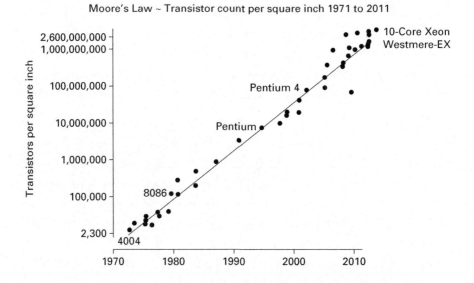

what we now know as the 'internet of things', when your fridge will tell you if it is out of milk and reorder it online and you can pro-gramme the heating and the dishwasher from your car, or whatever.

The rapid acceleration of both computing power and storage to $ ratio is represented in Moore's Law, which suggests, rather than proves, that speed and capacity in microchips and storage doubles roughly every 18 months. Figure 6.3 shows a representation of Moore's Law and indicates that current forecasts and experience suggest that doubling may now take three years as against 18 months.

This empirical phenomenon has the consequence of reducing costs and improving performance. This power has unlocked the potential for new applications with compelling customer propositions, and has been the foundation of new businesses and changed the way we all work. However, that power and capacity would be of much reduced value if the internet had not also been getting faster and faster with more capacity to enable connectivity. The investment in fibre-optic broadband is like the rails on which the 20th-century steam engines ran. Figure 6.4 illustrates the amazing growth in internet activity and capacity in the 15-year period 1997–2011.

FIGURE 6.4   The growth in internet traffic

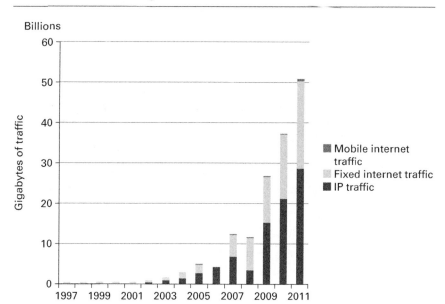

Combined, these long-term technical evolutions have made computing power and capacity more and more accessible and easy to use, leading to a whole range of market-disrupting services and putting traditional industries into structural decline. Consider these examples:

- iTunes has transformed the music industry, disintermediated traditional music retailers, allowed customers to pick and mix, lowered average selling prices and made publishers and labels rethink their businesses.

- Video streaming is eating away at the traditional cinema business with studio and movie-palace operations facing decline.

- Online newspapers and free news services are eroding traditional newspaper sales, which are in structural decline (in revenues).

- e-books and the growth of Amazon Kindle has driven the rapid decline in book retailing and caused publishers to rethink their distribution models, including more direct selling online.

- Uber is in the process of transforming the taxi industry (we return to its model later in the chapter).

- Countless apps and web services are impacting buying behaviours in travel, retail and services.

- The impact on business itself is burgeoning as companies exploit so-called 'big data'; notable actors such as Dunhumby are enabling focused marketing and increased customer intimacy.[2]

While such a list could continue to fill a book, it is the pace of change that is remarkable. Retailers are reporting that online buying is increasing at 15 per cent to 20 per cent per year while store sales are at best flat; this is eroding their traditional operational economics. From the technology perspective, the use of tablets and smartphones now accounts for as much as 50 per cent of online sales, up from 20 per cent in 18 months – suggesting a commercial parallel to Moore's Law.

The business operations model: Maxims for exploiting technological innovation

Let's look at the key lessons we can take from this simple overview and analysis of technology as a business disruptor (these generalizations will also provide the platform to understand three short case studies):

1 The first insight into digitization, and more conventional technology developments, is that technology supports explosive growth and marketplace disruption if it delivers extraordinary value. As we have seen in all the examples, the combination of end-to-end cost and convenience/service (which also has a value) for the buyer relative to the alternative is the decisive factor in creating explosive growth.

2 Disruptive businesses apply technology, but the technology itself is not the disruptor; it is the business model that leverages the technology that can deliver disruptive success. On our business operating model, technological disruption always

involves some combination of disintermediation of market channels, mastering complexity, optimized sourcing and fulfilment, and potentially the other verticals.

3 Disruptive technologies always have a combination of technical features. Steam and the Suez Canal disrupted tea-clippers; containers, ports and ships disrupted traditional cargo vessels; computer power, the internet and tablets have disrupted retail and publishing.

4 Disruptors change markets but they do not have to dominate them. Southwest Airlines hold only around 15 per cent of the domestic airline market, but it has become a reference point for pricing and service. The tea-clippers found alternative viable cargoes along different routes when the Suez Canal opened and steam ships became more efficient. Retailers continue to trade through their shops in streets and malls as e-commerce has accelerated. It is the price points that are set by disruptors and the consequential reduced returns for heritage operations that are the key; it becomes more difficult to maintain prices and margins as there is a new pricing floor that is attracting growing demand.

5 In the face of falling margins, there remains the potential for continued life after having been disrupted. Businesses may need to address alternative market segments, re-base their cost structures, find new value propositions, or adopt the new model wholeheartedly. This is about managing structural decline, when the lever of growth in Charan's model (introduced in Chapter 2) is no longer available.

6 Being a disruptor is not a guarantee of commercial return. Many technological developments cannot be fully protected by patent, and the development of challengers is encouraged by the visibility of market growth. Container shipping has never provided the consistent financial returns that its exceptional customer value would justify. Amazon in retail has recorded huge growth, disrupted the retail market, created astonishing shareholder value but has not recorded sustained profits, as we saw in Chapter 2.

7 The horizon of disruption can be cut short with new technological combinations overtaking disruptors. The accelerating rate of technological development, particularly with digitization, means that some technology-based business operating models may be obsolete in short order. If a company is in a segment that can be easily overtaken, its board would do well to be watching for such developments with cold objectivity.

8 Finally, as the saying goes, 'it can take many years to become an overnight success'. The case studies below show remarkable perseverance as the building blocks to being a disruptor are inched into place.

These maxims place technology as a disruptor clearly in the context of our business operations model framework. It is the business operations model that leverages the technology and drives growth and market value, both for customers and shareholders. Let's look now at three case studies, all of which have digitization as their technological platform for market disruption.

CASE STUDY   Uber Technologies

Uber is a technology company that is aiming to disrupt the taxi industry in major cities around the world. Based in San Francisco and started in 2009, it organized its first passengers in the city in 2010 and in September 2014 had expanded to 45 countries and more than 100 cities. Its innovative business model has made it a hot property with the media and with investors. Financials are hard to come by as the company is privately held. However, *Forbes* magazine suggested in June 2014 that gross revenues were $1.5 billion – that's what the customers paid to ride, and a net to Uber to run the business of around $300 million. The company and its app have caught the imagination of investors and the business press, attracting comment on its operating model and valuation. A recent private share placement is said to value the company at $17 billion. *Forbes* provided some useful analysis in June 2014, which suggests that this valuation may be more than 'full' based on a 10-year horizon of growth. It also points out that Uber is not alone; there is competition with a similar proposition in the form of companies such as

Lyft, Flywheel and Hailo, all of which help people to hail and pay for regular cabs from their phones.

Whatever the valuation, it is clear from the financials that Uber is in rapid growth through its disruptive model that leverages smartphone connectivity and sophisticated algorithms to give passengers a better experience. Through the customer lens the proposition gives compelling benefits. They can order a taxi from their smartphones, watch it make its way to pick them up, pay less than would be on the meter and have the charge go directly to their credit card account rather than having to find the cash or complete a card transaction at the end of the journey. Corporate accounts no longer have to process lots of expense slips and can see their city travel details on a regular basis across their whole team. This beats, hands down, the experience of standing on a wet and windy street corner wondering if the taxi you ordered on the phone will ever arrive, or waiting for a vacant cab to come by. It avoids having to find an ATM on the journey or being completely cleaned out of cash. Not only is it better and faster it is cheaper too, consistent with our maxim for a successful disruptive model. The *Sunday Times* on 8 June 2014 reported that the fare from Shepherd's Bush to Wapping in London was £24 versus a traditional London black cab at £44, which is quite a saving. However, Uber increases prices by a multiple and very quickly when the weather is bad or demand is high – this is called surge pricing and is something that the black cabs – by regulation – cannot do.

Unpacking how this is achieved using our framework and the maxims for technology disruptors is instructive:

1   Clearly technology is delivering remarkable customer value relative to traditional competitors – better, faster, easier and cheaper.

2   The business model involves getting new entrants to the taxi market to sign up with Uber and this is disintermediating the traditional regulated market for taxis. In the case of London, the new entrants don't have to spend three years learning the streets and then paying a large fee. They can simply pass the vetting process, sign up to be operational and use a satnav. The Uber taxis don't have to queue for hours at Heathrow or the London stations so their working utilization is much improved, as long as Uber gets to critical mass on its customer base so the work is available. In terms of business operations model, Uber has a much more optimal fulfilment network, courtesy of their algorithms, and has optimized its sourcing and supply; it has also attended to the basics in terms of safety and is continuing to work on regulatory compliance challenges.

    The operational, administrative and regulatory waste that is eliminated through the Uber model is the key to its disruptive business model. Uber drivers may well be working for less money but that is the result of the new model-cutting barriers for hungry entrants; there is no future in complacency, expecting 'the French Windmills' to be secure.

3   The technology combination that has made this possible is smartphones, a really nifty app, 3G mobile networks and some really clever algorithms back at Uber HQ; these bring together technologies, supporting our third maxim. The vehicle is still the vehicle and the driver is still the driver.

4   Projections for Uber, as assembled by *Forbes*, are for a market share of between 10 per cent and 20 per cent of the global taxi market; the upper end of this range would exceed investors' current valuations. This is a substantial but not dominant market share and supports our fourth maxim.

5   Other taxis – yellow, black or red – will continue to ply their trade but their net margins will decline, unless regulators intervene to support the traditional model – confirming our fourth and fifth maxims.

6   There is no guarantee for Uber on a 10-year horizon of a sustained commercial return. On the limited analysis available, the business can expect to be profitable, but the return on the premium paid for shares by later investors may disappoint. This mirrors many other high-tech investments where hype and expectation has trumped cold and calm common sense. It also supports our sixth maxim.

7   The competition may itself disrupt Uber with initiatives such as a better app, cornering the driver capacity in the market or persuading regulators to act; more extreme disruption could come from driverless (autonomous) cars: our seventh maxim.

8   It is just over four years since Uber first operated – a relatively short period in the life of a disruptor. As a result, our eighth maxim may not apply in this case.

Looking ahead, Uber's biggest challenge will be regulation. As of 2015: in Brussels the authorities have banned it. In Berlin the existing taxi network won an injunction against Uber, while in France the authorities are said to be considering a ban and Uber drivers have been attacked. Elsewhere from Melbourne to Madrid and Toronto and across the United States in Chicago, Boston, New York and Detroit the company has faced legal challenges. The strategy of raising a substantial fund now may be partly to put in place the war chest to take on those actions. The parallel with Southwest Airlines and its early legal battles is striking; at the time of writing there is no telling whether Uber will be as successful as Southwest Airlines.

CASE STUDY   Apple

Our analysis in Chapter 2 showed Apple as the company with the highest market value in the FT Global 500 for the three years to 2014 and the top supply chain performer in the Gartner rankings over the seven years to 2014. This number one valuation is driven by earnings, which our analysis showed is the biggest driver of market value. So although ExxonMobil and Walmart are more than twice the size of Apple in revenues, margin and growth expectations make Apple the more valuable business.

Apple is self-evidently a disruptor; it has transformed the music industry with iTunes and mobile phones with the iPhone. The iPad and iPhone technology took the tablet market centre stage and is the tablet of reference for most people, even if many then select the android option. Retailers now experience as much as 50 per cent of their online demand from phones and tablets. It is difficult to imagine life without Apple, which has become a serial innovator; the question often asked is what will they do next?

But the growth of Apple as a technology disruptor is a story of two halves with some setbacks in the middle. Its stellar trajectory only really started in 2006, as shown in Figure 6.5.

FIGURE 6.5   Chart of revenues and earnings for Apple

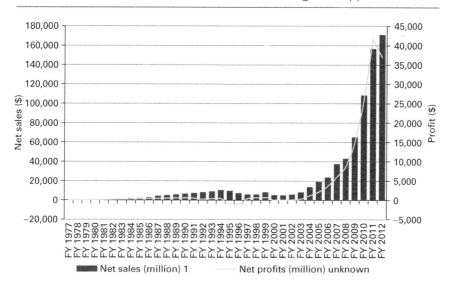

Phase 1 started in that famous garage in Los Altos in 1976 with Steve Jobs, Steve Wozniak and Ron Wayne developing, making and selling the Apple I. The company was incorporated in 1977 and launched the Apple II the same year. During the first five years, revenues doubled every four months and the Apple II became the platform for the VisiCalc spreadsheet, linking business and home use. In December 1979, Jobs and other Apple employees visited the Palo Alto research facility of Xerox and saw the graphical user interface (GUI). It made a profound impact on Jobs and was incorporated in two products that followed the Apple III – the Lisa and the Macintosh. The Lisa shipped in 1983 with the Macintosh in 1984. The Macintosh sold better than the Lisa due to its lower price point that still gave the magical user experience; it made computing accessible to people who had no programming skills. After a slow start, the prospects for Mac were transformed with the introduction of PostScript laser printing and available software for desktop publishing. The Macintosh Portable was launched in 1989 and the PowerBook in 1991. In the same year Apple introduced a major operating system upgrade and, as Figure 6.5 shows, revenues and profits grew very successfully until 1995.

The downturn in fortunes began in 1995 and was attributable to a series of failed developments including digital cameras, portable CD player, speakers, video consoles and the Apple Newton. The Newton was the precursor of today's tablets, including the iPad. There was just too much effort expended on too many developments, which for whatever reason did not land. Losses were incurred in 1996 and 1997 and revenues continued to fall, only recovering past 1995 levels in 2005. During that time Microsoft was in the ascendency and its version of the GUI took control of the personal computer market; Microsoft's Windows was the platform of choice for software developers and drove more than 90 per cent of the burgeoning PC market. Apple had lost out for a decade, which makes the current number one spot bring with it a certain schadenfreude – not that Microsoft is doing badly.

It is important to realize that Apple had the opportunity to license its operating system in the early 1990s to manufacturers but mostly chose not to. Instead it sued Microsoft in a case that lasted years and which Apple eventually lost. Possibly, had Apple chosen the licence route (channel in our business operations model) it might have stifled the acceleration of market growth of Microsoft's Windows operating system at adolescence rather than waiting nearly 10 years to beat it to pole position; readers should note that Microsoft was already the world's largest software company by 1988, so Apple would have been attempting to disrupt its further growth. Apple chose not to license and it is worth making the point that it would have likely changed the culture of Apple and restricted its ingenuity.

Steve Jobs had been ousted by the board in 1985 but returned in 1997, first as an advisor and then as interim CEO. But it took until 2004/5 for the company to land a market-beating trajectory as the iPod and iTunes took off. This was followed in 2007 by the iPhone, iMac and the iPad. The rest, as they say, is history; the revenues and earnings shown in Figure 6.5 tell it all.

Any survey of Apple's customers would report that its products are considered expensive but aspirational, because they are so good to use. It is this premium position that Apple has succeeded in maintaining in both phases of its development; while the business was going forward, margins were outstanding in relation to the competition for the sector. The contrast with the conventional PC could not be more striking, with the industry consolidating in the face of the struggle to make money as products became commoditized. Hewlett-Packard absorbed Compaq, which in turn had bought Digital; IBM sold out to Lenovo and Dell has been taken out of public ownership to reinvent itself. Many of the marginal brands have just passed out of sight. The list runs from Acorn, through Commodore to Wang. The parallel with airline industry consolidation and exits in the face of profitability challenges (as described in Chapter 1) is striking.

Looking at Apple's success in the context of our business operations model and the technology disruptor maxims provides a consistent picture; it is a narrative that is not usually articulated:

1   First, Apple has created a brand proposition that is really attractive and for which its customers are prepared to pay a premium. The brand aura and experience is in the same territory as the luxury clothing brands, a 'must have' and 'the thing to be seen with'. That is likely to be why it hired Angela Ahrendts in 2014 from Burberry to run their $20 billion retail operations. This is a high gross margin business, which carefully controls its own retail distribution and participates in that margin; the SEC 10K filing for 2014 shows a gross margin of 38.6 per cent compared to a 20 per cent benchmark for the sector and typically 70 per cent for luxury brands.

    To be a technology disruptor, Apple has designed great things that provide a real technological and in-use advantage. This fulfils our first maxim that it delivers real user convenience; for example it was the iPhone App that originally powered Uber as well as so many others.

2   However, its business operations model has been a key part of the success formula in two areas: channels and services and support; this aligns to our second maxim that it is not the technology that is the disruptor but its application. We said earlier that technical disruption almost always involves some combination of disintermediation of market channels, mastering complexity and potentially the other verticals.

For Apple the business operations model has focused on supporting its premium position. In the context of its gross margin, it has not had to be top quartile in the other areas.

3 The disruptive success of Apple has been driven by a combination of factors. This idea of combinations for success is our third maxim and in Apple it features: touchscreen and easy-to-use apps, 3G communications networks and ubiquitous Wi-Fi, seamless integration to both iTunes and the App Store. We would assert that these are not a single technology – hence its success is about how Apple has strung them together and exploited the moment of their evolution or development. It is worth noting that the original GUI concept came from Xerox Parc and was made available by a Xerox investment in Apple of just $1 million with software engineers moving across to Apple. From this it can be interpreted that Apple could bring greater dynamism to the development together with better manufacturing to sell at lower price points; the exponential development of Moore's Law made the timing right.

4 Our fourth maxim suggests that disruptors change markets but do not dominate them; again this appears to be the case. Apple has a 12 per cent to 23 per cent share of the world smartphone market (it varies by quarter as new models are released), 25 per cent of the tablet sector, around 6 per cent of the PC market. Only in music with iTunes is it a dominant player with 63 per cent. Android, Windows and other tablets thrive in the market but they do not hold the high ground on price and are positioned as commodity alternatives.

5 The narrative for Apple on the fifth maxim (life after being disrupted) applies to its period in a trough in the late 1990s and early 2000s when its fortunes waned; there was indeed life after that downturn while the business reinvented itself. Revenues did not collapse totally; survival is about managing for margin in the decline.

6 The sixth maxim, which suggests that being a disruptor is no guarantee of good returns, clearly does not apply to Apple. It has protected its leadership position with care and that has prevented followers getting too close; the reader should not underestimate the legal detail that has been expended to build and maintain barriers to copying and protect the quality of distribution, something all leading brands invest in heavily. In our business operations model terms this is part of managing the basics.

7 Our seventh maxim is about the horizon of disruption being potentially short. For Apple, the surge in market share of MS Windows and the Office suite as the de facto business standard was their case of the disruptor being

disrupted. Between 1993 and 2004, Apple's share of the PC segment declined from 9 per cent to 2 per cent on a market that grew by 570 per cent. Clearly the business market could not justify the premium that Apple was charging for a slightly superior experience, as GUI systems became universal and microchip power increased.

8   Our final maxim is that 'it can take many years to become an overnight success'. This definitely applies to Apple, as the chart of revenue and earnings in Figure 6.5 showed. There was a period of 10 years in the doldrums; more important, it is possible to look at the entire timespan from the introduction of the Macintosh as being a development and rehearsal for the current success. This observation covers particularly the user interface, channels to market, and service and support infrastructure that we alluded to a few paragraphs earlier.

Apple's channel strategy has evolved consistently to focus on exclusive distribution channels as a way to control the brand experience. In the early days this was done through independent Apple dealers, Applecenters; today it is achieved through Apple Stores (about 10 per cent of revenues), most of which are company owned and controlled; all the other channels are carefully managed to maintain brand identity and global pricing consistency. The selling environment is a key part of the brand experience, much like visiting a Burberry shop. This approach allows Apple to participate in a proportion of the retail gross margin and enables it to dictate trade discounts to other qualified retailers. It also provides first-level support and triage of problems that simply cannot be achieved without direct customer contact with trained support people. So Apple's channels, and service and support business operations model verticals, have been aligned together to be mutually supportive. But the service and support element of the business operations model is also distinguished by the App Store. This started with iTunes in 2001, but has moved on to be a comprehensive electronic retail store for music, apps and hardware. Using the cloud, Apple has enabled a seamless 'one account' approach to its customer interactions. This is both a revenue stream (more than 10 per cent) but also an operational element of the brand experience. It has created a virtuous circle with premium prices paying for excellent services, which reinforce the desirability of the brand and help to grow revenues and profits: their business operations model.

As we observed earlier in this section, Apple has held the number one position in Gartner's ranking of supply chain excellence for the seven years to 2014. Based on 50 per cent of the scoring for this assessment being based on growth, return and inventory turns (three of Charan's levers from Chapter 2), its leadership is hardly surprising. Looking at how Apple has organized its supply chain in terms of our business operations model we find:

- Market channels: powerful control of the retail channel and customer experience, including how it deals with international currency variations.

- Mastering complexity: a highly standardized product to help planning and avoid supply chain complexity.

- Optimized fulfilment networks: Apple takes skilful advantage of third-party logistics providers to give them flexible capacity to cope with launch peak volumes.

- Service and support: is mostly outstanding (as observed earlier).

- Inventory segmentation and deployment: is an issue mostly avoided by the low product variety and high volumes; however, Apple has a global ability to direct product to where it is needed and to balance supply and demand.

- Optimized sourcing and supply: over the last 15–20 years Apple has assertively outsourced its manufacturing to low-cost contract producers while retaining control of the intellectual property.

- Managing the basics: there is no case material that Apple has leveraged performance by managing the basics; optimized sourcing and supply have been enough to deliver super-performance in the light of the selling prices.

- Demand–supply planning: in the fast-moving world of electronic products, the importance of planning is paramount and clearly Apple makes those decisions well. However, the narrow range, the very fast rate of sale and a willingness to leave the market short of product, if necessary, all make the planning task easier than in other sectors such as consumer goods.

The challenge for Apple is 'what next'? As we have showed, Apple does not have dominance other than in iTunes. There will inevitably be challenger brands that get closer to the experience and for less money; also there will be a degree of market saturation. Apple has built significant barriers for competitors to surmount, but the stream of 'must-have' products will need to continue to build on the experiences that its loyal customers expect. Otherwise they will attract the 'incumbent's curse' – an idea we return to in Chapter 11.

CASE STUDY   Amazon

Our final case study of a technology-based disruptor is that of Amazon. The FT 500 classifies Amazon as a general retailer rather than a technology actor. Yet most think of it as a 'tech' innovator. It is now difficult to find anyone who does not use Amazon.com as one of their retail providers. It has become the reference point for online retail, which is a key feature of business disruptors (the scale of Amazon's achievement was highlighted in Chapter 2). The growth in both revenues and share price since the business launched in 1994–95 is remarkable and is shown in Figure 6.6. As we observed in Chapter 2, this remarkable trajectory has yet to deliver sustained profitability of the type seen at Apple, or indeed companies such as Walmart in the retail sector. Its market valuation is sustained entirely by the prospect of growth, waiting for when it is so dominant that value can be monetized. Our maxims suggest that valuation on such a basis is inherently risky.

Setting aside the question of profitability, even though it is a core part of our business operations model framework, Amazon's achievement through the customers' lens is remarkable. Its delivery through their operating model engages every single one of the verticals. We will unpack what Amazon has done in the context of the maxims and also the business operations model elements, but first look at Figure 6.7, which shows the technological timeline. It shows how Amazon has ridden the evolution of a number of technologies, particularly the internet,

FIGURE 6.6   The growth in revenues, market value and net income for Amazon since 2008

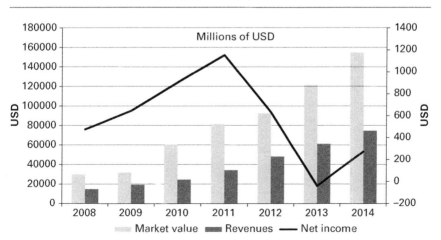

FIGURE 6.7   Timeline of Amazon's development in the context of technology

Year	Technology	Other Manufacturers	Amazon's Response
1992	GSM		
1993	Dial-up internet		
1994	Mobile phones		Amazon arrives
1996		Dell.com launches	Amazon books
1997			Personalized recommendations Subject-area browsing Prices lowered 1-click shopping
1998	WWW technology		Amazon.co.uk
2000		Cisco Systems starts	Consumer electronics Home Software Toys Videos Kitchen Cars Garden All products search
2001	Broadband started	Nokia 6210 Mobile Usage > 50%	Burst bubble $107–$7
2002	Optical-fibre		Free shipping orders over $99
2003	Blackberry		Apparel Jewellery Super Saver Shopping >$25
2004	Apple iTunes		
2005	Bluetooth		Shoes
2006	Flatscreen TVs		Amazon Prime (unlimited $79)
2007		Broadband widely available	
2008	iPhone		Amazon Ec2 services
2009	Cloud Google universal search	iPhone 3G	Fulfilled by Amazon services
2010	4G services		Groceries Video downloads Kindle
2011	Superfast broadband	iPad	Digital music
2012	Optical computing		Amazon price tracker
2013	Self-driving car		Kindle Fire
2014		Shapeways starts trading	Expanding footprint Sameday & Amazon Logistics Fashion Kiva Robots

mobile computing, Kindle and its portal design to build its successful business. It has also focused relentlessly on its customer interface and back office systems in terms of ease of use, one-click shopping, recommendations, customer intimacy (as far as that is possible down optical-fibre) and service responsiveness.

These technical combinations have delivered massive customer benefits in terms of:

- Ease of use: search, recommendations, one-click shopping with fast and convenient delivery through an increasing range of options.

- Remarkable variety and choice with more than 200 million products available through its own product sales, through 'Fulfilled by Amazon' and by independent vendors accessed through the portal.

- Low prices relative to the market: albeit probably too low for sustained profits and from our analysis it is not at benchmark levels in our business operations model verticals of optimized fulfilment networks and optimized sourcing platform.

This benefit combination arising from the technical combination is both compelling to customers and disruptive to other channels (that word disintermediation again as traditional routes to market are by-passed). Once again this supports our first, second and third maxims – compelling value; the technology is not the disruptor it is the model; and combinations are always present.

Amazon's global revenues were $74.5 billion in 2013, which is not the total value of goods sold since it only credits the sales commission for goods not owned by Amazon. This compares to Apple's $182 billion and Walmart's $473 billion; it bears out our fourth maxim that disruptors change markets without dominating them. For most retailers, Amazon is the price reference and it acts as a restraint on their commercial flexibility.

The fifth maxim points to life after disruption. Perhaps the most disrupted area of the market is book publishing and retailing, in which Amazon is particularly strong. There is evidence that publishers are adapting their business models to reduce their cost base and sell direct on their own accounts; our own publisher was selling direct in 2014, something it did not do two years previously. Book-selling retailers such as Barnes and Noble and Waterstones have been carefully adjusting their offer and customer experience, including emphasizing their own online offers.

Our sixth maxim suggests that being a disruptor is no guarantee of commercial return. This is certainly the case for Amazon. The question is the extent to which its current pricing policy is self-imposed as against what is essential for marketplace success. Certainly there are competitors in many forms, from eBay to many local operators. Again, there is evidence that these operators are fighting back by trying to increase variety through their own portals and match the Amazon customer experience.

The horizon on which Amazon itself might be disrupted is difficult to predict, so our seventh maxim cannot be confirmed. However, the timeline shows that it has taken 20 years for Amazon to reach its current scale, although its model has been a talking point since the late 1990s. This means that our eighth maxim (years to become an overnight success) is debatable. It clearly has taken many years for Amazon to get to the current point and may take many more for commercial returns on investment to be attained.

Looking at the key features of Amazon's business operations model, the narrative goes like this:

- Amazon delivers extraordinary value to customers through ease of access, low prices and huge variety – the company is easy to use.

- It delivers great service in the form of next day delivery, Amazon Prime, excellent packaging and good tracking information. Anyone who has queried a transaction will likely have found great responsiveness and attention to detail.

- The commercial costs and profitability are not yet benchmarked with other retailers; as we have observed, it operates on marginal profitability.

- To achieve its remarkable growth, it has disrupted market channels, especially for books and music, and given independent sellers wider access to markets where they can reach new customers and sell at low margins, giving great prices. The Kindle has disintermediated the traditional book-printing and publishing industry in the same way that iTunes disintermediated physical media.

- Perhaps key to Amazon's success is the way it has organized for complexity – adding range without adding stock and cost. Benchmarking analysis of its 10K report for 2013 suggest 56 days of stock, which compares well with many retailers at 70 to 80 days (it is not possible to be sure as the numbers require interpretation beyond what is visible). This would not be possible on 200 million items with every one being in stock; with limited inside knowledge, Amazon has combined wholesale supply on a just-in-time basis, bulk direct purchase and the use of the portal to extend the range of relatively slower moving products. This means that Amazon has made significant progress in its inventory deployment and segmentation vertical in our model framework.

- Amazon has added capacity in its fulfilment networks to accommodate its growth and is now attending to the basics of distribution centre automation with its acquisition of Kiva, a robotic warehouse automation system. Our benchmark comparisons suggest that Amazon is in the bottom quartile of its

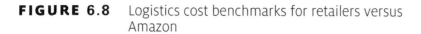

FIGURE 6.8   Logistics cost benchmarks for retailers versus Amazon

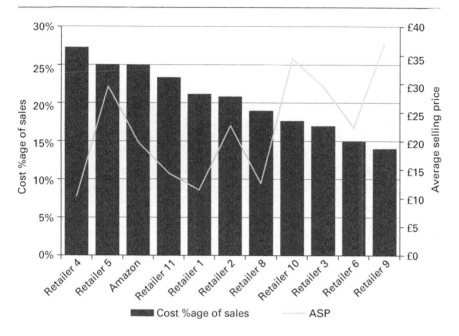

logistics cost-to-serve, as illustrated in Figure 6.8, based on public domain information and reasonable interpretation.

Overall this analysis suggests that Amazon has a way to go to get to a business operations model optimum. We will look at the opportunities for such improvement in Chapters 8 and 9: the basics and optimization.

Taking forward the framework in your business

Becoming a technology-based disruptor

From the analysis in this chapter, it appears that our business operations model framework and technological disruptor maxims have consistency in their application; not every maxim and model element comes into play in every case, but many do. If you aspire to be a tech-based disruptor, then taking it forward into your business involves answering the following questions:

- How can a technical development be converted into compelling customer value?

- What are the dynamics of the potential disruption? Through the technological development, who will be disintermediated? How will complexity be mastered? Where and how can costs be obliterated? What is the business and profit model to be?

- What are the combinations of technology that can really make the difference to the customer experience and the economics? The innovation is often in those combinations – so what have we got to harness?

- What is the scale of the market change that we need to create to become a disruptor? Is the potential really there and can we grow the market as well as change it?

- What will be the effect on other players in the market and how may they respond? Can they fight back, how and over what timescales?

- Can we really make money and over what timescale? How can we protect the innovation? Or will other entrants be able to join the party?

- How might we ourselves be disrupted and what do we have to do to stay at the front of the wave? How can we spot the trends?

- Do we really understand the timescales on which we may get breakthrough? Are we ready for the long haul and are the funds in place to get there?

When you have the answers to these questions, once again develop the narrative on how the technological development can be built into a 'money-making-customer-delighter' by defining the specific actions across the business operations model framework. Once again, you need to be thinking about narratives with numbers and timescales. Remember, it can 'take years to become an overnight success'.

Disruptive business models based on technology innovations are an exciting place to be. However, the dot.com boom and subsequent bust in 2000 should be a reminder that it is customer value and economic viability that matters. Defining the business operations model that leverages technology is as important as the technology itself.

Notes

1 The UK Dock Labour Scheme was established by the post-Second World War socialist government to regulate the operations of the ports in terms of hiring and firing of dockworkers. Funded by a levy on the employers it created an institutional barrier to the adoption of new technologies.

2 Dunhumby are a world-leading 'customer science' company using sophisticated analytics of retailer data to determine preferences and support the design of effective sales and marketing activities.

Market-changing models – driving transformation

07

We have seen from some of the cases so far that market channels and their economics are a key factor in becoming a disruptor; it is a pillar in our business operations model. Southwest Airlines avoided agents and the airline booking system; it sold direct to customers, first by phone and then over the internet. Apple, McDonald's and Amazon who are the top three in the Gartner rankings have all got their own distinctive channel models. Our fertilizer example in Chapter 3 used distributors to hold stock and service farmers. While in Chapter 6, Uber has built its own community of taxis and drivers and acts as an intermediary. That example was described alongside a fuller evaluation of both Apple and Amazon, with the distinctive choices they made in the course of their developments. Apple chose not to license its operating system but then took music and apps online as an integrated offer with its desirable and easy-to-use technology. Amazon was the pioneer of the e-retail channel – effectively taking on traditional retail shops.

In this chapter we unpack in more detail the ideas behind market channels and their economics – the first of our verticals in our business operations model framework.

Go-to-market choices – a key to overall economic performance and customer access

The choice of route to market is a key strategic decision which companies can easily take pragmatically or by default – without a full understanding of the true economics or with the right strategic intent. Gary Hamel and CK Prahalad (1989), referred to in Chapter 4, pointed to the strategic intent of Canon in the way it dismantled Xerox in the small copier sector. First they developed a great product at price points beyond Xerox's comprehension by innovating with disposable toner cartridges. Then Canon used the office distributor channel to reach and build this completely new segment, relying on the distributors' relationships, already established, with secretaries and office managers as strong influencers of the potential purchase. This helped both Canon and the distributors to build revenues as these influencers valued the convenience of the small desktop copier. It was within their financial compass to have one – so they did! This disrupted Xerox's pay-per-copy commercial model by taking volume away from the big copy-centre machines. Interestingly, Canon also helped Apple to gain share in the desktop publishing market when it made its laser printer available under the Apple brand – another channel that helped to build volumes to critical mass and lower unit costs.

Many companies maintain complex and multiple routes to market in order to capture all the available routes to use and consumption. These routes each have their own characteristics in terms of market access and economics. Figure 7.1 shows this diverse picture in the case of a company supplying health-care products across Europe.

The company shown in Figure 7.1 has two points of final delivery to the patient: the surgery/pharmacist and hospitals. Within the first, the product can be used at home or applied in the surgery; in hospitals it may be supplied in the operating theatre, on the wards or in accident and emergency. The company uses three channels: distributors, its own logistics and distribution and the wholesale channel, supplied through its own logistics. Each channel comes with its own requirement for services and with significantly different logistical effort and costs. In this case the commercial pricing terms need to reflect the respective costs and margin opportunity for the channel partners of:

- Customer-demand generation: large multinational companies very often have costly marketing programmes and sales forces that can only be cost-effective dealing with volume accounts – they struggle to be economic on accounts that only order in smaller volumes.

FIGURE 7.1   Channels to market for a health-care supplies company

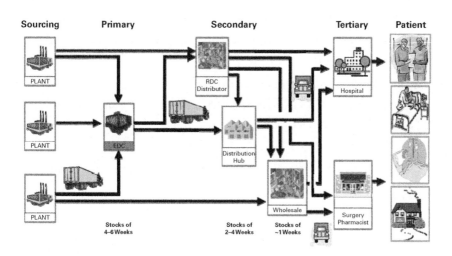

- Customer order capture: smaller customers are costly to serve through large central departments supported by enterprise resource planning (ERP) systems; such functions require large individual orders or sophisticated integration with customers to keep down the cost per order. Where electronic ordering is implemented with larger customers, the process is seamless and a large order can cost eurocents. Where a smaller order must be entered, credit controlled and validated manually, it can cost several euros. This can make the cost percentage to sales for processing an order of, say, €100 highly margin erosive – at as much as 5 per cent to 7 per cent.

- Order fulfilment: the cost of picking, packing, shipping and delivering is quite different if there is a pallet to go to a customer as compared to a mixed case of individual items that has to be assembled in the warehouse. Clearly the cost of picking and shipping smaller quantities in relation to the lower sales value can easily drive up the cost of logistics as a percentage of revenues from 2 per cent for volume to 15 per cent for packages.

- Stock holding: this is a cost that is often overlooked but reflects the balance sheet investment in buying and financing the stock, the risk that it may be spoilt or become obsolete as well as the cost of storing it. If the supplier provides big discounts for bulk purchases, the temptation is to buy and hold more, which can put a severe strain on the balance sheet.

- Credit control, cash collection, financing debtors and absorbing bad debts: these costs again are dependent on scale and control; infrequent, small-purchase accounts will carry a disproportionate level of cost.

In the case of the health-care supplier shown in Figure 7.1, the cost of dealing directly with thousands of small pharmacies in very small quantities is prohibitive; these outlets have no capacity to hold much stock and need servicing several times per day. In response to this need, the sector has developed very effective wholesalers who create scale with each account through selling many suppliers' products as well as minimizing delivery costs through local and efficient multi-pick depots. In the UK, the wholesale channel is the mandatory route to surgeries and pharmacies because of the process of managing health care free at the point of delivery; it is also driven by the huge variety of demand in small quantities that requires a shared logistics capability. The difficulty for suppliers in using wholesale channels is that there are competitors' products in same catalogue; suppliers' marketing therefore has to create demand by getting customers to pull the product through the wholesalers as well as incentivizing the wholesaler to prefer and promote the product.

In some national markets, surgeries and hospital departments are relatively autonomous in their buying and there is advantage on the selling side from using a distributor who knows the market well and is promoting complementary products to bring down the cost per transaction. This creates a level of exclusivity in distribution and increases the expertise at the point of sale. As such, it reduces the need for the direct marketing and incentives found in the wholesale channel.

Finally, the larger customers such as hospitals and public national health-care distribution channels can accept products in relative bulk, which makes selling and delivering to these large accounts cost-effective. These customers hold some stock to accommodate the daily and weekly variations in demand; they are also vast and sprawling institutions such that only their internal skills can actually get the product to the point of use.

For the company shown in Figure 7.1, the hospital channel was the largest by volume and the company was anxious to service it directly. It was considered essential to maintain direct contact with real customers in order to understand their needs and maintain market position.

However, one of the product innovations from this company started to grow rapidly due to its therapeutic benefits (lower cost per patient due to faster healing, fewer applications and greater patient comfort). It was priced at a premium to reflect these benefits and was recording sales growth at 20 per cent per year. In technical terms this was a disruptive product as it enabled new business operations models within the health-care providers; using it they could treat patients less often and more effectively with a lower net cost. The question inside the business was whether they should use the distributor channel to leverage increased volume through better market access in some markets. This was a plan to effectively cut out the wholesalers and create a disruptive business operations model to exploit its distinctive product.

The relative economics of the different channels for this product and for the business as a whole are illustrated in Table 7.1. Readers should note that these numbers are illustrative, rather than the actuals in the case, and that they should not be applied in other cases without due diligence.

Table 7.1 shows the margin and cost components from left to right that lead to a net contribution margin on the right-hand side. The analysis is shown initially for the business as a whole across all channels and then split by the company's traditional products and the advanced new growth product. It then looks at the relative channel economics for wholesale, direct and distributors across the two product groups.

It shows that the contribution margin to the business as a whole from the new growth products is a multiple of the traditional products: 38 per cent versus 5 per cent. It confirms that the direct channel

TABLE 7.1 Example of relative channel economics

Current Business	Gross Margin	Marketing Investment	Order Captur	Physical Distribution	Stock holding costs	Account management	Contribution Margin
Traditional product	30%	8%	3%	9%	2%	3%	5%
New growth product	65%	20%	1%	3%	1%	2%	38%
Total	41%	12%	2%	7%	2%	3%	15%
Traditional product							
Wholesale channel	20%	3%	2%	7%	2%	2%	4%
Direct channel	37%	9%	5%	10%	2%	4%	7%
Distributor channel				Service not available			
New growth product							
Wholesale channel	50%	12%	1%	2%	1%	1%	34%
Direct channel	70%	22%	3%	5%	1%	3%	37%
Distributor channel	55%	8%	1%	3%	1%	1%	42%

is viable for the traditional products on larger accounts as it contributes 7 per cent versus 4 per cent. And it shows that for the new growth product the distributor channel returns a higher net contribution margin than either wholesale or direct. This is due to a much lower gross margin being more than offset by reduced marketing, distribution and account management.

Channels to market are immensely complex for the health-care sector in their choices and costings, as shown in Figure 7.1 and Table 7.1. The options are conditioned not just by cost but also by regulation due to the public provision of the final service. Based on analysis of the type shown (the numbers in Table 7.1 are not actuals), the company contracted to use distributors in some European markets. This was based on the judgement that it would improve market access through a dedicated focus with synergistic products and enhanced economic performance. But this approach was limited to just some markets as the buying behaviours in others did not favour distributors.

The lessons from this simple case describing channel options and economics are important:

1 Distribution channels, in the form of third-party agents or distributors as well as general wholesale, can be the most viable way to reach the market.

2 Alternatively they may be a necessary cost to get access cost-effectively to market segments that the company would otherwise find even more costly (or impossible) to approach directly.

3 There can be significant variations in margin by channel that are not reflected at the consolidated reporting level – understanding the channel cost-to-serve is an essential part of management information and channel choice.

4 Channel design and its ongoing management is a critical skill that can drive both sales and net margin.

5 Channels inevitably make the supplier more remote from the final customer. That lack of immediate feedback is a risk as the balance of customer priorities and competitors' capabilities can move very quickly; it is important to have relationship management processes that keep you close to the action.

Channels-to-market – effective intermediation or disintermediation

The example of the health-care products supplier in the previous section showed that the company had chosen to both sell direct and use wholesaler and distributor channels. The margin impacts for that company were quite finely balanced overall, but in some product-channel segments were significant. In some cases the use of channel was the 'least-worst' option, in others it was a positive benefit, giving access to customers at lower cost and increased net margin. The choice of channel is about using intermediaries or disintermediating existing channels and forming a direct relationship with customers.

The design of disruptive business operations models is generally about disintermediating existing inefficient channels and forming new and more responsive relationships with customers; this may involve reintermediating in a new channel structure to enable a compelling customer proposition (as we described in Chapter 3).

The role of the customer in disintermediating channels and redefining value in their terms cannot be underestimated. Disruptive low-cost airlines not only cut out the agents, they avoid replacing that effort internally – they rely on the customer to self-service their travel plans. The cost of their retail customers' time carries no infrastructure and payroll costs; they can spend hours of free leisure time firming up their travel plans. The Uber taxi business is effectively disintermediating sclerotic, traditional and high-cost city taxi regulation, providing a way for customers to connect to a lower-cost service. The point is that customers do it because they are empowered by the app, motivated by the prices and attracted to the service proposition.

Apple iTunes and Amazon e-books (using the Kindle app) have both disintermediated the physical media production and distribution industries, which are now enduring long-term market restructuring and revenue decline. They have reintermediated themselves between publishers and the consumer. Publishers are not themselves disintermediated by the new channel since they control the publishing rights. But they have lost control of their distribution and pricing terms to access the market; these two dominant forces in music and books have been able to dictate terms. At the time of writing, the inevitable accusations of bullying, lawsuits and anti-trust challenges are taking place. *The Economist* commented on 13 November 2014:

> The stand-off between Amazon and Hachette has triggered a heated discussion about whether the online giant is a monopoly... the authors' associations in America are planning to urge the DoJ to investigate the firm [Amazon] for abuse of market power.

In the end, this is all about margin and return for market access. Amazon has moved to further disintermediate the publishers by offering both print-on-demand and self-publishing services to authors. The publishers are responding by setting up to sell direct to consumers – something they would never have done to their traditional booksellers.

In the business operations model framework the core value proposition has not changed – a book is still a book and a song is still a song. The battleground is about availability, pricing and delivery mechanisms enabled by technology. As we have seen, in everything from flights to taxis and fertilizers, price is a major motivator if the service is also good. Exploiting technology to build new more cost-effective channels is a core part of being a disruptive competitor.

Disintermediating the old and reintermediating with the new is a recurring theme in transforming markets. A starting point for understanding the dynamics and potential is the kind of analysis we showed earlier for the health-care supplies manufacturer.

Indeed that same company recognized the undifferentiated nature of its traditional market and responded by designing pre-prepared surgical and treatment packs. These sterile kits put the entire consumables requirement for a surgeon or doctor to complete an operation or treatment into a single package. The packs are customized to the particular needs of each practitioner and contain both the manufacturers' own products and other supplies. This product strategy follows the maxim stated earlier of getting close to the customer as well as disintermediating the traditional hospital departments' specifying, buying, stocking and handling operations. It locks out the competition and reduces internal costs for the customer. In addition, it increases transaction value and in theory reduces operating costs inside the supplier. Indeed this has proved to be a disruptive business operations model as measured by sustained growth of 20 per cent per annum. We will return in Chapter 9 to the challenge this company faced in making a return from its innovation.

Service-dominant logic – transforming the proposition

The health-care supplies company cited throughout this chapter transformed a conventional customer proposition by putting their products into complete treatment packs and selling them on a customized basis directly to doctors and surgeons. The transformation of the proposition ticks all the boxes – value to customers is improved as it saves the costly time for the nurses and administrators of checking and ordering stock; it guarantees it is right and complete. In channel terms, it gets the company close to its customers and shuts out the competition. The company has effectively absorbed complexity and cost on behalf of its customers – by changing the way they do business together they have 'co-created' value.

While the practice of service and product integration has been in existence since the 1960s, the academic term for this concept – service dominant logic (SDL) – was first proposed by Stephen Vargo and Robert Lusch (2004), who we referenced briefly in Chapter 3. They argued that all goods are a service since their value is in the utility of their application by the buyer or user. Their observations on the co-creation of value-systems are entirely consistent with our idea of disruptive competition through business operations models and apply specifically to this chapter on market channels and the idea of disintermediation.

In summary, and slightly adapted, the key propositions of SDL and their implications are:

- Service is the fundamental basis of exchange – what we enable customers to do rather than the thing they buy is what is important.

- Goods, money and institutions mask the service-for-service nature of exchange; indirect channels impede the fundamental basis for value exchange – how we have traditionally done business gets in the way of creating customer value.

- Goods (both durable and non-durable) derive their value through use – the service that customers derive from their purchase is what matters.

- The comparative ability to cause desired change drives competition – if you can do things for customers that change their behaviours you will change markets and be competitive.

- Service is now becoming more visibly important with increased specialization and outsourcing – the trend to decompose cost structures and look to outsource expertise and functional excellence is exposing value opportunities.

- The customer is always a co-creator of value – so value creation is interactional. We need customers to collaborate to help build new services and drive better value.

- A service-centred view is inherently customer-oriented and relational – channel intermediaries create barriers to identifying value opportunities and insert profit stacking.

- Every commercial and social organization integrates resources with its suppliers, customers and clients – this implies a network economy in which service is 'assembled' from a range of players who may collaborate laterally rather than as a hierarchy.

- Value is always uniquely determined by the beneficiary, which may be idiosyncratic, experiential, contextual and meaning-laden – you can take customers to an opportunity but their response may not be the one anticipated.

The implication of these insights is that companies need to think about how they move from a 'goods-dominant logic' to a 'service-dominant logic' as illustrated in Figure 7.2, adapted from Vargo and Lusch. As one of their maxims observes, the SDL buying behaviour was always in place, just not supported by the practices and thinking of suppliers.

FIGURE 7.2   The evolution of service-dominant logic

Goods-Dominant Logic Concepts	Transitional Concepts	Service-Dominant Logic Concepts
Product OR Service Product = Value Service = Cost	Core Product + Added Service Product = Value Service = Differentiation	Product Service System Product + Service = Value

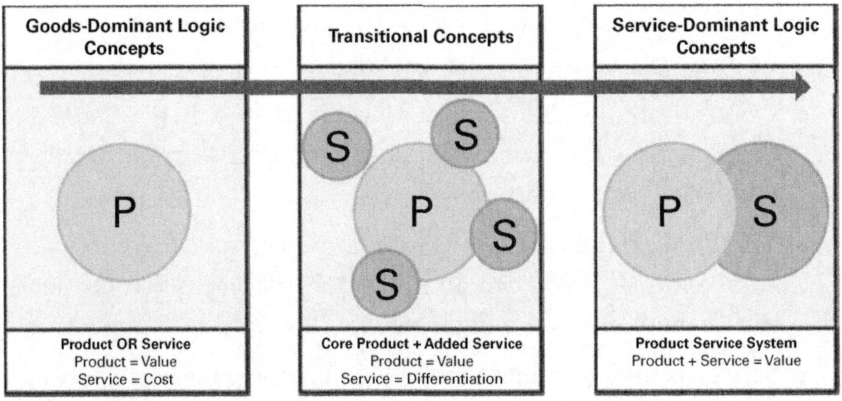

SOURCE: adapted from Vargo and Lusch (2004)

Figure 7.2 shows the idea that 'products' (what we supply) moves through the 'added value services' phase (what we can charge extra for) to a 'product service system' (the outcomes that we deliver for customers). There are many companies that are still trying to bolt on value-added services as an excuse to charge more and make up the margin lost to competitors through pricing. This reflects that they do not know what they really need to do for customers – our insight in Chapter 3.

So the big idea behind SDL in the context of our business operations model framework is that we need to reach inside our customers' value chains. We have to find the things we can do to release value for them and on which we can also make margin and grow the business. That brings us back to the idea of channels to market and their economics – it emphasizes that the customers' operations are in the economic mix; if a company can take in those costs and reconfigure the end-to-end operation, then transformation and growth is possible.

The examples of SDL are many and varied and we have already mentioned Apple's iPod and iTunes as well as the pre-packed and customized health-care service. There are a wealth of examples that can be identified from many sources:

- Hilti, the construction tools and consumables company, provide a rental service for equipment supplied to construction sites. This effectively avoids the need for the contractor to buy the tools, move them, maintain them and account for them; instead the contractor knows that he or she has eliminated investment, repair, loss, storage and movement. The contractor's costings can be done on a cost-per-fix basis with no hidden liabilities.

- City cycle rental and sharing systems are becoming common, with more than 600 cities in more than 49 countries having such schemes by the summer of 2014. One of the most high-profile services is in London where they are known as 'Boris bikes'. A city traveller can pick up a bike at a docking station and leave it at another; the bikes are repositioned around the city, maintained and are only accessible to registered users. The bike users do not have to worry about taking their bike on the commute, having it stolen or having to fix it when it goes wrong. For a rental fee at the time of use they get a trouble-free ride.

- A similar system is now being implemented by BMW using its Mini model – called Zipcar. Customers can rent a car by the hour with no hassle and without all the costs of ownership, parking and the like – just book, collect, use and leave back.

- The SDL model is being applied particularly in aerospace and defence. The term 'power by the hour' is trademarked to Rolls-Royce and the concept was originated by Bristol Siddeley who Rolls-Royce bought in 1968. Effectively an airline can avoid the need to invest in parts and engineering for its engines and instead contract for engine availability (power) at the moment (hour) when it is needed. This concept has driven the development of sophisticated measurement and monitoring of equipment during engine use, so that faults can be identified before they become operational issues. An engine over the South China Sea will be in constant contact with the engineering support centre in the UK so that when it lands in Hong Kong the support team will be able to immediately address any concerns as the plane is turned around for its next leg. This technology is known as 'through-life engineering' and is attracting considerable academic and industrial research investment.[1] It is important to note that all the major aero engine manufacturers, including GE and Pratt & Whitney, now offer this service delivery model.

- The defence industry has adopted the SDL model under the economic pressures of government spending constraints. BAE Systems and Babcock will now maintain warships and submarines on long-term contractual commitments – a kind of 'pay as you sail'.

- Outsourcing of institutional facilities (commonly called facilities management for offices, hospitals and other public buildings) by companies such as Emerson Electric and Johnson Controls effectively takes away the internal work of maintaining, cleaning, securing and powering a building. This translates into a 'cost per usable desk' deal, although it may not be quite phrased that way.

All of these examples imply a realignment of channels to improve value at the point of use and, hopefully, increase return for both supplier and customer. There may be a whole range of actors in the supply chains for these examples that are disintermediated in some way: eg the independent office cleaner, the local engineer and the internal departments for repair and servicing. SDL is a disruptive business concept because it realigns product–service delivery channels to lower end-to-end cost as well as improve availability and quality. At its heart, the SDL concept is about working with customers to co-create value by realigning channels.

Commercial focus – driving and leveraging scale through buying and pricing

The examples in this chapter so far have focused on the producer realigning their offer and channels to get closer to the customer. It has been about rebalancing the cost and value build in their own chain in order to extract better value for both parties through channel economics. However, the opportunity exists equally for companies to look back up their chains and exercise upstream channel choices and value creation potential. Every link in the chain has both customers and suppliers; the prerogative does not just rest with suppliers to co-create value.

This perspective moves the organizational focus from strategic product and service design (the marketing function) to procurement. It exposes the reality that for many companies the procurement function is not seen as being central to strategic redesign; rather it is seen as being transactional, based on a conventional view of supply markets. Nothing could be further from good business practice; supplier development and relationship management is the flip side of value co-creation with customers.

The transformation of retailing, led by companies such as Walmart, has been driven by disintermediation of wholesalers and importers. By dealing directly with suppliers and trading with them in volume, retailers have cut out the middle man, lowered the cost-to-serve and eliminated the intermediaries' profit margin. This has been replaced by slick internal distribution systems with large logistics centres, dedicated to delivering to large-format stores. In a similar but more radical way to our earlier health-care example, the whole of the economic balance between the channels in the chain has been realigned. It has exposed the potential to reduce the delivered cost to stores by as much as 20 per cent. Walmart then sell at a substantial discount to the market and this drives huge volume increases adding further circular value through improved operating economics. Smaller operators simply cannot follow this approach.

It has been a virtuous circle that has created a dependency with key suppliers for volumes at low prices. Procter & Gamble is said to be dependent globally on Walmart for as much as 25 per cent of its total revenues and has put in place strong customer-relationship management processes to manage that dependency.

The disintermediation of the traditional wholesaler through the strategy of dealing direct has led to some reintermediation with a new class of actor – the sourcing agent. Of this new breed, Li & Fung is the most notable. The company, based in Hong Kong, helps large retailers to identify suppliers across Asia, placing and administering orders on their behalf on a much reduced gross-margin basis since it does not take title to the goods, take any stock risk or pay for logistics. Their big customers for this model include Kohl's, Target and Walmart. It avoids the need for these companies to establish local sourcing offices. It is important to note that Li & Fung operate other parallel commercial models, including owning and distributing brands and acting as a traditional wholesaler.

The challenge for commercial and procurement functions is to recognize that they have a strategic role to play in identifying channel choices and their margin and competitive implications. This is where breakthrough value and true competitive potential is embedded, rather than in tactical negotiation.

We have prepared two cases to illustrate channel strategies in action, which is a crucial vertical in our business operations model framework.

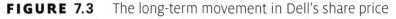

CASE STUDY   Dell

Our analysis in Chapter 2 included reference to Dell in both the FT 500 and the Gartner rankings. Over the past 10 years Dell has slipped in the FT 500 from a top 100 performer to nearly number 400 before being taken out of listed ownership in 2014. However, this apparent tale of decline does not tell the whole story. Figure 7.3 shows the Dell share price movement over the life of the business and, to use a sporting analogy, it is clear that Dell has had a game of two halves.

FIGURE 7.3   The long-term movement in Dell's share price

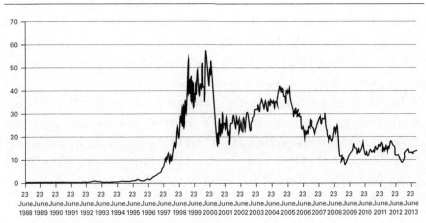

Figure 7.3 shows the massive growth in corporate value at Dell (started by Michael Dell in 1984) from its initial public share sale in 1988. As observed in Chapter 6, it can take a while to become an overnight success and the take-off in share price and market value was clearly in 1997 with a peak in 2000. Commentators are all clear, as we are, that the heart of Dell's success was its direct model. This was channel management at its disruptive best; it was very similar to Southwest Airlines cutting out the agents and dealing direct – and it was in the same decade. Dell cut out the dealers – specialist resellers; conventional high-street retail chains were not strong in the personal computer segment in the 1980s and early 1990s as they could not give the support people wanted. But Dell also built the machine to the customer specification – within 5 to 10 days you got the machine you ordered with the memory and drive capacity you wanted.

Based on what Michael Dell is on record as saying, the benefits of this model were:

- Bypassing computer dealers and avoiding related price mark-ups. Competition through the indirect channel between manufacturers was intense and this was driving up dealer discounts and incentives. The dealer channel's customer support was a major capacity constraint in a period when the customer community was learning how to use these new devices.

- Building each system to specific customer order eliminated inventories and allowed Dell to move faster to new technologies. As we saw earlier, the effect of Moore's Law on component costs was very rapid; clearing old stock through the chain is a potential liability as the dealer channel will require price protection.

- Communicating constantly with real customers allowed Dell to tap into what customers really need and appreciate. Dell was dealing with customers on the phone and then subsequently over the internet and through help desks – this enabled the company to get control of consistency of service around the world.

- Leveraging relationships with suppliers and technology partners to introduce the latest technology to products quickly – in 1991 Dell was the first to adopt the Intel 486 chip and thereafter was a leader in component introduction.

- Slashing order-to-delivery times to days through the use of cell manufacturing and working on just-in-time supply from local supplier parks. This not only gave Dell a very low inventory but also sheltered the business from both component and finished goods obsolescence – a major cost in the personal computer industry.

The implications of this channel and operating model were greater agility in the market. The business was protected from margin erosion through both the indirect channel and product obsolescence; it ran on cash-to-cash of minus 21 days in 2001 and had put huge focus on internal operating efficiency.

It is worth noting that in the early 1990s Dell tried to enter the retail market. This was unsuccessful due to the conflicts of running two competing channels; Dell fell foul of price protection commitments to dealers and posted its first loss in 1993. It is a generic lesson that companies struggle to maintain multiple channels due to the different disciplines and skills that are needed together with complexity of channel coordination.

The indicative relative economics of Dell's channel options is shown in Table 7.2; it has been prepared in order to illustrate the contrasts between the channel models – the actual numbers may have been slightly different but the direction is clear. It points to a 5 per cent gain for Dell over the traditional dealer channel, which is more than enough for the company to exert pricing power in the market; which indeed it did.

By 1999 to 2001, Dell had become the market leader with a global share of just short of 20 per cent. The share price graph tells the story of how this revenue growth drove market value; the reader should note that it was influenced negatively by the tech bust in 2000–2001, which affected everyone.

TABLE 7.2   Estimated relative channel economics for Dell as % to sales

	Dell direct	Dealer channel
Marketing	5%	3%
Dealer discount	0%	9%
Stock write off*	5%	8%
Delivery and Logistics	4%	2%
Inventory holding	1%	2%
Ordering	2%	1%
Customer support	4%	1%
Net model impact	21%	26%

* for Dell this is embedded in suppliers' costs

The second 'half' of Dell's history was a gradual share price recovery after the dot.com slump; it sustained market leadership until 2005. This was followed by a decline in the company's market share (to 11.6 per cent) and its market value until 2013. It was then bought out of public ownership by Michael Dell and private equity firm Silver Lake. The changes over that time with which Dell did not keep pace were:

- The shift from desktops to laptops – competitors such as Acer and Hewlett-Packard (HP) had essentially caught up with Dell.

- The shift from dealers to retail – in the mid 2000s the retailers caught on to selling PCs and disintermediated dealers. Retailers sold standard products without the need for configuration – and Dell had a history of not being successful with retailers.

- A series of quality problems took Dell some time to fix and cost a lot of money in compensation – the market got to know about this and switched suppliers – HP and Lenovo being the beneficiaries.

In terms of our business operations model framework, Dell won a significant advantage through disintermediating the dealer channel combined with some really effective manufacturing and fulfilment capabilities. It was worth at least 5 per cent in the cost structure but that was eroded as the competition caught up and customer preferences and their channel requirements changed.

The Dell case shows clearly that channel choice can be a disruptive competitive force; it makes margin available for powerful market pricing as well as being more attractive in service to customers. A relatively small (in percentage terms) improvement in overall economics can drive economic value disproportionately. It is therefore vital to understand the complexity of relative channel economics; also boards need to understand how difficult it is to live with two models in parallel. Of course it also takes us back to a conclusion we made in Chapter 2 that success can be ephemeral as channel preferences and costs change.

CASE STUDY   Kingfisher/B&Q

This case study looks at the supply side and the phenomenon of global direct sourcing.

B&Q is part of the Kingfisher Group, Europe's number one in the home-improvement retail sector (and also in China). Kingfisher operates through 600 stores in nine countries from the UK to China. The group generates more than

£7 billion in revenues. In the majority of its markets it is the number one retailer in its sector.

B&Q operates in the UK with around 26 million square feet of store space and generates revenues of around £4.5 billion. It has 25 per cent of the market. It is also a recognized internet retailer and owns the address **www.diy.com**.

In the 10 years from 1995 to 2005 home improvement was a growth sector, particularly in the UK, where it was fuelled by the increase in house prices. While the market was expanding rapidly, B&Q implemented an aggressive everyday low-price strategy (EDLP) to increase market share by delivering compelling value to its customers.

The growth in revenues and market share was exceptional with an uplift of approximately 70 per cent in revenues for 2004–5 over 1999–2000 figures. That growth concealed an even more dramatic uplift of around 125 per cent in volumes, with the company returning profits of more than £400 million per annum. Table 7.3 shows the trajectory of key metrics during this hot growth period.

Table 7.4 shows how EDLP works – selling for less while increasing margins. This table has been constructed from management presentations to analysts in 2004. It demonstrates that by removing promotional activity, goods can be sold for less at a higher contribution margin.

This approach is essentially about adjusting the commercial model internally – reducing the gross margin, taking out the in-store discounts and scaling back the advertising. By letting the value speak for itself, and getting less redundant

TABLE 7.3   Kingfisher B&Q UK sales growth and margin development, 2000–04

Metric	1999/2000	2000/2001	2001/2002	2002/2003	2003/2004
Revenue per sq. ft.	£143	£161	£162	£175	£171
Profit per sq. ft.	£14	£15	£15	£17	£16
Revenue per employee	£756,566	£873,754	£993,377	£1,125,000	£1,148,148
Profit per employee	£13,153	£147,441	£114,286	£105,714	£108,333
Profit margin %	10%	9%	9%	10%	10%
Revenue per SKU	£66,066	£75,051	£0	£92,500	£86,667
Profit per SKU	£6,420	£7,108	£7,500	£9,000	£8,267

TABLE 7.4 How EDLP returns a better margin

	Old retail	EDLP
Selling price	100	95
Product cost	65	65
Gross margin	35	30
In-store discounts	4	–
Advertising	6	4
Redundant stock	3	1
Achieved gross margin	22	25

stock and mark-downs through a tighter core range, the bottom-line margin actually increased.

B&Q Kingfisher combined this commercial strategy with a global direct sourcing strategy. This sourcing strategy effectively cut out the middlemen; these were the traditional importers and wholesalers, who often were looking for a 30 to 40 per cent mark-up as well as the local sourcing agents who also took their margin. The scale of the potential from this approach can be seen in Table 7.5; it delivered truly compelling value for customers. It is the combination of EDLP and the extra power from global direct sourcing that drives growth in sales, volumes and margins: the volume uplift being 125 per cent against a revenue uplift of 70 per cent.

TABLE 7.5 Some examples of sourcing and selling prices before and after global sourcing

Sourcing model changes		Original	Global direct
B&Q knife	Bought for	£0.88	£0.40
B&Q wood flooring/sq m	Sold for	£19.98	£14.07
Castorama wrench	Bought for	€8.50	€2.00
Castorama swimming pool	Sold for	€305.00	€129.00

* **NOTE:** B&Q is the trading name in the UK and Castorama is the trading name in France

From 2 per cent of purchases in 1999, global sourcing rose to 12 per cent by 2004 and is now around 35 per cent. This model does not just happen and has implications for the other verticals in our business operations model framework. Specifically, resourcing the disintermediation of traditional channels requires:

- Stock increases from 13–15 weeks to 15–25 weeks: that stock has to be held and financed, requiring investments in distribution centres.

- Suppliers in Asia and around the world need to be identified and managed, usually with overseas offices or agents (such as Li & Fung) – and this costs money and takes time to set up.

- Arrangements are needed with shipping lines and logistics companies to move the goods in containers from their origin to the warehouses in the markets.

This commercial model impacts on most of the verticals in our business operations model: commercial control, complexity, an optimized network, inventory segmentation, sourcing optimization and getting the basics right, including quality. Failure to address these aspects of the change will place additional risk on the supply chain in terms of product availability and quality, as well as cost.

Emerging maxims for using channels as a disruptive competitive capability

This chapter has introduced the concept of channels to market as a major strategic choice and a potential source of competitive disruption. We have assembled a set of maxims to guide thinking on how it might apply to other companies:

1 Channels to market have different characteristics in terms of market access and economics.

2 The choice of a channel can have a significant net margin impact through rebalancing the cost-to-serve across all the cost components – this analytical capability is difficult but essential.

3 Disintermediation of established channels is the key to being a disruptive competitor. In essence, dealing more directly takes out costs and profit stacking; it also gets you closer to the real customer and able to understand their needs and respond to changes.

4 Disintermediation does not always mean dealing direct; it can be the process of putting in place a new intermediary.

5 Disintermediation can involve radical product and service redesign, bundling the two and altering the commercial pricing model to price by outcome rather than by product; this SDL approach can replace or realign a whole range of actors along the end-to-end chain.

6 Disruptive channel control is the same as for technical disruptors – it does not have to be a dominant market share to be disruptive and it can be short-lived.

7 Disruptive channel design is not just an upstream concept; it can be applied downstream equally effectively to reshape the way that products are bought and distributed.

8 Effective channel disruption is not a strategy in its own right – it is dependent on the other verticals in our business operations model framework for its effective execution.

9 Above all, understand the cost build-up and margin impacts of the alternative channels to find the weak spots and the points of leverage – then you attack.

Taking forward the framework in your business

This chapter on the power of channels concluded with nine maxims. To take those insights forward into your business operations model you should:

- Identify the value chain from your suppliers to your customers and look for where there is margin stacking and double handling that can be disintermediated – if these exist then there is real disruptor potential and you need to consider how to configure a completely new business operations model to capture that opportunity: bear in mind the nine maxims.

- If your value chain analysis shows that channel partners bring value in your sector, such as consolidation and economies of scale, then look in detail at the economies and relative margin structures and make quite finely balanced choices about which customers to put through which channels. This requires detailed cost-to-serve analysis.

- In the context of the choices made between the two points above, consider how your business operations model can be configured to drive customer value and commercial viability. This may include measures to leverage value from several of complexity, service, networks, inventory and sourcing in an integrated package aligned to the channel choice.

- Once again, update your narrative and also your balanced scorecard.

Note

1   As an example, the Through Life Engineering Services Centre in the UK is based at the University of Cranfield and is funded by the EPSRC (Engineering and Physical Sciences Research Council).

Competing through the basics

08

Woody Allen is famously quoted as having said that '80 per cent of life is showing up' (*New York Times*, 21 August 1977). It is true that 'you have to be in it to win it' but the margin between success and failure is wafer thin; showing up is a qualifier for the game rather than a true criterion for success. This applies to both sport and business.

In the sport of cycling, Sir David Brailsford, who masterminded the British ascendancy to top cycling nation in the world, worked on the principle of the aggregation of marginal gains. He described this in 2012 as:

> The whole principle came from the idea that if you broke down everything you could think of that goes into riding a bike, and then improved it by 1%, you will get a significant increase when you put them all together.

The margins of victory between gold and silver are often measured in hundredths of a second, so the attention to detail embedded in his philosophy are worth hundreds of thousands of dollars in the professional world and continued funding in the amateur game. The training and development regime covers equipment, psychology, fitness, strategy and tactics. Weekly and monthly targets are set for performance improvement, measured in fractions of seconds, and riders train towards those goals for the big competitions, knowing what they have to be able to achieve to win.

This approach to sustained success is about microscopic attention to detail in support of great talent. Its attributes can be found in the business world – and in our business operations model we call this 'managing the basics'. This chapter unpacks this perspective on successful survival or, even better, becoming a disruptor. Managing the basics touches many of the other vertical elements in our business operations model, but it is worth a chapter in its own right.

Internal transformation and the 'power of 1 per cent'

In the same way that David Brailsford talked about a notional 1 per cent gain in each area building the platform for success, the same applies in business. We have been using the term 'power of 1 per cent' for nearly 10 years, based on simple financial modelling; we cannot claim to have originated it.

To illustrate the effect, we have prepared a worked example (using 2 per cent as the uplift for illustration) for a hypothetical company using a simple financial model based on the profit and loss account and balance sheet. This company's position is shown in Figure 8.1. It is a $1.5 billion turnover organization with a gross margin of 28 per cent and a net profit before tax of 2.7 per cent. It is running on extended inventories, debtors and creditors (58, 71 and 95 days respectively) giving a cash-to-cash cycle of 35 days (see Chapter 2 for a description of cash-to-cash). Using a figure of 2 per cent for the improvement in sales and a reduction in the cost of sales of 2 per cent, as well as for the SG&A (sales, general and administration) costs and those of distribution, the outcome for the company is a 74 per cent uplift in earnings before tax (EBT), moving from a margin of 2.7 per cent of revenues to 4.6 per cent.

The business is also highly geared (the ratio of debt to equity) with debts to overall capital employed of 108 per cent, including short-term debt netted against cash holdings. In general terms, a low margin and highly geared business with a lot of stock and debtors is a risky proposition. The CEO and board of our notional company would

FIGURE 8.1   Power of 1 per cent model for notional company

Profit and loss account		Current and %		Improvement %	Future and %	
Revenues	$'000s	1,500,000	100%	2%	1,530,000	100%
Cost of sales	$'000s	1,080,000	72%	−2%	1,079,568	71%
Gross margin	$'000s	420,000	28%		450,432	29%
Operating expenses						
SG&A costs	$'000s	205,000	14%	−2%	206,927	13.5%
Distribution	$'000s	105,000	7%	−2%	104,980	6.9%
Operating income EBITDA	$'000s	110,000	7.3%		138,525	9.1%
Depreciation	$'000s	20,000	1.3%	0%	20,000	1.3%
Interest	$'000s	50,000	3.3%		48,978	3.2%
Profit before tax EBT	$'000s	40,000	2.7%		69,547	4.5%

be highly motivated to increase the net margin before taxes to nearly 5 per cent as it would increase their resilience.

Yet the changes that are needed to make this happen are relatively small if they occur across the whole business. Looking back to previous chapters we observed that:

- Sales gains can be the result of improved service and better availability – from our experience, gains of 3 per cent to 10 per cent in like-for-like sales through this kind of improvement (Chapters 2 and 3).

- Reductions in the cost of goods sold and the corresponding increase in gross margin can be achieved by both improved procurement and an optimized manufacturing platform (to be addressed in Chapter 9).

- Increases in the gross margin can also be achieved through reductions in inventory waste and price markdowns to clear goods – selling more of the goods at full prices or reduced discounts (we touch on this in more detail later in this chapter).

- Savings in the costs of SG&A can be achieved by process redesign, as can the cost of distribution (a topic covered in Chapter 7 and which we will revisit in Chapter 9).

- Reductions in inventory holding reduce distribution costs as well as the direct financing costs (a point made in Chapter 2).

Figure 8.1 shows that the essence of the 'power of 1 per cent' concept is that small gains across the company can combine to be transformative. Radical and massive change is not always necessary; indeed it may be difficult and risky to do – even if the direction is clear.

This idea of transformation through incremental change is a recurring theme in this chapter – and provides a balance to the excitement of the previous chapters on technology transformation and market-changing models.

Obliterating waste

If you watch the top cyclists, on the track or the road, you will see them slipstreaming to save energy. The riders in the leading group will help each other by taking the lead in turns so that each rider will have the chance to recover by rolling in an area of reduced wind resistance. In a large group this can save as much as 40 per cent of a rider's energy; but even the leader gets a benefit of up to 5 per cent if he or she is being followed closely. In race riding, cooperation is often crucial within the team in order to bring home a winner.

The parallel with business is striking! Finding the opportunities to cut out waste along the supply chain in a coordinated way can be the difference between success and failure. But, like the aerodynamic vortices around the racing cyclists, business waste can be difficult to see and understand.

The best way to illustrate the potential is to introduce some data from fashion retailing where the biggest single waste is the lost margin when goods have to be sold at discounts to clear the stock. In one high-fashion producer and wholesaler, this represented as much as 40 per cent of the full price-target revenues. In general fashion retail, the picture can be difficult to analyse due to the many departments

FIGURE 8.2   Plot of markdown % versus stock commitment in
a retailer

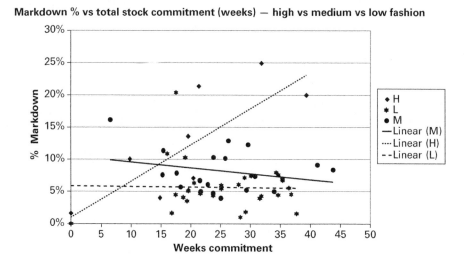

Markdown % vs total stock commitment (weeks) — high vs medium vs low fashion

and product profiles. For example, T-shirts, socks and underwear are
universal products and will sell from one season to the next. However,
higher fashion items can experience significant markdowns to clear
the stock at the end of the season; depending on the mix of products,
the margin erosion through discounts can be as much as 10 per cent
of planned full-price turnover. This in turn is typically more than
twice the logistics and distribution costs as a percentage to sales, or
up to 20 per cent of the buying price of the goods.

Figure 8.2 shows analysis for a multi-department fashion retailer
where the correlation of discounts and markdowns with stock commitment was exposed. Stock commitment was measured as the total
of stock in hand, stock in transit and stock on order with manufacturers
and suppliers. The correlations show that departments classified as
medium or low fashion had flat (or slightly negative) correlations
between markdowns and the commitment to stock measured in weeks.
The strongly positive correlation between the percentage markdown
and stock commitment for high fashion is striking; essentially, the
more risky the stock on longer lead times, the greater is the markdown
as a percentage of turnover.

In Chapter 4 we introduced the case of Zara and its parent company
Inditex. We observed that Zara has some of its categories produced

on short lead times, from sketch to store, through workshops in Spain, while other product areas are on long lead times from Asian factories. This combination has given Inditex its disruptor status with growth and financial return well above the market (as pointed out in Chapter 2). Clearly a core part of the company's strategy is the elimination of the waste on high-fashion product. It enables it to sell products that customers really want at good prices without having much left over to clear.

Almost every business has these 'pockets of waste', which typically represent between 2 per cent and 10 per cent of all revenues depending on the sector. The potential for transformation by introducing basic disciplines and processes in the planning and control of the supply chain can be seen from the 'power of 1 per cent' model. But based on this example, in some cases, it is much more than the odd 1–2 per cent.

The cost of complexity

We maintain that the reasons for waste being difficult to identify is that it is often hidden by the scale and complexity of large companies. We have identified seven different forms of complexity that can generate margin erosion:

1 *Customer complexity.* The range of customers, their buying practices and role in the chain was developed in Chapter 7 where we looked at the channels to market and their respective margin structures. Making sure that the margins through these various channels do not erode the overall net profit is a complex task. Making sure that individual customers make an economic contribution in relation to their cost-to-serve can yield remarkable results; in simple terms, this is about the internal process of price setting in relation to costs.

2 *Demand complexity.* The profile of demand will contain the complexity of both fast- and slow-moving products and there will be variations in the volatility of demand in each group, impacting the ability to forecast with accuracy. Making sure that the appropriate planning and provisioning processes are

in place across the range is crucial to avoiding excess stocks and simultaneous shortages; a single planning algorithm is unlikely to be adequate to address this complexity.

3 *Network complexity.* Extended supply chains contain many nodes as a result of the trend to global sourcing (as we described in the B&Q case study in Chapter 7). This creates extended lead times, increased stock holding and the risk of interruptions along the chain, leading to lost sales and missed promotions. Making sure that the extended supply chain is fully risk assured and that appropriate controls are in place is vital to securing continuity of supply; this is a complex task.

4 *Product and range complexity.* The variety that is offered in a product range almost invariably conforms to Pareto's 80:20 rule, as illustrated in Figure 8.3 where 20 per cent of the products account for 80 per cent of the sales volume; this also applies to customers. Complexity in the range can come from different products and packaging variants as well as alternative

FIGURE 8.3   The Pareto curve for products (and customers) always has a long tail of low yielders

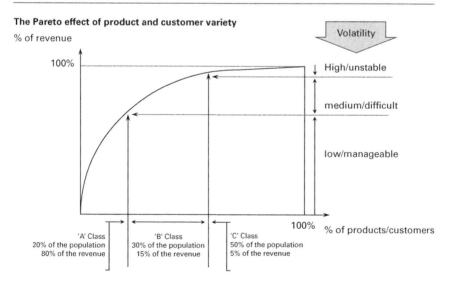

The Pareto effect of product and customer variety

% of revenue

Volatility

100% .... ↓ High/unstable

medium/difficult

low/manageable

100%   % of products/customers

'A' Class
20% of the population
80% of the revenue

'B' Class
30% of the population
15% of the revenue

'C' Class
50% of the population
5% of the revenue

service delivery models. Making sure that the interactions between materials, capacity and manufacturing process across products do not drive in excess cost is critical in the context of our 'power of 1 per cent'. We have seen slow-moving products clog up manufacturing with unnecessarily long runs and restricting availability on the faster lines.

5 *Process complexity.* The multiple steps or stages that are required to complete transactions with customers, suppliers and internally are built around the complexity in the four points above. Often processes are sequential rather than parallel, which adds non-value-adding time to the supply chain, which in turn induces variability, distortion and rework. Making sure that processes work in parallel and with minimum delay is a key to improving business performance and reducing waste; cutting out unnecessary process altogether is even better (a maxim from noted Michael Hammer in Chapter 4).

6 *Supplier complexity.* The number of supplier relationships that a company maintains can easily expand to the point of losing control, where the relationship becomes transactional rather than one of value co-creation. A myriad of suppliers often sit behind each actual supplier to the company and each of these is a potential point of failure. Making sure that the strategically critical suppliers and their chains are fully visible and that value-based conversations are taking place is key to reducing costs and increasing margin.

7 *Organizational complexity.* The scale and reach of business activity within an organization and between it and its suppliers and customers is extraordinary. Organizations generally run with complex functional structures to address these external and internal complexities. Making sure that goals are aligned so that waste is avoided is a critical task for senior management.

In all the dimensions of complexity there are opportunities to master its implications and improve margins. The blend of this focus will be specific to each company, based on its situation. The aim is to create

FIGURE 8.4 The virtuous circle of complexity management

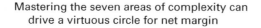

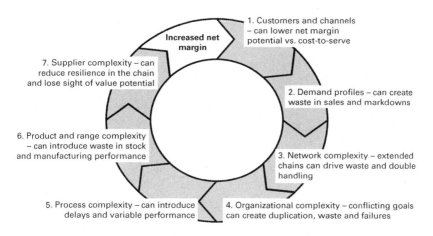

Mastering the seven areas of complexity can drive a virtuous circle for net margin

Increased net margin

1. Customers and channels – can lower net margin potential vs. cost-to-serve

7. Supplier complexity – can reduce resilience in the chain and lose sight of value potential

2. Demand profiles – can create waste in sales and markdowns

6. Product and range complexity – can introduce waste in stock and manufacturing performance

3. Network complexity – extended chains can drive waste and double handling

5. Process complexity – can introduce delays and variable performance

4. Organizational complexity – conflicting goals can create duplication, waste and failures

a virtuous circle in which addressing every element of complexity can contribute its 1 per cent or more to sales, margin and costs. Together the impact can be transformational, as the case studies later in this chapter will show. Figure 8.4 shows the virtuous circle of the elements of complexity all contributing to margin improvement with no compromise to service.

The bottom line is that almost every company can improve its service to customers (hence driving sales growth); reduce stock and manufacturing waste in the form of discounts, rebates and markdowns; improve manufacturing efficiency to reduce unit costs; and increase resilience through tighter relations with suppliers. As we observed at the start of this chapter, the individual gains can be quite small but still make a big difference; it may not be enough to confer disruptor status, but the improvements can be hugely valuable. Our case studies later in this chapter will show that, on occasions, the gains can be transformational and disruptive.

Lean and Six Sigma – a transformation concept

W Edwards Deming was a 20th-century American engineer, statistician, academic and management consultant who is considered the father of quality management. His work is widely credited as laying the groundwork of 'lean thinking' and Six Sigma analytical methods. Our consideration of managing the basics would not be complete without referencing him, the evolution of his work and specifically its application in the Japanese auto industry. The discussion of the impacts of complexity in the previous section pointed to many areas of potential waste within a business; the big idea behind lean and Six Sigma is the identification and elimination of waste.

The word lean implies what it says: free from fat – fit and efficient – with no spare flesh. Six Sigma is the term for high levels of statistical accuracy in process execution – six standard deviations or a failure rate of 3.4 defects per million against specification. Lean and Six Sigma combine with the idea that the elimination of waste through process accuracy will create a lean organization. As a concept, it is entirely consistent with Brailsford's approach to cycling perfection through the aggregation of marginal gains; it is also a process to access the waste driven by the complexities in the previous section.

Lean and Six Sigma have become a management process through a range of methodologies designed to apply statistical process control to business. The Shewhart cycle is called PDCA or PDSA (plan, do, check, act; plan, do, study, adjust). It was made famous by Deming but credited by him to Shewhart and is the foundation of the continuous improvement (kaizen) approach to manufacturing management. Kaizen is the Japanese term for continuous improvement, first established by Taiichi Ohno and Eiji Toyoda at Toyota; it is a core element of the Toyota Production System that made Toyota a disruptive competitor. It has been emulated by almost all the major automotive manufacturers in some form.

There is now an 'industry' of 'Lean Management' and 'Six Sigma' with qualifications in its use classified with judo-belt terms: yellow, green and black. The most recognized methodology has moved on from the Shewhart cycle to DMAIC, which is a circular process of define, measure, analyse, improve and control.

In essence, this process is about identifying potential areas of waste and then doing the appropriate data capture and statistical analysis to determine how to improve the value chain. It is then about taking action and controlling the results, where necessary leading to a further improvement cycle.

Taiichi Ohno identified seven wastes to be attacked. These are shown in Figure 8.5 with a short commentary on each. Some academics and practitioners have added additional wastes such as 'talent in the organization' and 'inappropriate product design'. Eliminating waste improves the value chain and drives improved margin and customer satisfaction. The case of how Toyota became a disruptor based on this approach is described later in this chapter.

FIGURE 8.5   The seven wastes in manufacturing

The seven wastes to be addressed in building a lean enterprise

Waiting — loses machine time and wastes labour — caused by parts shortages and poor scheduling

Overproduction — creates excess and obsolete inventory — blocks machine time for saleable product — caused by trying to optimize economics and poor scheduling

Rejects — faulty products cause rework and repairs, customer complaints and lost machine time as product is recycled rather than sold — caused by poor process control

Transport — time wasted on unnecessary movements — double handling and operator fatigue — opportunity for error — caused by poor layouts, overproduction and rejects

Over-processing — effort spent on activities that are not needed and do not add value for customers — caused by poor specification and production system design

Over-stocks — holding more products and work in progress than is needed leading to high holding and financing costs — caused by poor planning and incorrect batch sizes

Inappropriate design — making and selling goods that don't meet the real needs of customers — holding more products and work in progress than is needed leading to high holding and financing costs — caused by poor planning and incorrect batch sizes

The leading experts in this area are the team originally from MIT (Massachusetts Institute of Technology) and Cardiff University. We referenced Womak, Jones and Roos in Chapter 4; they have noted that lean thinking is primarily applied in manufacturing businesses. However, they do observe benefits from the adoption of lean management methods at the UK retailer Tesco, under the slogan 'every little helps'. The use of lean by this retailer supports the conclusion that wastes occur in all kinds of business and are open to improvement using the methodology. They also observe that there is no conceptual barrier to its application across the extended enterprise, including with customers and suppliers of the focal firm. The difficulty that arises is that a lean management programme requires collaboration and information exchange between the parties and functions in the chain; that free exchange is often inhibited by traditional business perceptions of the need to promote commercial self-interest.

We suggest that the future for business includes much greater transparency and collaboration between key trading partners. In future it will be supply chains that compete to create disruptive value rather than individual companies. We have already observed this model in the co-creation of value based on the concept of service-dominant logic (Chapter 7).

The importance of analytics in identifying the levels of waste and their root causes cannot be overemphasized (Figure 8.5); our experience of working with many companies is that their data can yield remarkable insights on the potential for process improvement to attack waste. Once again, time is the recurring theme; the preparation of value chain maps that allow a business to see and understand the cost and time build, from end to end, is at the heart of this discovery process and often leads to obvious but previously unasked questions: 'why can we not...?'

Case studies – introduction

This chapter has introduced the big idea that any company can take quite small steps to improve margins and competitiveness. This may be a platform for becoming a disruptor but, even if it does not, it will increase competitiveness. The fundamentals of aggregating marginal gains converge with the need to obliterate waste and manage complexity; techniques and methods associated with lean thinking and Six Sigma quality are appropriate across all sectors and help to increase quality and accuracy by identifying and eliminating waste. We have included three case studies to support the big idea of managing the basics to become a disruptor.

CASE STUDY   Aldi

Aldi is a hard discount supermarket chain that has been enjoying extraordinary success in the UK since 2012 (as well as in many other countries). It has without question become a disruptor. Kantar Worldpanel reported that its market share grew from 3.1 per cent to 4 per cent in 2013 and was 4.8 per cent in September 2014 after a continued strong performance in the year. Not surprisingly its success has attracted much analysis and commentary, largely because it has taken share from the established supermarkets including Tesco, as detailed in Chapter 2. Its success and the consequential impact on its much larger competitors reinforce some of our maxims for disruption:

- It has taken more than 20 years to become an overnight success – it arrived in the UK in 1990.

- It does not have to have a dominant market share to disrupt the market – with around 5 per cent share it is now setting prices for its much bigger competitors, so impacting their margin and returns.

- Market changes and timing is everything; as we observed in Chapter 3, customer preference can change. So competitors may fight back but they will have to do so in a different landscape. Aldi is reported to be making just less than 5 per cent profit before tax on a lower price structure against a sector benchmark of between 3 per cent and 5 per cent. This means that its competitors will have to cut prices and sacrifice margin in order to stay with Aldi as it grows.

- Aldi's success is not attributable to one single element of its business operations model – there is a unique combination of capabilities that have taken time to assemble and hone for the market as preferences have shifted.

We have included this case example under managing the basics because the Aldi model has addressed and reduced complexity. Let's look at the business operations

TABLE 8.1   The business operations model contrasts between hard discounters and supermarketers

Business operations model differences – discounter to supermarket				
		Discounter – Aldi	Supermarket	Difference %
Average basket size	Index	75	100	33%
Net margin of retailer	%	5%	3.50%	–30%
Private label share	%	95%	40%	–58%
Suppliers	number	250	1,200	380%
Lines per supplier	number	12	15	25%
Sales/store/supplier line	£'s	£52,000	£18,000	–65%
Supplier gross margin	% estd	30%	50%	67%
Below-the-line promotions	% estd	0%	15%	
Product lines	units	3,000	18,000	500%
Average store size	sq ft.	10,000	18,000	80%
Sales per sq. ft./year	£'s	£1,300	£1,200	–8%
Sales per line/year	£'s	£4,333	£1,200	–72%
Contribution margin/line/store	estd	£1,300	£510	–61%
Credit cards allowed	Y/N	no	yes	
Staff per store	number	15	50	233%
Sq ft per staff	number	667	360	–46%
£ sales per staff member	number	£866,667	£432,000	–50%

model elements that are really driving Aldi's growth in market share. Table 8.1 shows our compilation of a combination of public domain data, press commentary and experience to provide the comparison. The reader should note that these numbers are indicative rather than precise contrasts – nevertheless, the differences are striking and serve to show how disruptive value is being delivered.

Working through Table 8.1, the first point in relation to our business operations model is that the value to customers is compelling; supermarkets cost up to 33 per cent more for a comparable shopping basket. Aldi is achieving this at a net margin of around 5 per cent in 2014, which is now higher than its major competitors who are running at around 3.5 per cent – a figure that is in decline.

This is achieved in the main part by the differences in market channels and economics and the reduction in complexity. Aldi has effectively disintermediated the branded suppliers with 95 per cent of the products being private label as compared to around 40 per cent for typical supermarket chains. Normal marketing and promotional practice for branded suppliers is that as much as 15 per cent of their revenues is devoted to promotions and below-the-line marketing; Aldi effectively eliminates that activity with its everyday low-price formula. It makes this work for suppliers and its own operation through very tight control of the range of products that are sold – 3,000 versus 18,000. This means that the revenue per store per line is £4,333 in comparison to £1,200 for a general supermarket. Volumes are concentrated on few products and hence suppliers are not dis-advantaged or quality is not compromised. This means that suppliers who are part of the Aldi chain have a profitable opportunity along with growth potential; they are not under extreme commercial pressure.

The reduction in complexity in the range and the supplier base reduces waste, rebates, administration costs and double handling. The proxy for this benefit is the sales per staff member at £860,000 versus a supermarket at £432,000. Revenues per square foot are also slightly greater than a conventional supermarket. The costs of processing credit cards are eliminated by a policy of not accepting them.

These benefits extend back into the distribution system where the cases per employee per week are roughly double that in a conventional supermarket warehouse. As there are fewer products, they don't have to be spread over longer distances, increasing travel time and reducing productivity.

The use of fewer dedicated own-label suppliers allows the company to optimize its sourcing and supply platform and provide a profitable and economic challenge to its supply base. Because of the everyday low-price model and limited range, the demand volatility is much reduced and suppliers incur reduced manufacturing waste caused by less last-minute schedule changes.

This narrative relates to 'managing the basics' because every element that Aldi has engaged in their business operations model has had the effect of reducing waste, cutting complexity and creating lean streamlined and simplified processes. The question is, then, how can the conventional supermarkets respond to this disruptive competitor? The reality is that the heritage supermarket model has worked on blended returns for its range, space and complexity without recognizing the differential cost-to-serve for the slower-moving products (category C in Figure 8.3).

To compete on the core range, they will have to understand that cost picture with much greater detail and then find ways to maintain appropriate variety at an affordable cost and margin.

CASE STUDY   WH Smith

It is difficult to imagine that any reader will not be familiar with WH Smith. Its news and stationery shops are ubiquitous on the UK's high streets and at train stations, and it has outlets at airport terminals all around the world. This is a business operating in a declining marketplace for printed news, magazines and books, yet has delivered sustained value for shareholders as illustrated in Figure 8.6, showing the share price development since 1997.

This performance has been achieved in the face of continuous doubts expressed by the analysts and commentators on the long-term viability of the business; many others including Woolworths, Clintons and HMV have gone to the wall and the number of independent newsagents has declined by as many as 15,000. The results shown in Figure 8.6 have been achieved by a relentless focus on the basics in terms of margin control and giving customers what they want – and for which they are prepared to pay.

FIGURE 8.6   The movement in share price of WH Smith, 1997–2014

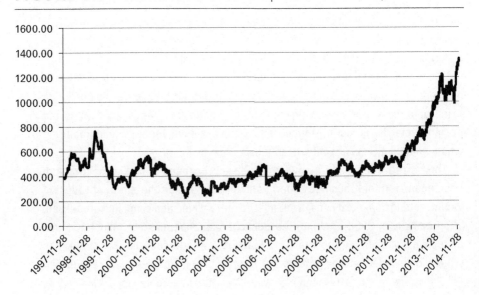

FIGURE 8.7   Revenues and margins for WH Smith, 2010–14

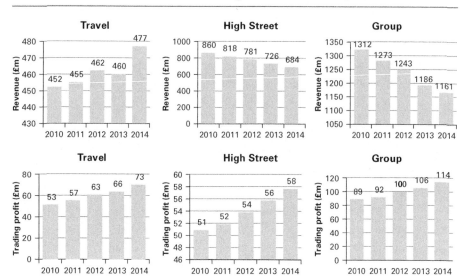

The decline in the early part of Figure 8.6 reflected group operating profits in 2001 of £11 million declining to a loss of £31 million in 2004 on revenues that were essentially flatlining. Kate Swann, the new CEO, presented her first interim results in April 2004, reporting a £72 million pre-tax loss. She warned that the business was uncompetitive and that 'she had found stock that was years out of date in the stockroom', which cost £45 million to write off.

Looking forward to the latest results for 2010 to 2014 inclusive, the story is of declining revenues but increasing margins, as illustrated in Figure 8.7. As the share price trajectory shows, it took some time for the market to believe that this trend was sustainable. Indeed, as we saw in Chapter 2, the analysts and commentators are fixated on growth; yet WH Smith had revenues in 2014 for high street and travel channels that were more than £200 million less than in 2001 but the business's value had increased by 300 per cent. As we observed in Chapter 2, margin trumps sales most of the time.

What did Kate Swann do that secured this transformation? The list is a remarkable catalogue of getting back to basics on which the business could give customers value and at a margin:

1 In 2006 Swann was one of the first PLC CEOs to close the final salary pension scheme – an extremely controversial move. However, continuing with the scheme would have been a millstone, when the deficit in 2003 was more than the entire value of the company.

2   Swann abandoned the sale of entertainment products and focused the business on newspaper, magazine and stationery products. At the time, the entertainment category accounted for 25 per cent of revenues but at very low margins. Analysts questioned how the company would replace that revenue but in fact the category was wasting space in stores by generating an inadequate return and blocking the sale of more profitable products (a classic lean – Six Sigma dynamic).

3   Swann floated off the news distribution business – creating additional shareholder value that is not visible in the graph and eliminating conflicts of interest on priorities at the boardroom table.

4   The fourth key decision was to focus the business more on travel outlets (channels) where the value to customers is that 'time and place utility' where margins can be sustained and competition is reduced. This is the only segment of the remaining business that has grown since 2001. Indeed the high-street retail business in 2014 was only 60 per cent of the revenues that were recorded in 2001!

5   Finally, Swann introduced a relentless, and now legendary, focus on cost and margin. This is a continuous improvement culture that is entirely consistent with the principles we have proposed in the chapter.

The *Daily Telegraph* echoed the analysts' sentiment when it commented in 2013 that: 'Concerns remain about the long-term health of WH Smith, particularly given its presence on struggling high streets across the UK. However, Swann insists the company is in 399 of the top 400 retail locations in the country and does not have a tail of loss-making stores.' In essence, Swann has dealt with the tail of the Pareto curve in Figure 8.3 and breathed margin into the company. Her successor, Steve Clarke, will need to maintain that ruthless focus while looking for new channels that leverage the scale of the business in its product area.

CASE STUDY   Toyota and the ascendency of the Japanese auto industry

In Chapter 2 we charted the performance of Toyota over the last 10 years and noted that it was number 18 in our subset of the FT 500's most valuable companies. It has achieved this in 60 years from a standing start and was the spearhead for the Japanese auto industry's leadership of the sector; that leadership and their operating methods have been carried all around the world. The chart in Figure 8.8

FIGURE 8.8 The development of global automotive producers by company origin

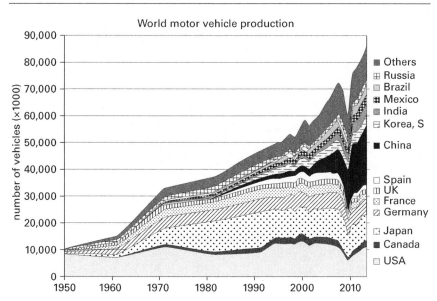

shows the evolution of automobile production from 1950 when the industry was dominated by mass production methods developed in the United States while the rest of the world was working on more of a craft basis. Following the evolution of volume it is clear that by the mid 1980s Japanese manufacturers controlled around one-third of the global market and that US auto makers had not advanced at all. This was a truly disruptive competitive event with Japanese cars pouring into the United States and European markets, where they were cheaper and more reliable than the locally produced cars, albeit somewhat smaller than the US standard. Governments and industry were anxious to understand this phenomenon and what was behind it, leading to the seminal work of Womak, Jones and Roos (1990) and their team to which we referred earlier in this chapter and in Chapter 4. Their book, *The Machine that Changed the World*, describes just how Toyota and the other major Japanese auto makers changed the rules of competition in the sector – and is the definitive story of 'lean' thinking.

Table 8.2 contains an extract of some of the key statistics that are presented by Womak, Jones and Roos (1990) across a number of tables. The comparisons show benchmarks of Japanese auto makers in Japan, Japanese auto makers in North America, North American auto makers in North America and European producers. The table is blocked out into three broad areas of measures: plant performance, new product development performance and supplier performance. We will develop below the narrative of disruption for each area.

TABLE 8.2   Key performance metrics for automotive production by origin (1989)

	Japanese in Japan	Japanese in N. America	American in N. America	All Europe
Plant performance				
Man hours/vehicle	16.8	21.2	25.1	36.2
Defects/100 vehicles	60	65	82	97
Sq m/vehicle/year	0.57	0.91	0.78	0.78
Repair area % of assembly space	4.1	4.9	12.9	14.4
Plant inventory days	0.2	1.6	2.9	2
Suggestions/employee	61.6	1.4	0.4	0.4
Training for new production hours	380.3	370	46.4	173.3
Development metrics				
Million engineering hours/new car	1.7		3.1	2.9
Average months development	46.2		60.4	57.3
Body types per new car	2.3		1.7	2.7
Supplier share of engineering	51%		14%	37%
Lifetime model production	400,000		1,750,000	1,250,000
Average annual production volume	125,000		200,000	190,000
Supplier performance				
Die change times (minutes)	7.9	21.4	114.3	123.7
New dies lead time (weeks)	11.1	19.3	34.5	40.0
Machines per worker	7.4	4.1	2.5	2.7
Inventory levels (days)	1.5	4.0	8.1	16.3
Suppliers per assembly plant	170	238	509	442
Proportion of parts single sourced	12.1%	98.0%	69.3%	32.9%

SOURCE: compiled from Womak, Jones and Roos (1990)

Looking first at plant performance, in terms of man hours per vehicle Japanese productivity was 33 per cent better than in the United States and 54 per cent better than in Europe. Defects were similarly 27 per cent and 38 per cent less respectively – meaning that there is no productivity cost to quality. Production could also be done in less space – avoiding unnecessary movement, one of the seven wastes. The benefits of this are apparent in the area required for repair and rework, which was 68 per cent and 72 per cent less – which implies that the faults were less significant in Japanese manufacturing as well as being fewer of them. Japanese plants operated on 90 per cent less inventory than their US and European competitors – another explanation for the reduced space and better productivity. The final metrics in this block relate to suggestions and training, where the culture in the United States and Europe leaps off the page. The Japanese were getting 15,000 per cent more suggestions and devoting 800 per cent more time to training than their US counterparts. With labour, space and rework being the main costs in auto assembly it is not surprising that Japanese cars could be 30 per cent cheaper as well as being more reliable. That was a truly compelling proposition for customers who were fed up with their cars breaking down.

The second block presents some metrics around the development of new cars. Once again, on all counts, the Japanese were able to develop a new car with 45 per cent less effort in 25 per cent less time and provide more body types. In production, the Japanese could accept much lower average annual production volume and lifetime model production. This meant that they could offer more vehicle choice and refresh the model range more frequently. The benefit to customers was that they could have the latest model and not have to be seen in the same car as their neighbours – and without paying a premium. This block of the table gives one major clue as to how the Japanese achieved this rapid development cycle – the supplier share of engineering was at 51 per cent compared to 14 per cent for North American producers and 37 per cent for the Europeans.

The final block in the table relates to supplier performance; it shows just how crucial is the role that suppliers played in the disruptive business operations model. Die change time was 90 per cent less than the United States and Europe and new die production time was around 70 per cent faster. The Japanese suppliers ran with more machines per worker, less inventory and fewer suppliers per plant; yet the Japanese were not single sourcing their parts. These statistics reveal a much tighter relationship with a more responsive supplier base and are redolent of the service-dominant logic concept of value co-creation in the supply chain.

Table 8.2 says it all in terms of how the Japanese, and especially Toyota, disrupted the dominance of mass production with lean thinking. This was all about managing the basics with true excellence and it served as a wake-up call to the global industry, which has had to play catch-up.

The column in Table 8.2 that shows the performance of Japanese plants transplanted to North America is much closer to the performance achieved in Japan; the lesson is that the methods and processes are replicable. Looking back to Figure 8.8, the picture of development since the late 1980s and early 1990s has been of globalization of the industry driven by the need to protect against currency fluctuations. The growth market has been China with its increasingly affluent population. In 2013, Toyota was the world's largest auto maker, making 10.3 million vehicles globally, followed by General Motors (GM) and Volkswagen both making more than 9 million. Toyota may have just 12 per cent of the global market but it is still the pricing reference point as its profit margins are running at around 8.75 per cent to revenues compared to 3.75 per cent for GM and 5.5 per cent for Volkswagen.

Now, that is the power of 1 per cent! It demonstrates the strategic value in managing the basics and just how difficult it is to recover after having been disrupted.

Taking forward the framework in your business

This chapter on exploiting the basics takes us back to the balanced scorecard. There is nothing magical here, it is about lots of incremental change and this should be landing in your balanced scorecard. Here are the steps that we recommend you follow:

1 Answer the question: 'does your business have a strong continuous improvement culture where suggestions are welcomed and goals are set bottom up as well as top down?' If not, that is your first task.

2 Is your business actively measuring hidden waste such as lost margin opportunities, incorrect pricing, inventory markdowns and customer disappointment? If not, then that is your next task as it will give you the areas on which to focus your process redesign – it is always process that conquers these wastes.

3 Does your business really understand its true cost of complexity? If not, then this is likely to yield a big prize and you will need to mount a very detailed analysis of your Pareto curve and its implications for capacity, stock, losses and customer value.

4 Depending on which of these applies to you (it may be all of them), think about your strategic narrative yet again and start to hardwire the emerging goals into your balanced scorecard.

Optimization of the business operations model   09

A t a lecture to executive MBAs at the London Business School, the point for discussion was inventory and its optimization. One student started to fidget with irritation and when asked for his point of view said: 'Why do we need to know about this? There are computer programmes that deal with it.' There are indeed computer programmes that work with optimization algorithms, but the well-known quote from Professor Paul R Elrich of Stamford University should provide a note of caution: 'To err is human – but to really foul things up you need a computer.'

Professor Richard Wilding has confirmed this adage through his research, which identified the inherent chaos that exists in supply chains and how the algorithms (formulae and programmes) that are embedded in computers can amplify that chaos rather than master it; such software algorithms are described as deterministic since they will make a single prediction from the programme and that programme is determined by the analytical relationships that the software designer applied. Optimization using this approach is about balancing trade-offs based on conventional wisdom; however, the experience in many markets is that a part of demand can be randomly disordered, effectively chaotic, and therefore requiring adaptive rather than predictive responses. Wilding observed that:

> Chaos is deterministic, generated by fixed rules that in themselves
> involve no element of chance. In theory, therefore, the system is
> predictable, but in practice the non-linear effects of many causes make
> the system less predictable. The system is also extremely sensitive to the

initial conditions, so an infinitesimal change to those initials may result in a completely different response. (Wilding, 1999)

He went on to state that the consequence of this view on endemic chaos in business systems is that the deterministic approach becomes invalid; he used the word 'reductionist' to convey the point of view that all problems can be reduced to a formula:

> The reductionist view argues that a complex system or problem
> can be reduced into a simple form for the purpose of analysis...
> The optimisation of the individual units, for example manufacturing,
> purchasing and distribution is believed to result in the optimisation of
> the global system. (Wilding, 1999)

Eli Goldratt, a renowned academic and entrepreneur who developed the theory of constraints (TOC), demonstrated that in manufacturing environments this is indeed often not the case. In the first, and most famous, of his many books, *The Goal*, he proposed the rule that:

> The sum of the local optimums is not equal to the global optimum.
>
> (Goldratt, 1984)

But the structure and scope of the optimization algorithms is not the end of this problem; the actual computing methods can introduce random effects in their own right. Heinz-Otto Peitgen, a prominent German mathematician and leading expert on fractals (the study of complex and repeating mathematical patterns), and his colleagues state:

> More and more massive computations are being performed now using
> black box software packages developed by sometimes very well-known
> and distinguished centres. These packages, therefore, seem to be very
> trustworthy, and indeed they are. But this does not exclude the fact that
> the finest software sometimes produces total garbage and it is an art in
> itself to understand when and why this happens.
>
> (Peitgen, Jurgens and Saupe, 1992)

Wilding conducted analyses and modelling that proved that chaos can be created within and from supply chain control systems, depending on the initial conditions, whether the system can be kept within 'islands of stability' and whether consistent but not repetitive patterns can be identified. If these conditions are not met, then the reductionist view fails and the accuracy of computing calculations becomes untrustworthy.

So the student was unwise in his complete faith in the system! It is necessary to understand the dynamics and take a cross-functional and total system view.

The new optimization – busting the paradigm or redefining the algorithms

The reader will have gathered by now that the use of the word optimization in the chapter heading should be approached with caution. Our point of view is that disruptors have found ways to break away from conventional wisdom: the ideas and relationships synthesized in so-called optimization. Rather we are looking for the opportunities to break the continuum to find new optima. The examples in the previous chapters all described cases where successful companies had deployed their business operations model to break conventional thinking; business operations models are disruptive if they are discontinuous. Technologies, channels and 'managing the basics' all provide the opportunity for transformation.

Designing a new business operations model is the opportunity to combine the verticals in our framework in new ways to create a fresh and super-competitive strategic narrative for the company. This is about breaking the existing paradigm, setting aside the established algorithms. The idea is illustrated in Figure 9.1.

Conventional wisdom is shown in Figure 9.1 in the solid curve, which suggests that an increase in service is secured by an increase in stock, with the ultimate of 100 per cent service requiring a very much greater investment in stock as the curve approaches maximum performance; but it never touches it and mathematicians call this the asymptote. The principle is that this is a continuous curve where management can make a defined trade-off as to where they position the business. Much of the inventory software that the above-mentioned student was relying on has this sort of model embedded in it.

FIGURE 9.1   Illustrating the maxim: 'Don't ride the curve – change it'

Our mantra is 'don't ride the curve – change it'. We argue that riding the curve is a limiting approach and that ways should be found to move the curve downwards, enabling the business to either increase service for the same stock or reduce the stock for the same service, or indeed some combination of the two. This is about stepping off one curve and onto another, as the dotted line and the arrows in Figure 9.1 show.

Elements of the business operations model that can leverage this approach

This chapter offers specific operational perspectives on how to transform the business or become a disruptor (please refer back to Figure 1.2 on p 5 for a diagram of the business operations model framework). To set this chapter in context it is worth a short recap on the previous three chapters, which together with this chapter form the framework in our development of perspectives around the business operations model:

- In Chapter 6 we looked at the technology dimension of being a disruptor, which found that disruptors tend to engage a range of our business operations model verticals, leveraging the technology with new delivery models.

- In Chapter 7 we explored the idea of market channels and their economics – this analysis showed that disruptive channel models are based on disintermediation and reintermediation of market channels, but are interlinked with support, optimized sourcing and inventory segmentation and deployment in our business operations model verticals.

- In Chapter 8 we looked specifically at the value to be gained from managing the basics. Lean management and the use of analytics to pinpoint opportunities for step change was the major feature; this development in our thinking linked to the management of complexity, optimized sourcing and manufacturing and touched lightly on inventory, sourcing and fulfilment.

It is clear from this recap that the narratives on disruptors (or, as a minimum, high achievers) always involve the combination of a number of elements. In this chapter on so-called optimization, in our terms breaking the paradigm, we look specifically at the potential for step change in fulfilment networks, service and support, inventory deployment, and sourcing and manufacturing. We also look at the integration layers in the framework of demand and supply planning and end-to-end commercial control. This will complete the examination of the model framework and lead into an exploration in Chapter 10 of 'what it takes to make it happen'.

In contrast to the excitement of technology, channels and the basics, the perspective in this chapter may seem more prosaic. But it is no less important and for some companies it can be the difference between life and death. The most important thing is to understand how executives and business leaders can think outside the box of 'trade-off thinking' and work out how to change the game rather than being constrained by convention.

It is the narrative of how operations can deliver disruptive performance that is important; we will have succeeded if readers can start to rehearse how they can break the mould in their companies' models and drive for transformation and disruption.

Fulfilment networks

Fulfilment and logistics costs can account for between 2 per cent and 30 per cent of turnover, depending on the physical nature of the product, its origins and the characteristics of demand; 5–10 per cent is the normal average range. Low-value bulk products such as some building materials are at the upper end of the extreme range and high-tech electronics and pharmaceuticals are at the lower end. This is dictated by the low to high value per cubic metre respectively. It is often the case that the lower end of the per cent to sales range places fulfilment in the non-strategic box, yet the actual impact on the business may be more about its ability to service customers in terms of lead time and order completeness (the perfect order from Chapters 3 and 4).

Figure 9.2 shows the contrast between conventional theory and the actuality of fulfilment network configuration. On the left is the classic model for calculating the optimum based on local delivery costs falling with increasing proximity to customers and being offset in a relatively linear way by increasing facility, inventory and primary freight costs. This gives a theoretical optimum number of fulfilment locations. The reality is on the right, which shows step changes in each function caused by factors such as the relative costs of transport by region, the costs of property and the relative scale by area of the sites in the network. This leads to a range of theoretical optimum site numbers in what we call a 'zone of indifference'. In line with the maxim from earlier, disruptive competitive advantage comes from 'moving the curve not riding it': let us explain.

The most effective way to achieve this step change is to leverage three complementary business model elements in order to change the role and nature of the requirement in the fulfilment network: inventory segmentation and deployment, mastering complexity and the customer proposition. We saw in Chapter 8 that there is a significant cost of complexity in the range of products offered. Many slow-moving products are bought in similar quantities to the faster-moving lines and this creates much higher relative levels of inventory measured in days or weeks of sale. This long tail of stock often clogs up warehouses and fragmenting stock into many sites makes no economic sense; it is almost always cheaper to hold it in a single

FIGURE 9.2 The key concepts of fulfilment optimization

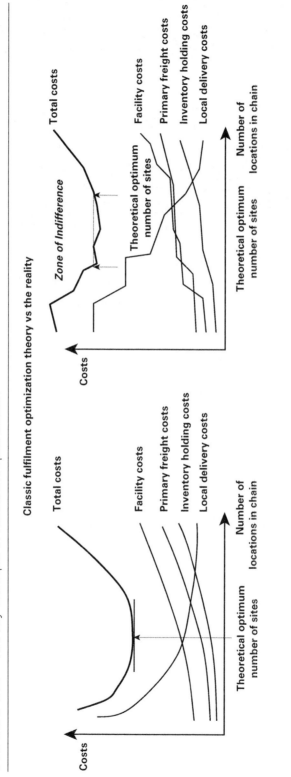

place and then ship it via express freight. This segmentation model reduces the capacity, and hence cost, required in many fulfilment locations and lowers the total cost of fulfilment. Such methods are now widespread in many sectors. UK supermarket chains have 'national distribution centres' for slow-moving stock. Many companies in the automotive sector have 'European distribution centres' holding hundreds of thousands of spare parts and regional centres holding only the fast movers; planes and trucks criss-cross the continent overnight making express deliveries. Amazon puts the responsibility for fulfilment back onto some of its suppliers as that avoids the unnecessary motion (one of the seven wastes of lean) from moving the product from one shelf to another before it actually goes to a real customer. This idea can be considered to reduce customer service but the reality is that express freight can overcome most of those concerns; it is important to understand what the customer really wants and is prepared to pay for.

A global leader in agrochemicals and crop protection had as many as 30 warehouses across Europe and wanted to rationalize the network to save cost and provide a platform for forecast growth. The conventional analysis identified a wide 'zone of indifference' with 12 sites having much the same costs as 19 locations. A more detailed inspection of the profile of demand found the entire network was configured to hold stock for major seasonal peaks, a role also intended to be carried out by its distributors and wholesalers. The step-change solution to their network was both fewer and smaller sites than the 12, but with much greater integration with wholesalers and distributors' stocks and the ability to package on a 'just-in-time' basis from bulk in the major distribution centres adjacent to the plants. This was cheaper and more adaptable to demand and avoided excess stocks and write-offs. It proved to be a competitive benefit to get more stock into the distribution channel since it impeded other producers' products from entering the channel. So the fulfilment network improvement needed to engage the channel economics, the inventory segmentation and the manufacturing organization in packaging.

Service and support

Customers' anticipation of service and support is often a critical part of their initial purchase decision. In industrial markets the availability of parts to keep equipment running is the key to maintaining production; any stoppage has a major economic impact. As we saw in Chapter 8, waiting time is one of the seven wastes to be attacked in lean operations. Caterpillar, the huge industrial, construction and mining equipment giant, has made a customer proposition virtue of this challenge by making the commitment to provide any part next day and, if it fails, you get the part for free.

However, providing parts and engineers on a 'just-in-case' basis when the probability of breakdown is remote can be a significant cost. Also having an engineer travel to a customer's site only to find that he or she has the wrong part is frustrating for the customer and costly for the company, which then has to make a second visit for which it cannot charge. Metrics such as 'first time fix per cent' and 'time to fix' are critical to managing the issue as they provide some insight into customer experience. In Chapter 7 we noted that Dell had suffered a market setback when its computers were perceived by the market to be unreliable; that kind of negative perception can take a long time to overcome.

Addressing the challenge of how to mitigate the costs of service and support while giving customers an acceptable response has spawned a whole range of initiatives that connect with our other business operations model elements:

- Design of equipment with in-built telematics and diagnostics enables a problem to be anticipated before it becomes unserviceable. This trend was observed in Chapter 7 in the case of Rolls-Royce and its provision of aero engines on a 'power by the hour' basis. As we observed, this approach impacts on channels and their economics; it opens up completely new business models.

- Remote diagnosis through internet-based investigation or skilled telephone support desks is designed to home in on the issue and in many cases the difficulty can be fixed without a visit. Even if an engineer is needed, they will be walking through the door with a very good idea of the problem – and hopefully the right parts.

- Making the parts economically available to reduce engineers' travel time and increase their productivity is part of mastering complexity, inventory segmentation and optimized fulfilment verticals. For example, one food equipment company has a mobile parts van in London that is in phone contact with the engineers and can meet them 'on the corner' to supply the part! The engineers can move from call to call by foot, on a cycle or a moped. Another solution is that parts can be delivered overnight to secure boxes near the location requiring service.

- The economic and service applicability of these solutions and others is dependent on the number of parts in the range, the customer turnaround requirement and the frequency of failure, among other factors. Where the scale is not sufficient to economically justify an engineer's visit from a core team, third-party repairers or walk-in centres are a way to meet customers' needs effectively. Some companies simply provide a complete replacement.

The key to service and support is a database to link the customer, the item requiring repair and the known faults with their associated fixes. The expectation is that in the next few years these capabilities will be increasingly online as the first point of call. Apple is particularly good at this; it maintains support teams at many of its stores who will prequalify the issue. If you have to visit a location, they have the entire catalogue of known problems and can fix most of them or provide a replacement.

All of these approaches take an unconventional means to satisfying customers' needs at a step-change reduction in cost. In our terms, it is a relatively fruitless exercise to try to optimize the engineers' routes when it would be better to try to avoid the visit in the first place.

Sourcing and manufacturing

We spent some time in Chapters 7 and 8 exploring the disruptive potential from sourcing and manufacturing in the cases of B&Q/

Kingfisher and Toyota. These linked optimized sourcing and manufacturing with market channels and economics, and the big ideas in lean thinking and managing the basics. But not every business either buys or makes to the criteria applicable to those segments – seasonal large batch sourcing or continuous flow assembly. There are other techniques in sourcing and manufacturing that can provide breakthrough and disruptive advantage where the need is to cope with complexity and variety in the factory.

The big idea in this is to carry the concept of inventory segmentation into the factory by streaming the planning and scheduling using a concept of fixed cycle – variable quantity scheduling based on the ABC Pareto distribution in Figure 8.3. The overall idea is illustrated in Figure 9.3, which shows 'A' items that are produced weekly, 'B' items that are made every four weeks and 'C' items that are produced quarterly. The A items are sometimes called 'runners', the exact quantity to be made being determined at the time of the run based on the stock and sales, and with a view on the planned closing stock, any orders in hand and planned promotions. The B items are called 'repeaters' and are produced every four weeks with the amount to be made determined just before the line is set up, based on stock and orders on hand and short-term forecast.

The C items, called 'strangers' are produced once a quarter, in this example, and are produced against actual customer orders that have been accumulated since the last cycle. At that time the company may also put in place a small amount of stock, with the aim of providing better but not perfect availability; other companies will only schedule production when they have an economic batch of orders.

One pharmaceutical company that deployed this approach reduced manufacturing costs by more than 10 per cent and saved as much as 40 per cent of its inventory investment. For them the move to a fixed-cycle schedule required reducing machine set-up times to much the same extent as observed in suppliers in Table 8.2 in Chapter 8 – days down to minutes. Achieving this was complex as it required simplification to and standardization of packaging specifications to cut set-up times; this impacted the manufacturing organization and engineering methods. Once again, conventional manufacturing planning and scheduling methods would have assumed change over times as fixed

FIGURE 9.3 Manufacturing optimization using the runners, repeaters and strangers concept

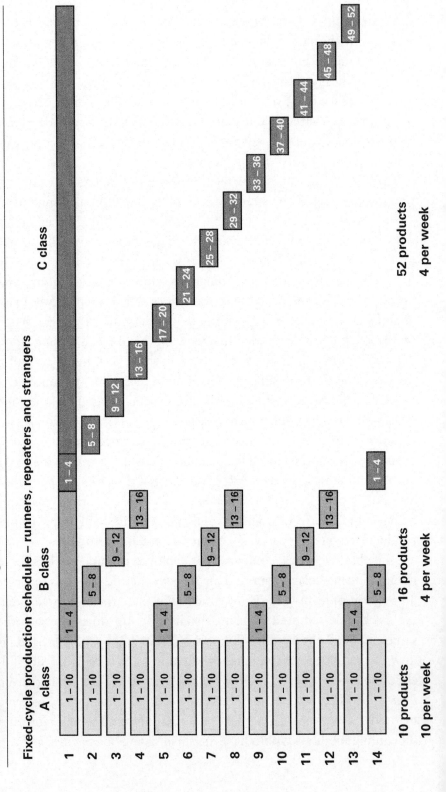

across the whole range and optimized manufacturing cost with no recognition of the cost of inventory.

The exact application of this streaming concept depends on the industry. One office furniture supplier set up a completely separate factory for low-volume lines, which were produced to order as compared to the volume lines that were made weekly to service a stock buffer.

These approaches to optimizing manufacturing apply the lean concepts introduced in Chapter 8 and reduce waste in terms of making only product that is needed, avoiding excess stocks and reducing waiting times by addressing set-ups. The pharmaceutical company found that these measures released manufacturing capacity, enabling it to cancel a planned investment and take on third-party packing contracts alongside its own products. It was truly transformational but barely visible to a casual visitor to the plant.

Demand and supply planning

Demand and supply planning is the first horizontal bar in the business operations model and is essentially an integrating capability across most of the verticals in our framework, but especially channels to market, range and customer complexity, fulfilment networks and segmented inventory and its deployment. We introduced the concept in Chapter 4, observing that it is commonly known as sales and operations planning (S&OP). As we said then, the aim is to create a workable plan that can meet the expected demand at an affordable operating cost and investment in inventory. S&OP as a process is about integrating the perspectives of meeting demand, financial budgets for revenues and profits, as well as capacity and inventory management. It has both a short-term and a long-term outlook; the short term is about meeting demand for the next few months and the long term is about informing business planning for capital expenditure and working capital management.

The idea is illustrated in Figure 9.4 as a jigsaw; the aim is for the company to converge on a single plan that meets the different functional priorities. Without it the tendency is for manufacturing to make

FIGURE 9.4   The sales and operations planning role: integrating plans and goals across the company

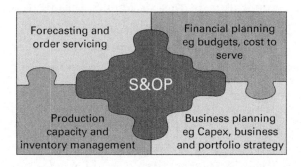

what is easy in order to meet its output goals regardless of customer demand; for sales to demand limitless inventory across an endless complex range while finance and business planning are unable to provide the resources for the company to function effectively.

Many large companies have very complex international supply chains with plants and business divisions and market territories in an extended matrix. A formal process is essential to consolidate validated forecasts of demand and development activity from the markets onto the plants in order to make both short-term decisions on what to make within the available capacity as well as the investments needed in capacity to service growth.

S&OP meets that need through a regular and rigorous monthly cycle that secures a single agreed plan across the corporation or business unit. If the plan has shortcomings or risks, those constraints are identified and how to deal with them is agreed; the business is working to 'one plan'.

Our experience of applying this process is that it delivers benefits across the organization:

- In the markets, product availability improves, often by as much as 5 per cent, which can drive sales increases through improved customer service.

- In the plants, there are fewer unplanned schedule changes, which drives improved operating costs and increased adherence to plan – in turn helping availability. The manufacturing benefits are often in the order of 5 per cent to 10 per cent of direct costs.

- In stock, distribution and fulfilment, the levels of inventory can be reduced by 15–20 per cent, which in turn reduces the need for warehouse capacity and stock financing, and reduces obsolescence and double handling with the fulfilment network.

Combined with the kind of fixed scheduling in manufacturing described in the previous section, the benefits can be as much as 15 per cent in manufacturing costs and 40 per cent reduction in stocks. That is rather more than a 'power of 1 per cent' leverage and is potentially transformational.

In a recent case, working with a fresh food supplier to British supermarkets, the benefits were focused on improved demand responsiveness, which increased from the low 90 per cent mark to as much as 97 per cent and at the same time freshness was improved, leading to a reduction in markdowns and waste of another 2–3 per cent on margin.

An integrated planning process is central to successful application of the business operations model; it engages and supports the benefits from the verticals in the model; once again, it is important to stress that disruptive models engage a combination of capabilities with a unique blend in relation to the products, markets and what customers find compelling. Just how much is available to the bottom line or for reinvestment in customer growth depends, as Wilding observed, on the 'starting conditions'.

End-to-end cost of service and supply and commercial control

The final horizontal band and integrating layer in the business operations model is about tuning the end-to-end cost structure of the company and providing the commercial feedback loop to price setting, the channel and investment focus for the firm. All the elements of our framework above this have been about improving service and reducing costs to create both a compelling offer and an economic business. It is underpinned by the need to understand the end-to-end cost build and consequential margin erosion along the supply chain: we call this cost-to-serve or net margin management. It is the central nervous system of the business operations model, connecting the question of financial viability with the compelling proposition and the operations model (as shown in Figure 1.1 in Chapter 1).

We have already seen that:

- The economics of channels can vary significantly – driving relative margin erosion (Chapter 7).

- Complexity in the product range and the customer base can drive cost disproportionately into both manufacturing and distribution (Chapter 8).

- Manufacturing management models and planning methods can cope with this complexity and drive significant margin gains (this chapter).

The reality is that both products and customers erode net margin as the goods and services flow through the chain; that erosion of margin is not consistent and conventional accounting based on allocations is invariably misleading. The starting conditions for inconsistent margin erosion are:

- The initial planned margin for the product – often some categories command (or are assigned) a higher margin than others in the overall product mix.

- The physical characteristics of the product in terms of cube and weight, batch size in production, stock levels, perishability and stock risk.

- The customer and channel characteristics in terms of channel margin allowances, customer order size and service demands (eg packing and delivery methods).

The discovery is that costs in the chain don't fall evenly across this mix and the range of margin erosion is unexpectedly large. Our earliest publication on this topic (Braithwaite and Samakh, 1998) looked at the combination of channels to markets and broad product categories for a computer manufacturer; the results are shown in Table 9.1.

It is immediately obvious from Table 9.1 that the monitors category was essentially unprofitable and the retail channel was the least

TABLE 9.1   Comparison of margin erosion by channel and product category

% Margin Erosion	Average margin erosion by category	Distributors	Large Accounts	Retailers	OEMs
Accessories	9.1%	9.4%	9.1%	7.7%	9.4%
Peripherals	13.3%	14.0%	13.3%	11.6%	10.9%
Monitors	88.5%	106.1%	99.0%	76.0%	91.6%
Processors	7.6%	8.9%	7.4%	6.3%	6.1%
Overall % of margin eroded	22.0%	18.0%	20.0%	27.0%	25.0%

profitable. Any attempt to average costs or control margin at a general level would almost certainly not maximize the financial potential and could easily lead to incorrect prioritization.

In more recent work with a fashion retailer we analysed every product/customer combination, classifying costs as variable, semi-variable and fixed based on activity-based attributions along the supply chain, rather than accounting allocations.

The graph in Figure 9.5 shows the output of this analysis in what is often called a whale curve. It plots the sales volumes and the attributable profit by product, sequenced in descending order of contribution from left to right. The graph for this case of the fashion retailer describes a situation we find to be quite common – the tail of the business generates significant loss-making volume.

The example in Figure 9.5 is quite extreme in that 40 per cent of potential profitability is eroded by the tail; once again this is rather more than the odd 1 per cent and deterministic formulae are unlikely to 'get at' the detail of the problem since they tend to rely on averages and generic algorithms. Analysis of the root causes of this margin erosion tends to expose:

- Inconsistent commercial control on planned margin in relation to the true cost-to-serve.

FIGURE 9.5   The chart of margin erosion against revenues by product for a fashion retailer

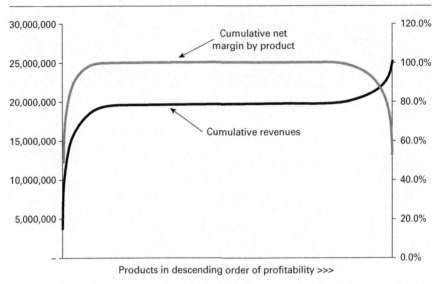

Products in descending order of profitability >>>

- Poor planning of the range, creating excess and slow-moving stocks that force margins to be sacrificed to realize the value of the stock investment.

- Excessive service commitments to customers in relation to the cost-to-serve – sometimes this is seen as poor control over the terms of trade that have been agreed with the customer.

In the example case the primary root cause was the second bullet point above. The change objectives were not to reduce the range and eliminate the loss-making products; rather it was to take out about half the problem through improved planning and forecasting processes combined with buying from suppliers in a more disciplined way in relation to overall planned volumes. As observed by Wilding and described earlier in this chapter, the system was predictable – success was about finding the subset and then managing that detail in order to avoid 'chaos'.

A relentless focus on improving process and control integrity over a 10-year period has recorded sustained growth; earnings have more than doubled and the share price has followed that general trajectory.

Case studies – introduction

The discussion in this chapter has focused on the improvement that is available from functional 'optimization' across the business operations model. We have cautioned against the concept of optimization as a trade-off; rather we have observed that breakthroughs in performance come from game-changing measures – finding a completely new optimum. The two case studies below provide practical examples of how this game-changing process works and how much value it can deliver.

CASE STUDY   Addis Housewares

At the time of this case study Addis Housewares was a family controlled business in the late 1990s – it was a business generating losses of about £1.5 million (about 5 per cent of sales) on a turnover of around £30 million. We have included this case study on a smaller private company to show that transformation and value creation are not the sole preserve of larger companies.

The product was injection-moulded plastic household bowls, brooms, mops, buckets, bins and the like. New management was installed to turn it around and the first step was a diagnosis of the business to identify the potential. The picture was of a company producing 700 different products, including colour variations, giving an average sale per product per week of £824 or around 400 pieces for each stock-keeping unit. The business was running with 14 weeks of stock cover but could still only achieve a 'perfect order' performance of 60 per cent. The actual individual product availability was around 96 per cent but, with orders containing many products, the statistical chance of having everything when it was demanded was much lower. The chief financial officer (CFO) commented at the time that being a 'little bit wrong' was enough to damage the customer experience.

And costs were high. Fulfilment and logistics were costing 14 per cent of turnover and finished goods were spread across three sites. This was necessary to hold the high levels of stock, but created double handling and contributed to the disappointing customer service.

The company was also being threatened by new cheap imports – albeit not to the same quality of product. On top of that, customers were demanding more variety; the supermarkets wanted their own specific colours and finishes and this would further fragment demand.

The improvement narrative at Addis was one of changing the game rather than conventional optimization in the areas of fulfilment, inventory, integrated planning and manufacturing. Together they turned the business around from a loss of 5 per cent to a profit of around 9 per cent – a 14 per cent swing. It enabled the company to be sold by the family and taken on its next journey by new owners.

Table 9.2 shows the 'before and after' situation at Addis. On entering the turnaround the first area of focus was inventory and fulfilment, since the cover and costs were perceived to be high. Establishing basic inventory controls took stock down from 14 weeks to around 8 weeks and allowed the closure of the external warehouses; previously manufacturing schedules had not integrated at all with either stock levels or market forecasts – they often made what they felt like in order to meet their unit cost goals, regardless of the need. As a result, the on-time in-full (OTIF) customer order achievement improved considerably to the mid 80 per cent level and costs in logistics came down to about 10 per cent. This brought the business close to break even.

TABLE 9.2   Addis housewares – turnaround story

Performance area	Before	After
Distribution structure	Intermediate sites	Single site
Stock in weeks	14 weeks	2 weeks
Inventory policy	None	Integrated stock policy
Customer service OTIF	60%	95%
Quantity availability	95%	100%
On-time delivery turnaround	3 days	1 day
Logistics costs	14%	8%
Manufacturing organization	Functional	Cell
Set-up time	8 hours	8 minutes
MRP system	Yes	None
Manufacturing sequence	Colour within line	Line within colour
Spare capacity	Little	25%

The question for management was then how to take more cost out of the system and increase reliability for customers. They argued that if they could achieve this, they could respond to customers' requests for increased variety. The focus then switched to manufacturing and the long set-up times on the big injection-moulding machines. A changeover could take eight hours, losing a complete production shift and creating labour waste while people stood around waiting for the change. This in turn encouraged longer run lengths for a product and created waste as colour changes were put through the moulds; it was common to see green buckets followed by buckets streaked green and red (unsaleable) until quality buckets came out red. The unsaleable buckets were crushed and reformulated with black colouring to make black dustbins; needless to say there were plenty in stock to be sold off cheaply.

An electromagnetic die-change development was introduced so that mould changes were just a question of a forklift manoeuvring the replacement die so that it could be clamped in place with the magnets. This reduced the set-up under the mantra 'from eight hours to eight minutes'; the actual time was generally less than 15 minutes! At the same time they introduced a cell-manufacturing organization so that the team responsible for the moulding press was also engaged in the final assembly and packing. This required a major layout change, but obliterated the high stocks of work in progress.

The outcomes of this change were not fully anticipated but were the result of connecting this new more flexible manufacturing model to real demand. The lead times were now so short that a customer order for which there was no stock could be made the day it was received, ready for despatch the following day; there was little or no cost penalty for the change.

The result of this capability was that demand planning and forecasting was simplified to a weekly process of creating production orders to build to a stock target of no more than two weeks. The complex manufacturing requirements planning (MRP) system was taken out and the cells were left to decide what to produce and when. If they wanted to work extra and have Friday afternoon off they could; if there was no work, the deal was an annual hours arrangement and product was not made unnecessarily.

The die change was so rapid that it was quickly discovered to be better to produce by colour rather than by product. This eliminated the 'streaky bucket' problem and avoided that product having to be crushed and reworked into black dustbins – the only product where it could be reused and which ran on more than 20 weeks of stock and low prices.

Manufacturing costs fell by more than 10 per cent, stock came down to two weeks or less and the business released capacity for new product introduction. Perfect order achievement was close to 100 per cent because of the short lead times. The only place where stocks increased was in packaging and finishing materials. The exit net margin was around 9 per cent for a commodity product.

The change to cell manufacturing did not just involve the shop-floor layout and establishing teams. It cascaded through the whole organization as much of the traditional planning of manufacturing was made obsolete; the short lead times simplified the planning process and placed the responsibility for demand generation and fulfilment firmly on the commercial function. There was a significant realignment of roles and the business had to learn to work with new key performance indicators (KPIs) both in terms of what was measured and the targets. While the results speak for themselves, it was not a completely comfortable process.

We like this case because it shows that a relatively small company can embrace step changes in its business operations model and drive transformation. It proves the maxim 'don't ride the curve – move it'.

CASE STUDY   Health-care consumables manufacturing and distribution

---

We touched on the case of this health-care manufacturer in Chapter 7 when we introduced service-dominant logic and market-changing models. It was making sterile packs containing all the consumables needed for medical procedures and configured to the specification of individual surgeons and practitioners. This new model of supply was disruptive in that it was attracting high levels of demand and registering double-digit growth.

However, it was proving more difficult to turn a profit, with losses of 2–3 per cent of revenue being sustained over the early years. This short case builds on some of the step-change optimization opportunities introduced in this chapter.

Analysis showed that the company would produce the forecast requirement of the medical practitioner and hold it in stock, waiting for call-off by the hospital. This resulted in as much as 20 weeks stock in the warehouse and lots of double handling as all that stock would not fit into one building. Analysis also showed that the rush to get customers signed up had on occasion lost control of pricing and the margins were dangerously low in relation to the cost.

The challenges identified by management to realize profits from this growth segment were:

- Reducing lead times and increasing manufacturing responsiveness to enable stocks and operating costs to be reduced.

- Establishing improved commercial control to ensure that customers make reasonable commitments and meet them, and that planned gross margins reflect actual costs.

- Encouraging product standardization between practitioners – many of the local variations were found to be costly and not really needed and the sales people could guide some surgeons towards a more standard pack.

The business operations model changes started with work on inventory segmentation and deployment. This approach reflected the 'runners, repeaters and strangers' approach described earlier, with some products justifying production to stock and others placed on a slightly longer lead time and supplied in smaller quantities on a make-to-order basis. The implications for the plant were much tighter integration between assembly and sterilization and much-reduced batch sizes – down to a lot size of one in some cases. This in turn reduced stock and saved money in distribution. The trajectory in this turnaround is targeting profits of 9 per cent with some constraints on growth; the company has understood that it can leave competitors to sustain unprofitable growth and eventually go out of business.

In conclusion – optimizing is about finding a new model

Transformation in all our examples and case studies has been about finding a new business operations model that improves operating economics and, through that, the customer value experience. Our cases both involved turnaround from decline or losses; the improved performance helped to re-establish growth or delivered growth at a profit.

Relating the achievements in transformation to the business operations models, recurring themes for readers to take away are:

- Mastering complexity is often about overcoming self-imposed concepts of how things should be organized – think about how you can tear up the old rules.

- Optimized fulfilment networks are enabled by a new approach to complexity and the segmentation and deployment of inventory – get it right and cost just falls out of the business.

- Service and support is a prime area for radical thinking because the costs are so high – but avoiding the need is even more satisfactory for customers, as well as costing less.

- Segmentation of inventory as a concept flows back into manufacturing where different planning concepts, combined with availability commitments, can radically reduce costs.

- Planning and end-to-end cost and commercial control are key skills – they can both inform the radical approach and also support it.

In summary: 'Don't ride the curve – move it.'

Taking forward the framework in your business

Optimizing is a potentially flawed concept in the light of our analysis, but that introduces the opportunity to change the game and potentially become a disruptor. To take this scenario forward you need to answer the following questions and take the appropriate measures:

- Can you be confident that the solutions and analysis conducted within your business are looking for game-changing opportunities rather than just riding the trade-off curve? If the answer is no, you need to find a way to challenge the embedded wisdom.

- Have you thought about radical ways to manage variety in your business by segmenting flows in both inventory and the sourcing and fulfilment platforms and networks? Again, if the answer is no, there is a latent opportunity and you should find a fresh way to do the analysis and design.

- How good is your planning? Do you spend a lot of time arguing about plans and forecasts? If that is the case then you need to update the planning process because that will be driving hidden waste in stock, obsolescence and markdowns.

- Do you know which customers or products destroy margin (because some certainly do)? If not then you need to initiate a process of net margin management to find the big losers and cut them out as best you can.

When you have answered these questions, then you need to look back at the business operations model framework and once again update your narrative for transformation or becoming a disruptor.

Making it happen – becoming a disruptor

10

When Pelé, the legend of South American football, was asked for the secret of his greatness, he said:

> Success is no accident. It is hard work, perseverance, learning, studying, sacrifice and most of all, love of what you are doing or learning to do.

This is consistent with our observation in previous chapters that it can take years to become an overnight success. It is when a company's business operations model comes together that the business takes off; there is indeed no silver bullet. And disruptor status may be transient, as is the success of football teams, when players leave or competitors improve.

In this chapter we explore the challenge of making transformation happen – be that turning around a business, as we described with Addis – the plastics homewares company – or becoming a fully fledged disruptor, as observed with Amazon. In Chapter 1 we introduced this book and its foundation in our research into the characteristics of disruptors. We have been influenced by a series of meetings of LCP Consulting's thought leadership panel, our consulting and teaching experience and an LCP-sponsored project at Cranfield's School of Management. That project by Chris Melton, who is now a consultant at LCP, looked specifically at the origins and triggers for business success from the application of supply chain thinking. As well as covering the academic literature he looked at the background to

TABLE 10.1   Case studies researched to build the framework

Apple	Coca-Cola	Dell
Ikea	John Lewis	McDonald's
Pret A Manger	Samsung	Tesco
Unilever	Walmart	

the success of 11 companies, through desk research and interviews, as shown in Table 10.1.

We have developed some of these cases in this book as well as including additional cases and examples that reinforce the conclusions and validate the business operations model framework for disruption. Chris Melton's report and thesis (2012) identified eight 'contexts' for radical change; these are shown in Figure 10.1, into which we have placed the business operations model. The work found that in any single case there is usually some combination of the contexts that trigger transformation, but certainly not all of them. So, the multiple triggers of the actions to becoming a disruptor are similar to the features of the business operations model where the narrative of success commonly engages a number of dimensions.

The actions for realization, shown on the right of the figure, include a range of perspectives that have to be brought through together to ensure successful change. Here we have built on our 'crystal for change', which we have used successfully with many companies over the last 10 years. Our experience is that successful change and transformation has to engage every facet of the crystal. We will look at each context in turn and then unpack the formulation of actions for transformation by describing the crystal:

- The most common context for transformation is *declining business performance*. This is normally measured in terms of the five levers described in Chapter 2: growth, margin, velocity, return and cash. For public companies, any decline across the five levers is quickly translated into a reduction in market

FIGURE 10.1   Contexts and actions for business operations model transformation

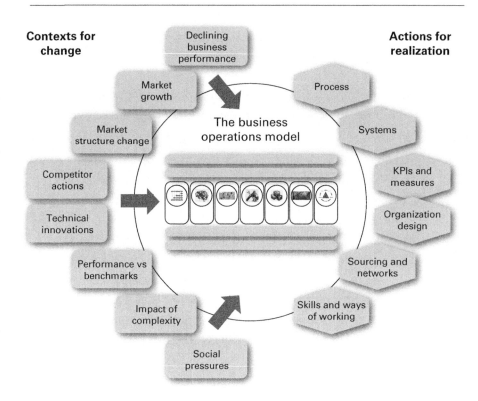

value, which in turn creates a loss of confidence among investors and triggers demands for change. The same is true of businesses controlled by private equity or which, although unlisted, have a widely held shareholding. In contrast, privately and tightly held companies can take longer to recognize and respond to poor performance. They don't have the relentless focus of the analysts, the media and private equity investors; and their people are more deeply embedded.

- *Market growth* is also a context for triggering change, when a company sees an opportunity to exploit growth in demand by changing its business operations model to respond to that growth (Figure 10.1). Examples in construction would be the introduction of prefabrication methods in response to major investments, or events such as the Olympics where service models had to change because of timescales and logistics. The growth in the container shipping sector was a response to the growth in global trade in manufactured goods, which was itself triggered by the new model shipping capacity becoming available. As described in Chapter 6, liner companies have vied to commission ever larger ships in search of greater economies of scale.

- *Market structure change* is about channels and delivery, as discussed in Chapter 7. The growth in internet retailing is a case in point; it is now the major channel for retail growth and has opened up opportunities for many, not just for Amazon, and left some laggard retailers at a disadvantage. Also the development of 'service-dominant logic' delivery systems for aero engines and defence equipment is a market structure change that requires all the major suppliers to develop an offer. The 'internet of things' will provide further potential for channel disruption that is currently difficult for us to imagine.

- *Competitor actions* are about the need to respond when some combination of competitive pricing and service initiatives make the company's positioning less attractive. The example of Aldi's disruptive impact on the major supermarkets is a case in point that is now demanding changes by three of the major UK chains: Tesco, Morrisons and Sainsbury's.

- *Technical innovations* are a major trigger for business operations model change and we provided examples in Chapter 6. In that chapter we pointed to the fact that the application of technology is commonly the platform for new models as much as the technology itself.

- The causes of decline are often elicited by *performance measurement and benchmarking*; concerns about competitors may arise before a full-blown decline is visible. In Chapter 9 we described some findings from Womak, Jones and Roos (1990); that benchmarking initiative was an automotive and government response to the disruptive changes brought in by the Japanese manufacturers. The work showed clearly the deficiency in the business operations model of the US auto makers at the time. But the Japanese themselves had contexts that led them to develop their unique model that is now copied around the world; the disrupted and the disruptors are two sides of the same coin but driven by different contexts (we will return to that idea shortly).

- *The impact of complexity* on performance can also be a trigger. In Chapter 4 we commented on Hamel and Prahalad's (1989) maxim of strategic intent and how that had undermined full-range full-service suppliers. In Chapter 7 we gave the example of Canon disrupting Xerox by carving out a simple niche that avoided much of the cost of complexity of the full-range manufacturer. It is also a factor in the progress of discount retailers such as Aldi, who can operate at much lower costs than the major supermarkets, as observed in Chapter 8.

- *Social pressures* is the eighth and final trigger identified by Chris Melton. The research found that Pret A Manger (one of his focal companies in Table 10.1) had made great progress in its market by responding to its customers who wanted to be confident in the ingredients and freshness of their lunchtime sandwiches. The business model was built on 'made on site, no stock carried over and waste given to the homeless'; customers are prepared to flock to this position in droves and pay a little more. The pressure of social media in some markets is now so great that companies will have to adjust their models to avoid risk of failure and the social approbation that could go with it. The social card may be stronger in the future.

The search for excellence or, better still, disruptor status is not about ticking off this checklist, it is about how the pressures on a company come together across these factors. It appears to us that the narrative of contexts divides broadly into four groupings:

- *The burning platform*: this is where business performance is declining, sometimes rapidly. At the same time the company's markets may be changing sharply or aggressive competitors may have established new offers, possibly with the help of new technology. Alternatively it will be where performance benchmarks badly against the leaders. For a business facing a burning platform, the change in business operations model can be either a story of recovery or leapfrogging the competition. The fashion retailer example in Chapter 9 with the high-margin erosion was a company on a burning platform that recovered well. The success of Tesco started from a burning platform in 1984 when market share was 12 per cent and declining and the financials were disappointing; but from there it leapfrogged the competition to reach nearly 30 per cent.

- *The model opportunity*: this is where a change in approach to the market can lead to becoming a disruptor. It is most likely to originate from market structure changes or the ability to create them. This in turn may have a technical, complexity or social context. It may also be accompanied by market growth, or drive it. Early adopters of model change can get what is called a 'first mover advantage'; others will be followers and their success will depend on the capacity of the market to accommodate 'me too' players and just how well the 'first mover' did their work. Examples of disruptors through the model opportunity include Rolls-Royce aero engines, Ford for mass production and then Toyota for lean manufacturing; in Chapter 7 we gave the case of Canon leapfrogging Xerox – but before that Xerox had leapt ahead with its own copying and printing at the time.

- *The market opportunity*: this is where market growth is driven by some combination of economic trend and technical development. In turn it may engage with questions of complexity, performance measures and benchmarks. Once again, the 'first movers' may be able to engage with this opportunity by changing models in terms of channels as well as delivery capabilities. An example here would be the packaged holiday business, where increased family affluence created completely new demand as families wanted to travel with convenience. Another is the growth in the logistics services market from the middle of the 1980s, based on economic growth and core competence strategies that drove the outsourcing boom.

- *The hybrid opportunity*: this is where the burning platform combines with either model or market opportunities. It is about companies being in some trouble and then being able to grasp the opening presented by some structural or technical change. A generic example here would be catalogue retailing, which was itself a disruptor in the 20th century through companies such as Sears Roebuck in the United States and GUS in the UK. These companies experienced a decline in favour of retail malls but are now reinventing themselves as digital retailers competing with the likes of Amazon, embracing a new model.

Clearly, if a company is on a burning platform, it has itself been disrupted, either by the market or competitors or its own poor performance. In contrast, the other three narratives are the potential disruptors, creating burning platforms for others.

It is instructive to look briefly at some narratives for disruption of some of the cases in the previous chapters using this model:

- Irish Fertilizers was eventually disrupted by low-cost competition based on market structure change as new cost-efficient international plants came on stream. The company was behind on all the performance benchmarks except quality. For the company it was a burning platform; for the competitors it was mostly a market opportunity.

- Zara has become a disruptor through its approach to fast fashion, exploiting growth, market structure changes as well as innovating in its production and distribution system to deal well with complexity. In line with most disruptors it is now a price point reference without holding a dominant share of the market; its disrupted competitors have to find ways to become more agile or face declining business performance.

- Apple was disrupted for a period by the power of Microsoft based on declining performance, market structure change and Microsoft's technical innovation. It then became a disruptor through its own technology and how it drove market structure change through its business operations model.

- Amazon has disrupted many through its development and exploitation of market structure change that has then driven growth in its channel. It has achieved this through the exploitation of technology and how it has mastered complexity.

- Dell was a powerful disruptor as it changed the market structure and disintermediated dealers; through its close relationship with suppliers it was able to exploit technical innovations and its performance was well above industry benchmarks on key ratios. But Dell was then itself disrupted by lower-cost competitors, the move to laptops, the resurgence of mass retailing in the sector and the decline in prices, which made Dell's customized specification and online channel less competitive. Dell is now back in the retail channel, having made an abortive attempt to use this channel many years ago.

- Toyota transformed the world auto industry in response to a market opportunity in the post-war recovery period in Japan. It had to build smaller cars for the Japanese roads and do it in a way that was more economic due to constrained capital. Having learnt to do this, it disrupted the US and European industry through its low-cost cars, based on its technical production innovations. That in turn drove market structure change, which also drove growth. The disrupted auto makers, who simply did not believe what was happening, have spent years catching up. Their below par historical performance made them vulnerable during the global downturn triggered in 2008 and there were bankruptcies at GM and Chrysler – a real burning platform.

Actions for realization – the 'crystal for change'

On the right-hand side of Figure 10.1 there are six hexagons, which we have classified as actions for realization. These are based on the crystal for change, which is a framework we have used successfully to guide management teams to an integrated set of actions to deliver transformation. Unlike the business operations model and the contexts, where in any one case only some of the points may be applicable, our observation is that effective change requires specific actions in every facet of the crystal.

The reason for visualizing change as a crystal is that it is multifaceted. If you hold a large crystal to the light and turn it, you will see different refractions and colours; yet every facet of the crystal is needed in order to secure the effect you see. Managing transformational change follows the same concept; you have to take in all the facets to get the full effect, but the way you turn it can be specific to the case. Where you start and how you sequence actions can be the difference between success and failure; and we are also very clear that cherry-picking detail is a formula for disappointment.

Figure 10.2 shows the crystal for change; each facet is briefly described below:

- *Business processes*: the importance of business process design was stressed in Chapters 4 and 9. Large organizations, particularly, require high levels of process excellence to deliver effective operations. We have seen, as we unpacked the

FIGURE 10.2   The 'crystal for change'

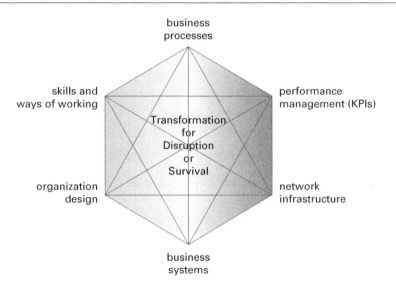

business operations model framework, the importance of process in planning as well as in channels, complexity, inventory and service. Good processes strip out time and waste, and hence cost; they improve responsiveness to customer demand and increase service. Process is always at the heart of any transformation.

- *Business systems*: these mirror processes; our organizations are mostly so large and complex that having that complex information consistently available and processed in a timely and accurate way is a crucial role for systems. Many organizations have made the mistake of trying to drive change through systems and, in our opinion, nothing could be more wrong. We have seen declining business performance blamed in companies' accounts on systems changes over repeated years. Process and organization should always lead systems change. Systems are essential but they don't need to be gold-plated; the kanban concept at the heart of the disruptive Japanese auto-industry disruption was entirely manual and card-based.

- *Network infrastructure*: this is about the facilities for manufacturing and distribution. It is about: Who (subcontracted or owned)? Where? How big? How equipped and operated? How flexible? How resilient? This is where the money gets spent with suppliers and inside the company's own facilities. It is where the business operations model becomes physical and tangible. The configuration of the network to deliver disruption or survival is often seen as a functional role, as we remarked in Chapter 4. Nothing could be further from the reality; the characteristics and attributes of the production system are at the heart of the business operations model and effective transformation. The John Lewis case study later in this chapter will illustrate this point and the link with processes and channels.

The final three facets of the crystal for change reflect the 'how' rather than the 'what' of transformation:

- The *performance management* system is how the organization constructs its performance measures to evaluate, recognize and reward its people for doing the right job and doing it well. The adage that 'what gets measured gets managed' is always true; if the business has understood its shortfall in the marketplace, it can focus its teams on the changes and trajectory needed. KPIs do not exist in isolation of processes and organization design, and they are generally dependent on systems for their reporting.

- *Organization design* is at the heart of any change but is often underestimated; new processes, network and KPIs almost always require new organizational lines and accountabilities.

- Finally, there is a need to focus on the *skills required* to make the change happen. In Chapter 4 we talked about T-shaped people having the attributes to manage a particular function with great depth but also to understand and respond to the wider issues for the company: being able to respond to the end-to-end improvement agenda.

Our experience of working with companies through transformation initiatives is that starting with organization and performance measurement provides clarity and focus rather than ambiguity and tension. If you set out on the journey of change with clarity of organization, roles, responsibilities and the required measures of performance, people will know where they stand and what is expected of them. In the short term they may not have the skills, resources and processes to carry that through, but if that is treated with some sensitivity it is better than asking people to do new things via old structures. And it is important to note that some people will not want to take the journey.

In the 1980s when Xerox was fighting back against the low-cost disruptors, Fred Hewitt, the global vice president of logistics used to reorganize and reset the KPIs on day one of any change. It sent a powerful message that it was serious – and removed any ambiguity. Another example was our work with a large catalogue retailer that was trying to reverse structural decline; we again agreed that the starting point was the organization and the measures. It took them at least six months to get all the measures flowing and during that time they worked to change the processes and the supplier base; but the organizational change signalled clearly that the die was cast. Within a year the business was on a restored trajectory and, 10 years on, profits are double what they were at the start of the change process.

Overcoming disbelief

If executive sponsorship of a major change is lukewarm, it is 'easy' to fall back on process and network change or rely on systems as the 'answer'. This will seldom place accountability firmly where it needs to be and the goals will simply not be believed.

Disbelief and inertia are commonplace in the face of change. A major US health-care company that was moving to a European structure discovered this when it started, by trying to redefine its processes in a way that was 'organizationally agnostic'. For over a year the arguments raged, with most of the heat and emotion being driven by individuals' expectations of what their turf would be at the end of the transition. No agreements were reached and the project stalled. Their president for Europe said one night over dinner with us: 'The problem is they don't believe me.' Nine months later he finally made the changes to set up an appropriate organization and within two years it was delivering remarkable results.

This theme of disbelief and rejection of change is the story of humankind – and the famous quote from Machiavelli from the 16th century in his book *The Prince* says it all:

> It must be considered that there is nothing more difficult to carry out, nor more dangerous to handle, than a new order of things. For the reformer has enemies in all those who profit by the old order, and only lukewarm defenders in those who would profit by the new. This arises partly from the incredulity of mankind, who do not truly believe in anything new until they have actual experience of it.
>
> Machiavelli (1513)

Gary Hamel, who we referenced with CK Prahalad in Chapter 4 for their idea of strategic intent, also recognizes the challenge of inertia as well as the importance of step change. He wrote:

> The most powerful defenders of strategic orthodoxy are senior management and strategy making needs to be freed from the tyranny of their experience. (Hamel, 1996)

My argument is the more difficult the economic times, the more radical innovation becomes the only way forward. In a discontinuous world, only radical innovation creates wealth. (London Business School, 2015)

The truth is that most people struggle to understand the implications of change until they have experienced it.

The implication is that once the change has gathered momentum and is delivering results, people will mostly step in behind it. Hamel is indeed right when he points to radical change needing powerful champions who take no prisoners. Peters and Waterman (1989) in their book *In Search of Excellence* called them 'monomaniacs with a mission'.

It is, of course, much easier to take people along with radical change when they are on a burning platform. The key in today's complex business environment is for the change to be appropriately designed and that entire teams need to share the passion for the new direction; initiative fatigue is a real risk.

Don't underestimate serendipity

As we have observed, disruptors can work hard for long periods without much progress or recognition; they are kept motivated by their vision and belief together with a measure of obstinacy. They are watching for the evolution of opportunities to bring elements of the model together and readying themselves to take advantage of them.

While it is often said that you make your own good fortune, our research with Chris Melton pointed to the element of serendipity in many success stories. Serendipity is defined as 'making desirable discoveries by accident' or a 'fortunate happenstance'. Seasoned executives would probably use more down-to-earth terms such as a 'stroke of good fortune' or 'when events and conditions come together'. It is a repeated theme in our cases that people and companies that put themselves in the path of good fortune – and grabbed it – made the breakthrough. Each of the examples below contain an element of serendipity as well as some combination of passion for what people are doing, dogged persistence or just plain hunger and desire to succeed.

It should never be too late – but sometimes it is

The ethic of business-school teaching is one of pointing to super-performance and success based on cases; the narrative of failure is seldom a topic. As we showed in Chapter 2 and throughout this book, disruptor status can be transitory and even a sustained disruptor, such as Southwest Airlines, will experience volatility in results. A few years later, for many, their companies' value and position will have declined for whatever reason and the magic will have faded. Sometimes this is just about the competition catching up, but on other occasions the market changes radically, technologies enable new business models or other contexts take effect.

The wisdom of Charles Handy, the distinguished author and philosopher specializing in organizational behaviour and management, pointed to the challenge of renewal when he gave us the idea of the sigmoid curve for organizational (and personal) evolution in his book *The Empty Raincoat: Making sense of the future* (1995). This is shown in Figure 10.3 and points to the stages from inception, through growth into maturity and then the decline.

FIGURE 10.3   The sigmoid curve and finding future breakthrough

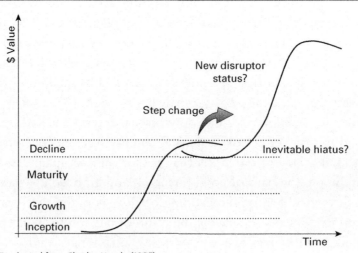

SOURCE: adapted from Charles Handy (1995)

The challenge is how to initiate a new state of inception and growth while still in the maturity phase of the old model – or moving towards decline. Overcoming disbelief in that situation is an even more difficult task. That was indeed the situation with the health-care company mentioned earlier; the president was initiating change based on his view 'over the hill', anticipating the arrival of low-cost competition for their core suture product and the arrival of high-tech non-invasive surgical tapes. He knew that they needed to adjust the business operations model but his team did not believe him when he said the change would happen; also they were not ready to accept the oncoming challenge to their profitability that necessitated the changes.

There is likely to be a hiatus during any transition from one sigmoid curve to another, regardless of whether it is clearly foreseen – and that is shown in Figure 10.3. The question is how severe the downturn will be and whether a business that does not make the adjustment will survive.

We introduced the case of the downturn at Tesco in Chapter 2 and have returned several times to its challenge, and that of its fellow UK supermarkets, from the hard discount operators such as Aldi and Lidl. Given that Tesco's market share is still over 25 per cent at the time of writing, it is unlikely that Tesco will go out of business but it will likely have to take some tough medicine to adjust its cost base and this will probably involve the sale of some business units and assets.

In the end, a business fails or loses its independence when it runs out of cash as well as being unable to borrow more or raise new funds from shareholders. If the management of the business can summon the courage to make the jump from one curve to another, the decline in the fortunes of most companies can be restored by assertive actions in managing the basics, as outlined in Chapter 8.

To support the conclusions of this chapter we have prepared four short case studies. The case of Woolworths, which went down at the hands of its suppliers and banks, is introduced as a case study in order to show that it is never too late, until it is.

CASE STUDY   Southwest Airlines

We covered the case of Southwest Airlines in detail in Chapter 1 but it is important to pick out some aspects of the 'context' and its disruptive capabilities in the light of our observations in this chapter.

First there was growth in the travel market in Texas, with Houston, Dallas and Fort Worth being among the fastest growing in the United States in the mid 1960s. Second, there was a KPI context as the established airlines were running fully loaded on routes between these cities and it was difficult to book a seat. Indeed it was a truly dreadful service. Third, those flights were often part of much longer routes crossing the state, which impacted reliability and restricted capacity (as we discussed in Chapter 1). As a result there were three powerful contexts in play from our Figure 10.1 – the opportunity from rapid growth, the potential to change the market structure and the value from reducing complexity.

Southwest Airlines also ticks the two boxes of 'endless determination and perseverance' and 'serendipity'. The endless determination story is told in the legal battles it went through just to operate. The airline was founded in 1967 and it applied to the Texas Aeronautic Commission to fly the intrastate routes between Dallas, Fort Worth and Houston. Because it was flying intrastate, it judged that it did not need permission to operate from the Federal Civil Aeronautics Board. Local permission was granted and the immediate response of Braniff and Texas International (neither of which still existed by the early 1990s) was to apply to the courts to challenge the issuing of the certificate.

The ensuing court battle went all the way to the Supreme Court and Southwest Airlines eventually won in 1971. It started operations on 18 June 1971, more than three years after the original certificate had been issued. That can only be described as dogged perseverance. But it did not stop there; the early schedules did not attract enough business to support its four aircraft and it was loss making; by April 1972 it needed to act.

It had already experienced a measure of serendipity in the timing of its aircraft purchase and leasing deal as it negotiated with Boeing for four aircraft that had been overproduced before an industry downturn. It saved 13 per cent on the purchase price and was able to secure favourable financing. The second stroke of good fortune was the realization that it could turn its aircraft on the gates in 10 minutes and that this would enable a nearly comparable schedule with one fewer aircraft – a massive reduction in the cost base for no sacrifice in income. The good fortune continued with the easy disposal of the fourth plane at a net profit of $533,000, as the industry had picked up and prices had hardened. By 1973, Southwest had broken through the clouds and was in relatively blue skies.

Case studies and commentary all point to an integrated focus by Southwest all around the crystal to make change happen and grow the business. Perhaps the most significant emphasis is on skills and ways of working, performance measures and operational effectiveness; it is a great place to work and clearly delivers effective performance through knowing what it has to achieve.

While various sources of turbulence have demanded continued determination and perseverance, the simple narrative shows how the company became a disruptor. Some might say riding its luck; we would say making it.

The case reflects the conclusions of this book perfectly:

- Dogged early persistence to overcome legal challenges and then a period of 10 years before the business value started to grow rapidly.

- Disruptor status achieved through a strong and sustained vision of the new operating model as well as serendipity.

- The business operations model gives customers extraordinary value.

- Success has been sustained – and there is still growth potential providing that Southwest Airlines stays focused and avoids complexity.

CASE STUDY   Christie-Tyler

Christie-Tyler (CT) manufactures upholstered furniture and originated in South Wales. During the Second World War, the company made seats for planes and buses and in the period of post-war austerity it returned to its roots in domestic furniture. In the 1950s and 1960s the company flirted at least twice with bankruptcy and was dragged back from the brink; furniture can be a volatile sector because of the discretionary nature of demand in a cyclical economy. We have included such an old case because one of the authors worked in the company during the mid to late 1970s and CT's rise to prominence is a story of achieving disruptor status. Indeed it was a tale of dogged perseverance, pure serendipity and (as set out in Chapter 8) transformation through the basics.

Following yet another downturn in the late 1960s the chairman and CEO, George Williams, made quite a number of production staff redundant as the demand was not there. When it picked up again he was quite reluctant to increase the staffing as he had so nearly been burned twice before and cash was an issue. However, he was approached by some of the personnel he had let go, who offered to work on a pure piece-rate basis if he would set them up in one of the barns on his estate. Making upholstery is a low-asset business. The company already had most of what was required: cutting tables, sewing machines, an air compressor to drive the staplers and upholstery benches. All that was needed was clean dry space. He negotiated a rate with the team that was less than his direct costs in the main factories and set them up. He supplied the frames for them to upholster from the central wood mill – the capital intensive part of the operation. In the short term he could sell the product and there was no long-term commitment.

The results from this self-organizing team were electrifying; the workers were quickly earning double the wage that Williams was paying in the factory and producing more than double the output from less space. He had discovered cell manufacturing, as we described it in the Addis case in the plastics industry. Having made this discovery after sustained perseverance, Williams acted quickly to change the business operations model. He figured that CT could cut prices in the market to hit spectacular value 'price points' with better products. It was the Walmart concept – sell more at a lower price with a slightly lower gross margin but from less space. If you do that you can grow fast while making much the same level of profitability. CT could make a suite (sofa and two chairs) that retailed for between £199 and £299. At that price the product quite literally sold itself in a market that was emerging from post-war austerity and was keen for style at great value. Adding capacity in South Wales was not a problem and the business grew from less than 5 per cent market share to around 30 per cent in less than 10 years, a rate of gain that marketers will tell you is exceptional.

Around the crystal, the combination of process change (moving to cell manufacturing) with the manufacturing change (moving to many small plants) and aggressive productivity goals were the platform for a changed business operations model. The monthly accounting process was as good as we have seen since and was entirely manual. Williams was able to bring in staff who were completely inexperienced in upholstery making, reducing dependency on craft skills and apprenticeships. Organizationally he hired young energetic managers, many short-commission army officers, and that created a cadre with a particular style, quite different from what had gone before.

The company floated, was a stock market star and attracted a lot of commentary on its application of cell manufacturing. But 30 per cent is a market share threshold at which you are there to be challenged, as we have seen with Tesco. The combination of learning by competitors with the inevitable economic cycle, the impact of which cannot be avoided at a 30 per cent share, meant that in the mid 1980s it started to go backwards. It lost its independence to a takeover by Hillsdown Holdings, which itself got into trouble and the business was picked up by a venture capital firm. Then, in 2005, CT went into receivership when two of its customers went bankrupt within a year. The brand still exists today but many of the subsidiaries are now in separate ownership.

The case reflects the conclusions of this book perfectly:

- A period of 20 years or more of persistence to reach take-off.

- Disruptor status achieved through serendipity, which was grasped with both hands.

- The business operations model changed to give customers extraordinary value.

- Success was transitory – especially in a cyclical sector with low barriers to entry.

CASE STUDY   John Lewis Partnership

John Lewis is a remarkable business because it is the largest employee-owned company in the UK. It has two core businesses: department stores and the upmarket Waitrose grocery brand. The company's website says: 'We are now one of the UK's top ten retailers with 43 John Lewis shops (31 department stores, 10 John Lewis at home and shops at St Pancras International and Heathrow), over 300 Waitrose supermarkets, an online and catalogue business, a direct services company, one production unit and a farm.'

It is a legend and reference point for customer service and quality in the UK and is recognized around the world; we have found it referenced for excellence as far afield as South America. It retained the title of the UK best retailer in the Verdict customer satisfaction survey for 2014. It sells under the strapline of 'Never knowingly undersold', which comes with a price match commitment if others are selling at a lower price.

The recent growth has been remarkable, as is shown in Table 10.2. It shows that the total revenues grew by between 3 per cent and 10 per cent per year and profits grew much faster, with the exception of 2012 when the company made pension adjustments, carried the cost of commissioning new stores and invested in quality for the future.

This story of growth and margin has been driven by significant business operations model change; the business is now a disruptor just because it is a reference point for range, price and customer loyalty. The figures show that the online growth has been between 18 per cent and 40 per cent year-on-year and

TABLE 10.2   John Lewis department stores trading history, 2009–13

	FY 2009	FY 2010	FY 2011	FY 2012	FY 2013
Total revenue £m net of VAT	£2,327	£2,417	£2,662	£2,790	£3,050
Online sales £m	£333	£394	£538	£681	£959
Total revenue growth		3.9%	10.1%	4.8%	9.3%
Online growth		18.3%	36.5%	26.6%	40.8%
Operating profit	£144	£166	£201	£158	£217
Profit growth		15%	21%	–21%	37%
Average selling space (calculated)	3,664,928	3,904,054	4,001,238	4,156,055	4,523,353
Number of stores	27	29	32	35	39
Average sq ft per store	135,738	134,623	125,039	118,744	115,983
Average sales per store £m	£73.9	£69.8	£66.4	£60.3	£53.6
Store sales per sq ft	£544	£518	£531	£507	£462

SOURCE: compiled from John Lewis Partnership report and accounts

that the effect on stores has been for revenue per store and revenue per square foot to be in steady decline. The company has added smaller stores in anticipation of this decline; the average turnover per store has declined by 27 per cent compared to just a 15 per cent decline in sales per square foot.

Financially, the growth in online sales has more than offset the reduced productivity in the stores themselves and John Lewis has cleverly integrated the store and online offer to increase customer interaction and grow sales and loyalty; this is sometimes called omni-channel retailing. In our opinion, omni-channel is the backbone for future retailing success.

Looking at the 'context triggers' for its achievement, they were the realization of the growth potential in online and the market structure shift towards it; the technical innovations associated with online retail; and the opportunity to manage complexity in new stores by integrating them with the online service.

To jump the sigmoid curve, John Lewis experimented with johnlewisnow.com in 1999, bought buy.com in 2001 and launched johnlewis.com that year using the platform experience it gained from the learning period and the acquisition. In its first year the website took £24 million across 5,000 stock-keeping units (SKUs), 10 years later it took more than £600 million plus (net of VAT) across 219,000 SKUs.

In 2003 the company decided to begin an expansion plan that would see 10 new stores being opened in 10 years. The implications of that expansion and the growth plans were the need to reduce the complexity of store operations, releasing backroom space to sales area. This involved a change to sending most products to stores in single-item quantities rather than packs and stopping suppliers delivering direct. The company had experienced a large warehouse malfunction in 2001, which led to it losing 3 per cent of its sales that Christmas; so the expansion plans required improved central distribution capacity.

It proved particularly challenging to change mindsets across the business to seeing the supply chain as more than a necessary cost. Ultimately they succeeded and a major project got under way to build and equip a 750,000 square foot semi-automated warehouse to replace a number of existing sites and provide increased capacity to pick and ship single items to both stores and the online market.

Until that facility was up and running the disbelief remained latent. But once it was, and the business was able to implement the process changes in store service and replenishment, the benefits were immediately apparent. The company was quickly saving as much substantial operating cost in stores from the new central facility combined with stock reductions, and it proved hugely valuable in serving the spiralling online demand. The integration of the store and online offer, and its accommodation in the distribution system, has proved to be a huge advantage. The general manager of the new site is quoted as saying: 'We had built it for 10 more department stores and modest online growth; instead we are opening fewer stores but are seeing massive online growth.' While the design was highly flexible, there was also an element of serendipity; events combined successfully to support the online growth with very high service levels. At the time of writing the company is commissioning another 750,000 square feet of capacity in distribution. The strategy, as of 2014, is to add smaller department stores and integrate them with the online offer and its supermarket business.

In the context of the actions around the crystal, the change was led by a combination of facilities and network but with the supply chain organization repositioned to ensure the change landed. Supply chain was made central to the planning of inventory in stores so that the responsibility for replenishment, in-store and online availability was clearly positioned. To achieve this there were parallel and major changes to systems, skills and KPIs. It was indeed a successful integrated change.

Once again, the key conclusions are consistent with the maxims of becoming a disruptor:

- It takes time to build a huge success.

- Disruptor status has an element of serendipity, as nothing happens quite as planned.

- There was an element of disbelief because of previous failures and the change in how stores would be serviced – that was until people experienced the service and how it coped with the online growth.

- It was not even close to being too late – but they'd had problems in 2001.

- The business operations model changed in order to reduce costs and provide a platform for the market structure change.

- Success in this case is likely to be as sustained as at Southwest Airlines, since the brand is held in such affection by its customers.

CASE STUDY   Woolworths

Woolworths in the UK was a household name in general retail with 900 stores: one on almost every high street. The company entered administration in November 2008 when suppliers refused to supply it after their trade credit insurance was withdrawn and the banks withdrew their loan facilities. The business found no buyers, other than for packages of stores, and went into liquidation.

This is a narrative in the category that 'it is never too late until it is'. Woolworths was disrupted by a whole range of market change and competitor actions. In the retail space, Argos was a powerful competitor and Tesco launched a major catalogue on toys and other categories that directly challenged the core Woolworths range proposition. Market channels were changing, with e-commerce starting to grow rapidly. The business had a real burning platform – it had been marginally profitable, at best, for some time; there were plenty of contexts for change.

Some two years before it went to the wall, the company did the analysis on profitability; Figures 10.4, 10.5 and 10.6 show a sample of that work. It exposed a huge erosion of net profit at the tail of the range, with a substantial part of the volume not making any useful contribution (Figure 10.4 shows the example of just one department). Root cause analysis pointed to the larger stores being over-ranged with products that attracted higher levels of discount and markdowns

FIGURE 10.4   A whale curve from the analysis for a sample department showing net margin erosion

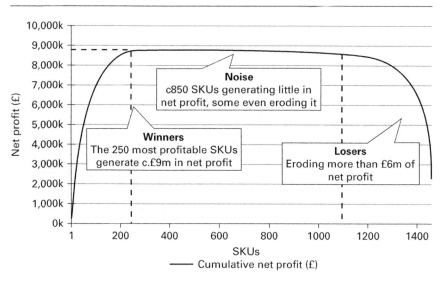

FIGURE 10.5   Chart showing larger Woolworths stores were less profitable

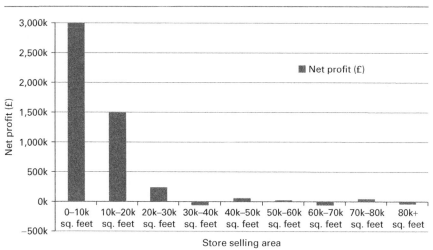

FIGURE 10.6   Woolworths analysis – showing poor stock position on hot Christmas sellers

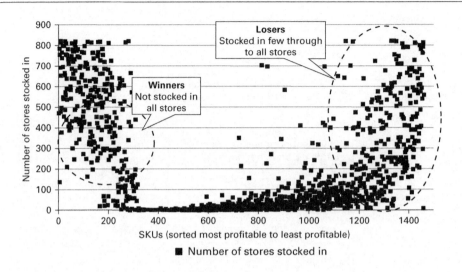

Number of stores stocked in

(Figure 10.5) and that the better-selling and more profitable lines were not placed in all stores and were not bought in sufficient quantities. As a result the hot lines in toys were out of stock at the end of November and the shelves were full of gaps (Figure 10.6).

The answer to this challenge was exactly the same as that taken by WH Smith – 'trade for margin not for revenues'. This should have involved closing or re-merchandising the bigger stores as well as applying a ruthless buying and ranging focus to the departments that were losing money. Such an approach would have included buying more of the products that could easily have been predicted as 'winners'; the analysis had shown that they were actually quite predictable and previously had been undersupplied. This was termed 'buying deeper on the sure-fire winners'. It also meant cutting ranges and avoiding products that were less likely to sell well. This is a meticulous retailing process that is tough to embed. It requires some faith to take a leap that can be perceived as sacrificing sales; retailers are often heavily focused on the top line rather than margin. In this case the management team was not able to overcome its disbelief and uncertainty over the risks of change. It did not need to eliminate all the issues implied in the whale curve; reducing it by 25 per cent would have been sufficient to turn the business. For whatever reason (most likely a strong measure of disbelief), action was not taken and it was eventually too late; but closure was not inevitable until that last season.

Once again, the case reflects the conclusions of this book perfectly:

- A long-term historic success can be disrupted by changes in the market and the channels – Woolworths was overtaken by new channels.

- It is really difficult to jump the sigmoid curve – overcoming disbelief.

- It could have been turned by a focus on managing for margin rather than for revenue – the WH Smith example.

- It's never too late until it is – in this case it was.

Taking forward the framework in your business

This chapter focused on what triggers the strategic move to transformation or, better still, disruptor status. To take the framework forward you need to consider which of the triggers (more than one is likely) apply to your business and which scenario applies to your business. Answer the following questions as a team:

- Are you on a burning platform? You will know this from your analysis in Chapters 2 and 3 – and if you have not already found an answer, then you probably need to focus on 'managing the basics'. Go back to the relevant chapter(s) and answer the questions at the end.

- Is there an emerging model, market or hybrid opportunity that your capabilities will be able to adapt to and exploit? If so, then develop your narrative and integrate it with the business operations model framework.

- Are you at risk of being disrupted and do you have any appropriate response? This will most likely require a radical approach to the redesign of your operations model – but it will be better sooner rather than later if you are to jump the sigmoid curve.

- Are you able to organize for change by taking an integrated perspective around the crystal? If not, you need to work on the management culture or you have little chance of overcoming disbelief.

Rehearse the completed narrative – it will never be exactly right but if it engages across your business operations model and is consistent then you have a starting point.

You have to make your luck – but then take it as a team.

Guiding principles to building a competitive edge through business operations models   11

Edward de Bono, who is famous for his promotion of lateral thinking, said:

> Creative thinking – in terms of idea creativity – is not a mystical talent. It is a skill that can be practised and nurtured.

He also said:

> Most executives, many scientists, and almost all business school graduates believe that if you analyse data, this will give you new ideas. Unfortunately, this belief is totally wrong. The mind can only see what it is prepared to see. (De Bono, 2009)

De Bono (1985) used the idea of 'thinking hats' to describe different thought processes by the colours of the hats of the wearers. So for example:

- White hat thinking is based on information and deduction; it is derived from the facts.
- Yellow hat thinking is based on optimistically exploring the opportunities and looking for value and benefit.
- Black hat thinking is judgemental; it looks for the negatives and why something may not work, spotting the difficulties.

- Red hat thinking is about intuition and emotion; it expresses likes and dislikes, loves and hates, what you most want but also what is feared.

- Green hat thinking is the creative approach to problems; it explores opportunities and new ideas.

- Blue hat thinking is the hat used to govern the thinking process alongside the other hats.

While Peters and Waterman (1989) described a key source of success as having a 'monomaniac with a mission' (see Chapter 10), our experience is that really successful teams usually have at least two leaders with different thinking styles. You need the eternal optimist (yellow) and creative (green) balanced with facts (white) and hard judgement (black). If a team has spent many years trying to become an overnight success, emotional thinking (red) is never going to be far from the surface and can colour (pardon the pun) all the other thinking dimensions.

Our aim in this book has been to provide a fresh pathway (blue hat) to creative strategy definition – and potentially disruptor status. It includes all the thinking dimensions and points to where emotion and judgement are so important.

We have focused on the narrative of operations and its context in value creation, and have stressed that it is an insufficiently recognized area of strategy development and execution. Yet as we point out in Chapter 4, Johnson *et al* (2008) reported that 11 out of 27 new Fortune 500 entrants in the last 25 years were business model innovators. Our framework is not the only perspective on achieving business success, but we would argue that the operations dimension is often underestimated in strategy formulation.

We also argue that it is possible, using our framework, to define transformation or disruption measures. It is not purely an analytical process; in de Bono's terms its needs creative tensions within the team, and some moderation – the blue hat.

Stepping through each chapter in turn, the essence of the business operations model is to help executives to develop narratives for disruption. The key points are summarized below.

In the first five chapters we introduced the overall business operations model concept, the potential for value creation at the corporate level and how that is driven by compelling customer value. We also distilled key points from the literature to pick up on our core theme; the key points from these four chapters are:

- Business operations models are about a unique balance of customer value, the operations to deliver that value and the commercial viability of the value proposition (Chapter 1).

- The business operations model framework is built around customer value and organizing to secure the commercial viability of delivering that value. That in turn is achieved through seven vertical capabilities of which some, but seldom all, will be central to success in any given situation. The capabilities are integrated through both a planning 'layer' and end-to-end cost management and visibility (Chapter 1).

- Super-performing businesses – disruptors – outstrip market indices by a factor of thousands; rapid growth in market value can be achieved in just a few years when a business model goes 'hot'. The strongest driver of value is earnings or profits (Chapter 2).

- The value of disruptors can also be perceptual and in some cases may be relatively transitory – there should be no room for complacency in any boardroom (Chapter 2).

- There are clear levers that connect financial performance to business operations model choices, which will improve performance and through which boards can explore the potential for transformation (Chapter 2).

- If a company delivers exceptional value to its customers it will succeed, subject to sustained profitability; customers decide what is valuable to them and make quite refined judgements on what they appreciate (Chapter 3).

- Customers are interested in lowering the overall cost of their purchase, including their internal costs; alternatively they are interested in increasing convenience, reliability and aura, some of which may also lower their total cost of ownership (Chapter 3).

- Business strategy thinking contains a 'gap' in its strategic valuation of operations; too often the assumption is that it is about choices and trade-offs. The idea that things can be done radically better and that such an approach might inform strategy is unusual (Chapter 4).

- The established management thinking that does bridge the 'gap' comes from work in the areas of process improvement, performance measurement and the idea of business models (Chapter 4).

- The theme of disruptors transforming markets is part of current parlance; being a disruptive innovator is recognized as a potential source of market value and investors are attracted to such businesses. We propose four core scenarios for disruptive business operations models: technology, market channels, managing the basics and 'optimization' (Chapter 5).

In Chapters 6 to 9 we unpacked the four scenarios to understand how the attributes in our business operations model come together and can be used to build a narrative for successful transformation. Key insights are:

- In Chapter 6 – the technology scenario:

  - Technical innovation is less about the technology than the business model changes that it enables – technical innovations only thrive if they enable both businesses and consumer to obtain compelling value.

  - Disruptors do not have to dominate a market to control them – a growing share and high visibility can be sufficient to set the agenda of the whole market.

  - For companies that have been disrupted, there can still be life, but continued survival invariably requires radical change.

  - Commercial returns from winning technical disruptor status are not assured and the half-life of some businesses can be short.

  - It can take many years to become an overnight success – perseverance and careful cash management is needed while the elements come together.

- In Chapter 7 – the channels scenario:

  - The choice of channels to market can have a major impact on net margin and has the potential to be transformational.

  - Disintermediating established market channels to transform business economics is a key source of disruptor status.

– Disruptive channel design can be applied both downstream and upstream of the focal company.

- In Chapter 8 – managing the basics:
  – Managing the basics can be an underestimated source of transformation and, on occasion, disruptor status.
  – Relatively modest gains in several areas of the business, achieved simultaneously, can propel a company to the top of the pack – the power of 1 per cent.
  – The key leverage from managing the basics comes from mastering complexity as well as identifying and obliterating hidden waste.

- In Chapter 9 – the optimizing scenario:
  – Optimizing the business operations model should not be considered as a tuning process – the big opportunity is to change the paradigm to achieve transformation rather than accept trade-offs.
  – Radical operating model shift is available in many of the model verticals: networks, service and support, complexity, and optimized sourcing and manufacturing. The key is to combine these opportunities through end-to-end planning, cost and margin visibility.

- In Chapter 10 we identified that there are eight possible context triggers that may lead to a company moving towards disruptor status. Once again it is combinations of these that are the motivations for action; scenarios include the burning platform, the model opportunity, the market opportunity and the hybrid opportunity. Key conclusions were:
  – Successful disruptor status is always secured through a balanced set of actions around the 'crystal for change'; it is usually best led by changes in organization and the associated team performance measures.
  – In evaluating the potential for successful transformation, never underestimate the need to overcome disbelief, the power of endless determination and an element of happenstance or serendipity.
  – If you are on a burning platform, it is never too late until it is.

Building a new business operations model by selecting from the elements

Our business operations model framework, together with the cases, provides a means for teams to develop their own narratives for transformation and potentially achieving disruptor status. It is not a formulaic process where you can plug in the situation and the answer will fall out; as we saw with the comments on optimization, that approach is potentially flawed. Rather, it requires creative thinking and inductive logic leaps, based on a broad appreciation of the situation for the company and the environmental changes that are taking place.

From our perspective, the starting point is always to understand the nature of and opportunities to create compelling customer value. We covered in some detail the approach to eliciting what customers will find compelling; it can be applied both to established markets and to innovation opportunities. Having understood the goal, it is possible to identify the broad underlying cost structure to secure both the pricing and service of the target proposition. From that an understanding can be gained of the difference that needs to be bridged. There may be a circular refinement process here, but that can then be informed by the potential in the verticals of the business operations model. At that point, the key areas of focus can be determined from channels through complexity, networks, service, inventory segmentation, and sourcing to managing the basics. There are likely to be two or three of the verticals that will provide the necessary leverage.

Integration through the planning process and the end-to-end cost and margin control brings the whole picture together.

We cannot stress too highly the need to develop the narrative of change so that people can see the dynamic that is to be attempted. Building that word picture or diagram is part of the process of overcoming disbelief. Figure 11.1 shows an example from the fashion sector. The company was in structural decline and needed to reverse its fortunes by giving customers better value and securing that value by eliminating waste.

The fashion company in Figure 11.1 needed to switch from a financially focused approach to maximizing gross margin to thinking about customer value – and how the product and the process of managing

FIGURE 11.1 Building a narrative for change at a fashion business

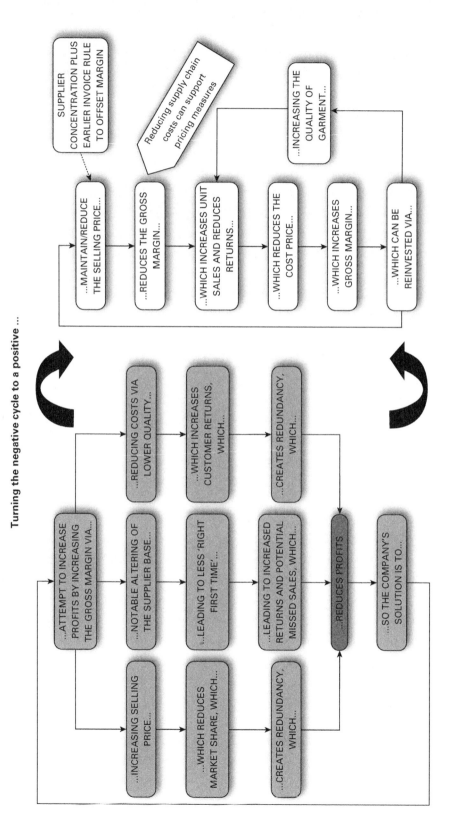

Turning the negative cycle to a positive ...

redundancy could be changed to support that. The discovery was that sacrificing a little bit of margin to reduce the selling prices and put improved quality into the product more than covered its cost, generating savings in returns and a return to growth in volumes. Then serendipity kicked in! The team discovered that the increased volumes on key product lines enabled them to negotiate reduced buying costs and there was no sacrifice in margin. Furthermore, increased velocity reduced markdowns and discounts. Margin was restored alongside a return to sales growth: it was a win-win-win.

The experience is that the initial narrative is never quite what actually happens but is sufficient to overcome disbelief and get the change rolling. As we saw with the John Lewis case study, the outcomes can easily exceed expectations when a radical approach is adopted.

The importance of analytics in design

At the start of this chapter we quoted de Bono decrying a dependence on analysis as a means to determine solutions. He said it is wrong to think that 'if you analyse data, this will give you new ideas'. He went on to say: 'The mind can only see what it is prepared to see.'

In our terms, this does not invalidate analysis of the kind we have described in the previous chapters. Without analysis, how can you tell which customers and products are eroding margin disproportionately? Or how can you tell which products should be segmented in their inventory across the distribution chain? The complexity of many businesses with tens of thousands of products and customers is such that analytics are essential; the process of interpretation of the analysis to develop narratives for transformation or disruption is the crucial skill. Our experience of this work is that different dimensions of analysis are best brought forward in parallel to create a wall-board of key facts for the team to consider together. From this the scenarios for change can be described. Then further modelling and analysis may be carried out to test their validity and value. Figure 11.2 shows this process in concept, which is a crucial part of overcoming disbelief. The process is sometimes called inductive thinking, where different facts are lined up and the team makes 'logic

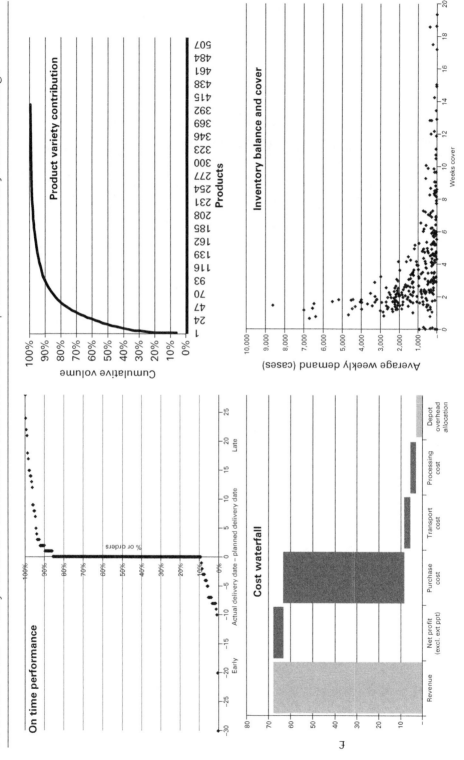

FIGURE 11.2 Analytics across the business inform an inductive process to build a storyboard for change

leaps' towards new opportunities. In contrast, deductive thinking is the process de Bono criticized; you do not get good answers by relying purely on the analysis.

Driving change through the crystal, building road maps for the journey

In Chapter 10 we introduced the 'crystal for change' as a means to describe and plan a successful integrated set of actions. The point was made that a balanced set of actions is needed across the facets of the crystal that recognizes not just the assets, processes and systems but also the organization, performance measures and skills. It is crucial that initiatives are not cherry-picked as this often breaks the interdependence of the facets. Our experience is that describing the major changes on each of the facets in a single diagram helps to ensure that the links are visible; once again it is about narratives. This is illustrated in a simplified form in Figure 11.3.

FIGURE 11.3   Describing actions around the crystal to 'land' major change

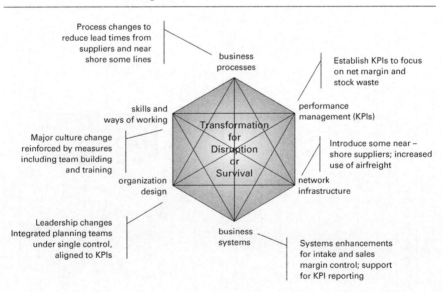

We described in Chapter 10 the European president of the health-care company who only got the programme moving when he changed the organization; starting with process was just not going to work. The John Lewis case was dependent on a change in organizational ownership of store stock replenishment. The Addis plastics recovery nearly stalled from resistance inside manufacturing management and needed both organizational change and new performance measures.

The story at Xerox was that the measures in people's personal goals were the thing that changed on day one of any programme. Fred Hewitt was clear that he needed to send clear signals to his team and the organization, both that he was serious in holding them to the new targets and that the team would be supported in reaching those goals.

This was mirrored at Heineken, which needed to improve its customer service and reduce inventories and the amount of beer wasted; individually these were small changes, but remember the 'power of 1 per cent'? The brewer took a long-term view to improvement as there was no burning platform. They put in new KPIs and that got the whole business thinking about the issues; then they formed a new central team to help with process changes and the supporting systems.

Creating highly visible road maps is an important part of communicating the programme for teams to see and understand. Complex project management diagrams with hundreds of tasks are important for control and resource allocation, but they are unreadable and unintelligible to the average person. Building road maps that align to the crystal – and the priorities and sequence – is important to the organization. Figure 11.4 offers a simplified example that aligns to Figure 11.3. Clearly, programmes of change have to be aligned to the financial year, the resources available, the investment–return ratio and the degree of risk. Changes to burning platforms will look quite different from a more measured and structured change.

Symbols for change

Symbols for change are an important part of overcoming disbelief. If the senior team is serious about the changes it wants to see, it is

FIGURE 11.4 Communicating the road map for change

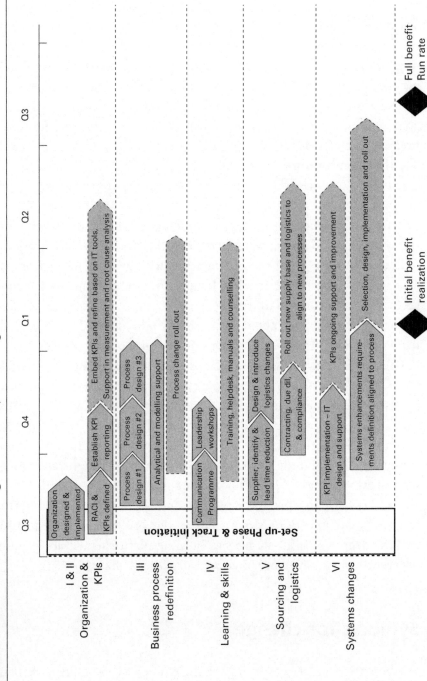

essential to send signals to the people with whom it means business. In Chapter 10 we quoted from Machiavelli – this quote from the 16th century is true today. Too often a group of organizational saboteurs will emerge who have decided that they don't want, need or believe in the change. Symbols of change are needed as clear statements of intent that things are going to happen. Typical of these are:

- Changing the organization structure (as we discussed earlier).
- Changing the leadership.
- Formally adjusting the performance measures and building them into people's reward structures.
- Moving people or offices, including opening or closing facilities.

Process and systems changes on their own have a high risk of failure unless the other facets of the crystal are clearly defined. The time taken for processes and systems to be designed in a potentially disconnected way affords organizational saboteurs the opportunity to extend the scope, raise doubts and simply filibuster.

Forbes magazine reported in December 2013 on a systems implementation failure at Avon Products, the global home-selling cosmetics company. It reported that:

> Avon Products Inc. is halting a massive multi-year software project...
> Avon balked when the software rollout not only disrupted regular
> operations, but when implemented was so difficult to use that
> representatives left the company 'in meaningful numbers'.

The report went on to say that Avon was being forced to write down its investment of more than $100 million since the proposed new system (a combination of SAP and an IBM e-commerce front end) for customer order management would not be used globally as had been intended. It is a reminder of the quote we used in Chapter 9: 'to really foul things up you need a computer'.

The internet and company accounts are littered with such stories. Our experience is that such problems are seldom the fault of the software but of its alignment with the processes in the business. If the new processes are not clearly defined and the people have not signed up to the changes, the outcome is generally an excessively complex software set up and, in Wilding's (1999) terms, a measure of chaos. Of course people blame the system but it is usually the organization, KPIs skills and ways of working that have failed to secure the right, and simple, process definition. The road map in Figure 11.4 based on the crystal shows systems following rather than leading and processes tied to KPIs; this is how it should always be.

Finally, under the heading symbols for change, even when a comprehensive programme has been defined, there will be people who will not make the trip for reasons of skills, attitude, self-image, personal animosity, or whatever. While letting such people go is one of the hardest things for any executive to do, they cannot be retained as their disbelief is corrosive.

Challenges and risks for innovation and change

As we have seen in the cases of the US automotive industry being disrupted by Toyota and the Japanese, and more recently Tesco being disrupted by the hard discount chains, a dominant share of a market presents competitors with their own opportunities to disrupt. Our discussion of Handy's sigmoid curve made the point that it is difficult to make the jump to a new trajectory, yet radical innovation is needed when a company's position is challenged.

This is a recognized phenomenon, which Rajesh Chandy, now Professor of Marketing at the London Business School, described as 'the incumbent's curse' (Chandy and Tellis, 2000). It is indeed really difficult for a company to reinvent itself when it is the marketplace leader, incumbent, because lower-cost operators can cannibalize its market, picking off segments – in our terms, disrupting. The company is usually heavily invested in the assets of production and distribution, together with the systems and processes to apply them. The organization structure and KPIs will also have been aligned to the former model. The psychology of abandoning the old model and taking the financial charges for changing the assets is really difficult to stomach. The case of Aldi in Chapter 8 showed how its business operations model could cannibalize the conventional supermarkets. Dell is another case in point and we told the story of its decline in market share as its direct channel model became less relevant to the market. The inertia arising from a reluctance to take the pain early is an advantage to the incoming disruptors, who can gain momentum before a coherent competitive response is forthcoming. The scale of the earnings decline, debt re-rating and the financial charges to write down assets can be traumatic for a public company. It takes time to summon up the courage to do it and all the while the situation is deteriorating. This reduces flexibility to mount an effective response.

At the other extreme it is easy to be complacent, overconfident or overambitious and this too carries a risk of failure. This has been described as the 'Icarus paradox' by Danny Miller (1990), an economist and Professor of Entrepreneurship at HEC Montreal. The essence of the idea is the paradox of successful businesses failing after a period of success and where the decline is the consequence of the things that led the organization to its original success. Like Icarus in Greek mythology, whose wings had enabled him to escape imprisonment, the same wings melted when he flew too close to the sun. The business parallel is that if you become complacent, overconfident and blind to the dangers, you may be heading for a fall.

As we see it, the idea in business has two perspectives. First, the company may or may not recognize that it is close to the top of the sigmoid curve, but still try to drive more performance out of the existing operating model; these companies generally realize too late that they have tried to exploit the model for too long – and face a rapid downturn. The second perspective is a surfeit of ambition and hubris leading to unwise investments and initiatives; this may apply either to the incumbent or a potential disruptor. We saw plenty of overconfident potential disruptors fail in the dot.com boom and bust for just this reason.

Avoiding risks such as these requires clarity of vision and business operations model integrity. In de Bono's terms, the management team needs to be able to represent all the thinking styles, above all balancing creativity and ambition with facts and critical objectivity. The narrative that comes from that process is the vision, mission and means for success.

In conclusion

De Bono was clear that creative thinking is a skill that can be developed and nurtured. By implication, innovation can be a controlled and managed process, even if serendipity plays a part. Such a process will always benefit from a framework to guide teams in their development. In this book we have described our business operations model framework and we offer it as a way for executives, academics and students of management to understand and move to exploit the undervalued potential that operations can bring. It is not a formulaic approach; it requires lateral thought, analysis and the application of structure alongside perseverance, intuition and occasional happenstance. We have shown that the value potential can be extraordinary. But both the 'incumbent's curse' and the 'Icarus paradox' make the point that change is really difficult; the stories about 'overcoming disbelief complement that insight.

Alongside bold and radical game-changing initiatives we have also shown that the power of 1 per cent can be transformational through the aggregation of individually quite small changes. We hope that just a few of our insights have connected with each reader and may promote an innovation or prevent a mistake. In the end, teams will take from our thinking what works for them. If that can have been even slightly informed by our thinking, we will have succeeded.

Thank you for taking this journey with us and allowing us to share our experience. We leave you with one final maxim: 'never underestimate the strategic potential from your business operations model!'

Taking forward the framework in your business

Don't argue – find the strategic keys from this and the previous chapters and just do it.

REFERENCES

Braithwaite, A and Samakh, E (1998) The cost-to-serve method, *International Journal of Logistics Management*, **9** (1)

Brown, T (2009) *Change by Design: How design thinking transforms organizations and inspires innovation*, HarperCollins, New York

Chaffee, E (1985) Three models of strategy, *The Academy of Management Review*, **10** (1), pp 89–98

Chandy, R and Tellis, G (2000) The incumbent's curse? Incumbency, size and radical product innovation, *Journal of Marketing*, **64** (3), pp 1–17

Davenport, T (1993) *Process Innovation: Reengineering work through information technology*, Harvard Business School Press, Boston

De Bono, E (2009) [1970] *Lateral Thinking: A textbook of creativity*, Penguin, London

De Bono, E (2009) [1985] *Six Thinking Hats*, Penguin, London

Fleming, J and Asplund, J (2007) *Human Sigma: Managing the employee-customer encounter*, Gallup Press, New York

Ghemawat, P (1991) *Commitment: The dynamic of strategy*, Free Press, New York

Gladwell, M (2009) *The Story of Success*, Penguin

Goldratt, E (1984) *The Goal: A process of ongoing improvement*, Gower Publishing, Aldershot

Grundy, T (1995) *Breakthrough Strategies for Growth*, Pitman Publishing, London

Hamel, G (1996) Strategy as revolution, *Harvard Business Review*, July/August

Hamel, G and Prahalad, CK (1989) Strategic intent, *Harvard Business Review*, May–June, pp 63–76

Hammer, M (1990) Reengineering work: Don't automate, obliterate, *Harvard Business Review*, July–August, pp 104–12

Handy, C (1995) *The Empty Raincoat: Making sense of the future*, Random House, London

Johnson, MW, Christensen, CM and Kagermann, H (2008) Reinventing your business model, *Harvard Business Review*, December, pp 50–59

Kaplan, R and Norton, D (1996) *The Balanced Scorecard: Translating strategy to action*, Harvard Business Publishing, Boston

Levitt, T (1974) *Marketing for Growth*, McGraw-Hill

London Business School [accessed 10 February 2015] Inside the innovation lab, *Business Strategy Review* [Online] http://bsr.london.edu/lbs-article/181/index.html

Martin, J (1996) *Cybercorp: The new business revolution* (1996) Amacom, New York

Melton, CM (2012) *Development of a framework to determine business success from supply chain management*, Cranfield University, MSc thesis

Miller, D (1990) *The Icarus Paradox*, Harper Business, New York

Naveen, J (2012) [accessed 10 February 2015] [Online] http://www.inc.com/naveen-jain/10-secrets-of-becoming-a-successful-entrepreneur.html

Peitgen, H-O, Jurgens, H and Saupe, D (1992) *Chaos and Fractals: New frontiers of science*, Springer Verlag, New York

Peters, TJ and Waterman, RH (1989) *In Search of Excellence: Lessons from America's best run companies*, Bloomsbury, London

Porter, ME (1980) *Competitive Strategy*, Free Press, New York

Porter, ME (1985) *Competitive Advantage*, Free Press, New York

Schumpeter, J (1942) *Capitalism, Socialism and Democracy*, Harper & Bros, New York

Sheth, J and Sisodia, R (2009) *The Rule of Three: Surviving and thriving in competitive markets*, Free Press

Treacy, M and Wiersema, F (1993) Customer intimacy and other value disciplines, *Harvard Business Review*, January/February, pp 84–93

Vargo, SL and Lusch, RF (2004) Evolving to a new dominant logic for marketing, *Journal of Marketing*, 68 (1), pp 1–17

Welch, J and Welch, S (2005) *Winning*, Harper Business, New York

Wilding, RD (1999) The supply chain complexity triangle: Uncertainty generation in the supply chain, *International Journal of Physical Distribution and Logistics Management*, 28 (8), pp 599–616

Womak, J, Jones, D and Roos, D (1990) *The Machine that Changed the World*, Simon and Schuster, New York

INDEX

Page numbers in *italic* indicate figures or tables

Printed in Great Britain
by Amazon